Twenty-first Century Anarchism

Twenty-first Century Anarchism

Unorthodox Ideas for a New Millennium

Edited by

Jon Purkis and James Bowen

CASSELL

Cassell
Wellington House
125 Strand
London WC2R 0BB

PO Box 605
Herndon, VA 20172

First published 1997

British Library Cataloguing-in-Publication Data

A catalogue record for this book is available from the British Library.

ISBN   0 304 33742 0 (hardback)
          0 304 33743 9 (paperback)

Library of Congress Cataloging-in-Publication Data

Twenty-first century anarchism : unorthodox ideas for the new
    millennium/edited by Jon Purkis and James Bowen.
         p. cm.
      ISBN 0-304-33742-0.—ISBN 0-304-33743-9 (pbk.)
      1. Anarchism. 2. Subculture. 3. Subversive activities.
    4. Anarchism—Forecasting. I. Purkis, Jon. II. Bowen, James.
    III. Title: 21st century anarchism
    HX833.T86 1997
    335'.83—dc20
                                           96-43321
                                         CIP

Typeset by Ben Cracknell Studios
Printed and bound in Great Britain by Biddles Ltd, Guildford and King's Lynn

Contents

Part III: If Not Now, When?

Acknowledgements

First, we would like to thank David Goodway for initiating the idea of the book, and Steve Cook and Jane Greenwood at Cassell for being so encouraging, helpful and flexible regarding its production.

We would also like to thank the contributors for producing what we regard as a very fine collection of essays, and for providing helpful general comments and having a very cooperative attitude to working with us. A big thank you to those in and around the anarchist 'scene' in York and beyond in the late 1980s for planting the seeds for many of our ideas, and for remembering to have a good time too.

We are particularly indebted to Jude, Joseph, Poly P. and Colin for intellectual and practical support far beyond the call of duty. Finally, thanks to everyone who has helped in any way in getting this book together, from sorting out computer problems and printing, to making cups of tea and generally keeping us relatively sane: you know who you are!

JB & JP.

The Contributors

James Bowen lives in West Yorkshire and spends his days in the pursuit of total self-actualization by means of literary translation, academic research, dubious musicianship, football, homebrew, hitchhiking and obsessive linguistic analysis, some of which he even occasionally gets paid for. His cartoons and biting political analysis have also been published in *Lib Ed* magazine and the sadly now-defunct *Northern Star*.

Jude Davies teaches in the School of Cultural Studies at King Alfred's College of Higher Education, Winchester. Among his publications are articles on Hollywood films and American Literary Naturalism, and he is currently working on a book about identity in contemporary American cinema. Somewhat exiled in the South of England, he follows GM Vauxhall Conference football via teletext.

Mo Dodson is Principal Lecturer in Communications at London Guildhall University. His *New Statesman* and *Edinburgh Review* articles and reviews, written during the 1980s, about anti-authoritarian art and anti-art interventions, helped introduce these to the mainstream press. Mo has survived the Thatcherite years with his libertarian socialists ideals intact.

Karen Goaman is currently engaged in writing a PhD thesis in Anthropology on contemporary radical anarchist currents, part-time lecturing in Communications at London Guildhall University, and raising two children outside of the school system. She lives her life as closely as possible to her anarchist and ecological ideals, and refuses and opposes car ownership and travel. She has written many reviews and articles for the *Bulletin of Anarchist Research* and *Anarchist Studies*, and produces a newsletter for the Anarchist Research Group.

Judy Greenway works at the University of East London in the Department of Cultural Studies and Innovation Studies, where her teaching includes undergraduate courses in utopias and utopianism, and lesbian and gay cultures. Involved with anarchist, feminist, and lesbian and gay activism for many years, co-founder of the women's liberation paper *Catcall*, former contributor to *Peace News*, *Spare Rib*, *Wildcat* and *Zero* as well as academic journals with more boring names, she is now researching the history of anarchist women in Britain, which she suspects will turn out to be a lifetime project.

Lindsay Hart has been involved in a wide range of social change groups, some of which have used tactics of direct action in their campaigns. He is a trained Traditional Chinese Acupuncturist and circus skills performer and tries to balance all three with writing and researching about popular protest movements.

Steve Millett divides his time between his family, a part-time job, and a PhD in eco-anarchist political theory. He lives in York.

John Moore is an anarchist theorist and writer. He is the author of *Anarchy & Ecstasy* and *Book of Levelling*, as well as contributing editor of a forthcoming festschrift *Lines of Resistance: Essays for Fredy Perlman*. His work has appeared regularly in the *Bulletin of Anarchist Research, Social Anarchism* and *Green Anarchist*. The writings of Fredy Perlman have been a lasting influence upon his works and days.

Dave Morland has been sympathetic towards anarchism since the middle of the 1980s and spent seven years researching the ideology as a part-time student at the University of York. His involvement with anarchist networks centres principally on the Anarchist Discussion Forum and Yorkshire Anarchists. He lives in Sunderland with his partner and two small children, and is employed as a lecturer in politics at the University of Northumbria at Newcastle. He is currently working on a book on anarchism and human nature, having previously written papers for British anarchist periodicals.

Jon Purkis is a part-time lecturer in Sociology and PhD student who feels most at home playing music and hitching around the Highlands and islands of Scotland. He has participated in a number of ecological, peace and anarchist groups, and has recently been active in and written about Earth First!, campaigned for sustainable consumption and tried to keep quiet about his interest in horror films. He lives in the Colne Valley near Huddersfield with his partner and their border collie.

Paul Rosen was closely involved in many of the activities discussed in his chapter, and has recently been gratified to find his first band's second single advertised for sale in *Record Collector* magazine. Disillusionment with the mainstream music industry led him to get involved in more explicitly political activities during the 1980s before getting somewhat burnt out and retreating into academia. He now tries to bring his politics into his academic work, and resists worrying about the contradictions this involves. He's currently working on a book based on his PhD thesis, about technical, economic and cultural change in the bicycle industry, and is also looking beyond that towards questions of transport and urban development.

Colin Wisely lives and works in Huddersfield. Early contact with the great radical educationist, Stephanie Drury, introduced him to the principles of libertarian thought but never did improve his punctuation; despite, her efforts. He is currently working on a film script based on the life of Buenaventura Durruti and also on a novel from which the last essay in the collection here is drawn. Desperate publishers and film producers may contact him through the editors. He hopes that the financial success of this book will enable him to purchase a soft-top Mercedes.

CHAPTER 1

Introduction

The masks of anarchy

In Dario Fo's play *The Accidental Death of an Anarchist*, the chief protagonist – the madman – manages to change the course of the play through his bold and innovative adoption of different disguises and personas. Throughout the play, his real identity is elusive, but somehow his irreverent, provocative and canny presence exudes from whichever costume he has put on.

In the late twentieth century, anarchy is back in action, donning more disguises than ever before: sometimes as a latter-day Ned Ludd, lying in the mud, chained to a huge earth-moving machine; sometimes sharp-suited and pristine-clean at a tenants' association meeting; and sometimes bleary-eyed at a computer terminal riding the electronic waves. In the face of diversity, the redundant black-hatted and caped stereotyped anarchist runs forlornly from place to place, desperately trying to make sure that he is there – bomb at the ready – when the television cameras arrive. But he is nearly a hundred years old now, less nimble than ever, and his words sound out of place among the colourful and creative men and women who have traded in the old models of subversion for new weapons of cultural diversity, individual and collective responsibility, and a sense of humour.

Anarchism as a political theory may be much maligned, but it keeps coming back with a vengeance. As we approach a new millennium, it is certainly more diverse than it has ever been and perhaps even more relevant amidst the complexities and contradictions of an increasingly fragmented world. Anarchy has many masks which are all important, and this diversity cannot be united under one banner. It is not so much that anarchism offers blueprints for a liberated egalitarian and sustainable future for all of us, but that it poses difficult questions right now about power, the relationships of human beings to each other and to the rest of the world, and about culture and identity. Traditionally, anarchists have been primarily concerned with the political issues of economics, class and workplace struggles. These issues *are* encountered in the following pages, but the writers have sought to approach the world from new, controversial and interesting angles, particularly in relation to how society, culture and technology interact on different levels, and ways in which we might look to developing them in the future.

In essence, the real strength of anarchism lies in its critiques of power relationships which exist interpersonally and between people and institutions and in its inherent mistrust of any person who would wish to wield such power. In acknowledging and criticizing these power relationships, however, anarchism is not merely reactive, but also seeks to develop new ways of organizing and relating based on the principles of equality, freedom and empowerment for the whole human race.

Anarchists oppose capitalism and any other political or economic system in which one person, region or culture can thrive while another suffers or starves, and anarchists are therefore often at the forefront in criticizing Western economic imperialism and exploitation wherever they manifest themselves. Anarchists are not, however, a new breed of Puritans who would seek to eliminate all aspects of modern living for some primitive, isolated, rural idyll. Indeed, anarchism has an essentially hedonistic aspect which advocates the promotion of pleasure above pain in all things and the full use of appropriate technology and invention in the pursuit of that pleasure. However, this hedonism is tempered by an acute sense of responsibility in both individual and collective action. The feminist slogan that 'the personal is political' coupled with A.S. Neill's observation that 'freedom is not licence' combine well to sum up these faces of anarchism.

Bearing this in mind, anarchism and the environmental movement also draw a great deal of inspiration from each other, since both recognize the long-term unsustainability of consumer capitalism, the necessity for individual reponsibility and the fact that collective action really does work. However, individual and collective empowerment, like knowledge and freedom, is not something that is given and passively received: it is something which has to be actively sought and achieved. This book endeavours to highlight and understand active and powerful ways in which people (including anarchists) take control of their own lives, to subvert oppressive power relationships, and develop their interpersonal and wider relationships.

A new idealism?

Anarchist theory works on a number of different levels. Because it proposes radical changes in society, it is essentially idealistic. However, on another level, it is firmly rooted in the here and now with regard to practical examples of people on all sides actively undermining power and authority, sometimes in weird and wonderful ways. The terrains of theory and action have changed, and now there are generations of activists operating in many fields of protest for whom the works of Kropotkin, Malatesta and Bakunin are as distant in terms of their description of the world as the literary classics of writers such as Charles Dickens. The industrial age from which anarchism emerged operated on very different temporal and spatial levels from the present one, spawning political movements that addressed mostly issues of economic injustice and the instrumentalism of making sure that everyone had enough to eat. The dominant anarchist political vision of change was an insurrectionary one (the Revolution, on the barricades) and only a handful of women had the wherewithal to suggest that politics extended to personal relationships too. Anarchist theory also rarely travelled beyond the confines of the nascent industrial West.

Modern anarchism has long since needed a major overhaul, and this book is part of a new theoretical and practical tradition which has started to develop over the last few years. Anarchists have been quick to take an interest in the emergence of postmodernism, chaos theory, ecologism and feminist post-structuralism – all philosophies which celebrate the breakdown of absolute and mechanistic interpretations of society. In this collection we see these ideas adding their voices to old arguments and at the same time being used to fuel new debates. Our intention is to use those aspects of anarchism which are still relevant, while happily rejecting much of the historical baggage which seems to accompany most political thinking. As Judy Greenway succinctly states in Chapter 11:

> If anarchism can after all be thought of as an approach, a critique, a set of questions to be asked about power relations, rather than a theory or set of answers, then perhaps it can escape the fate of yesterday's discarded ideologies.

How to read this book

We have tried to make this book as accessible as possible for both the specialist reader and the interested browser. To this end, we have included a Glossary of names, terms, theories and events which might not be immediately obvious, particularly to the non-specialist reader. There is a problem within much anarchist theory that it tends to get bogged down in irrelevant academic gobbledygook, which perhaps stems from a tendency for anarchist theorists to be far removed from the activists which they write about. All of the contributors to this collection, whilst coming mostly from academic backgrounds, are also activists in their different areas, and are thus writing from both a practical and theoretical position. We have tried to avoid problems of inaccessibility wherever possible by making explicit (either in the Glossary or in the text and notes) exactly what is being discussed or inferred. This is not to say that this, as a book of ideas, does not contain some difficult and challenging theories, but we have tried to present these in as accessible a way as possible without simplifying the arguments. As the editors, we would also suggest that all of the chapters warrant a second, third, even twenty-seventh reading in order to understand some of the nuances of the arguments presented. We do not necessarily agree with all of the views expressed herein (the contributors do actually contradict each other on numerous occasions), but we believe this fluidity and flexibility of approach to be essential in order to understand and theorize about the world in all its complexity on a variety of different levels.

The main body of the book is divided into three parts, based on three main themes, but with a common thread running through all of them regarding their relevance to the present and ways in which these can, will and must affect the future.

The first part, *Old Dogs, New Tricks* contains three chapters which address some of the old chestnuts of political argument and debate, but offer new and interesting perspectives on these. Dave Morland addresses the problem of human nature, arguing that anarchism, despite a century of debate on the subject, needs to develop a revised concept of human nature rather than attempting to go down the existentialist road which ultimately offers nothing to anarchists. Instead, in accepting that history is not fixed, a theory of human nature is developed from a synthesis of individualist and collectivist interpretations of the subject. Steve Millett's chapter on the Welfare State criticizes this bastion of the post-war democratic consensus, arguing that the State is unsuitable as an institution for administering welfare, and that it is not the most needy who benefit from it. He rejects notions of individualism currently fashionable in New Right thinking, and goes on to outline ways in which welfare has been and can be collectively owned and controlled in order to benefit and empower all of society. In Chapter 4 Lindsay Hart looks at radical direct action, with particular reference to the British environmental movement, and argues that anarchism can and does sit comfortably within some aspects of this movement, particularly in terms of non-hierarchical organization and decision-making. However, he insists that concepts of violence, non-violence and the commensurability of means and ends must be addressed and clarified if radical direct action is to fulfil its potential in changing the world.

The second part, entitled *Culture and Anarchy!*, identifies a number of spheres of popular culture in which anarchism demonstrates its subversive nature in order to smash some icons, to question some accepted anarchist readings of culture and technology, and to have some fun into the bargain. In Chapter 5 Jude Davies provides a retrospective analysis of the 'Anarchy in the UK' festival held in London in 1994, with a view to examining the ways in which British anarchism extends its influence right from the margins to the mainstream. Representations of Mr Blobby in particular are examined with a view to assessing the large and pink one as both potentially truly subversive and as a recuperated media image of subversiveness. In Chapter 6 Karen Goaman and Mo Dodson trace a current of anarchist and subversive cultural intervention from the late 1960s to the present. Their focus is very much on the cultural margins, but they look at ways in which this subversive current has developed a proud tradition of self-expression, iconoclasm and humour while seeking to change the world on a variety of different levels. They argue that such a current is creative and proactive, and thus rejects Foucault's notion that oppositional movements are inherently reactive.

Paul Rosen's chapter is something of an autobiographical journey through the murky underworld of late 1970s and early 1980s punk, with specific reference to the self-directed, self-managed, and eventually self-destructive activities of bands around that time. He looks specifically at the relationships which developed between the bands, recording organizations and the technology of the time, identifying a number of their self-directed and cooperative activities as 'anarchy in action', as well as pointing out a number of mistakes that were made. Lessons for the present and future in music and technology are thus drawn out. In Chapter 8 John Moore looks at how the idea of a subversive text has been understood historically, in a number of legal, political and academic contexts. He argues that to write a truly subversive text, both the structure and the content must constantly challenge the reader's perception of the world. To illustrate that this can be done, he examines the work of the anarcho-primitivist writer Fredy Perlman, drawing on the work of French feminist philosopher Julia Kristeva.

The third part, *If Not Now, When?*, looks at some everyday features of modern life (transport, consumption, work, sex, drugs, punishment) and proposes ways in which anarchists might look to liberating these areas in a sustainable and responsible future. In Chapter 9 Jon Purkis takes up the issues of transport and consumerism, identifying them both as areas of unsustainability in our modern world, but also as areas under-theorized by anarchists. He offers a wide-ranging critique of modern capitalist modes of travel and consumption, and proposes that individually and collectively responsible attitudes to these may be socially liberatory in themselves, as well as being essential for a sustainable future. In Chapter 10 James Bowen turns his attentions to the problem of work in the late twentieth century and in the future. He argues that, since there is less work for people than ever in our society and that much of the work is for useless ends and the profit of someone else, it would be better to reinvent ourselves as creatures of leisure and self-actualization. By using appropriate and accountable technology to relieve us of the scourge of useless toil, he proposes a complete rethink of the ways in which we construct our own identities, spend our time and fulfil human needs.

Judy Greenway's chapter maps out some of the ways in which lesbians, gays, feminists and others have sought to break down, transgress and subvert the sexual mores of our society. She suggests that such groups have been instrumental in questioning interpersonal and sexual relationships and in redefining and realigning sexual identity. Technologies from contraception to surgical transformation offer the potential to liberate people in terms of sex and identity in the future, but although the possibility for redefinition exists, she argues that it is essential not to forget about questioning and liberating our personal relationships on a basic human level. In the final chapter Colin Wisely proposes a series of alternative futures from the terrifying to the insurrectionary to the gently subversive. He describes five possible outcomes for our society in the next century, taking into account current social problems such as crime, drug use and the division of labour and projecting them into these proposed future scenarios. His fictional representations of possible anarchist futures seek (like the BBC!) to inform, to entertain and to educate.

We, the editors, believe that this collection makes a valuable contribution to contemporary anarchist literature. Its variety and innovation are intended to move social and political debates forward, while addressing a number of seldom-explored subjects from challenging, unorthodox and controversial angles.

Part I

Old Dogs, New Tricks

CHAPTER 2

Anarchism, Human Nature and History

Lessons for the Future

Dave Morland

Human nature is one of the most important concepts employed in political argument. Whether in everyday conversation or academic discourse, it is used as an evaluative tool to embrace or reject political ideologies. Traditionally, anarchism has been attacked on the basis that its conception of human nature is excessively optimistic. Anarchism, reputedly, will simply not work because human nature is not as good as anarchists like to think it is. This chapter aims to correct this erroneous apprehension, and it intends to illustrate that anarchism offers a very realistic assessment of human nature that constitutes one of the greatest strengths of anarchist thinking. At the same time it highlights the dangers of adopting the philosophy of the New Right and cautions against a marriage with existentialism.

Introduction

Generally speaking, anarchism is dismissed in the public's imagination as being either too violent or simply unworkable. The former perception has much to do with the image anarchism inherited at the end of the nineteenth century, with which it remains associated. An anarchist, it would seem, is someone who operates incognito, armed with a dagger or a pocketful of semtex. This vision of the anarchist as a clandestine terrorist was cemented in novels like Joseph Conrad's *The Secret Agent*, set in the 1890s and published in 1907. Yet more recently Peter Marshall has commented, 'the very word "anarchist" continues to evoke a shiver of anxiety among the respectable and well-off.'[1] A detailed investigation of what it is to be an anarchist, or, more precisely, what anarchism means is beyond the remit of this chapter. However, in so far as it is concerned with the second assumption, that anarchism is unworkable, some elaboration on the nature of anarchism itself will undoubtedly emerge.

At the heart of political argument lies the concept of human nature. Particularly in popular discourse, but also in academic analysis, the concept of human nature is the benchmark by which political ideologies are either embraced or eschewed. Human nature is invoked time and again in everyday conversation as testimony to the success or feasibility, or conversely the naïvety or utopianism, of social and political ideals. A conservative, for example, might comment that socialism will never work because human nature is not good enough. Humankind is burdened by original sin, and socialists would do well not to forget it when drawing up plans for future society. As Christopher Berry has remarked:

> 'human nature' has a prominent place in the repertoire of explanations and justifications that is embedded in popular consciousness. It is this consciousness that is largely responsible for the perceptions people have of their society and it is these perceptions that directly affect their political beliefs and actions.[2]

Inasmuch as political ideologies are instrumental in shaping the popular consciousness, then they are responsible for constructing a political programme that is partly underpinned by a set of assumptions about human nature.

It has often been said that people turn to ideologies to make sense of the world. By and large this appears to be true. But for ideologies to afford meaning and understanding they have to provide an account of the world in which their followers live. The more convincing their explanation of events, the more converts they can hope to attract. Ideologies do this by enunciating an argument that transcends all three dimensions of time: past, present and future. Not only do they pronounce on the past and the present, but they offer a view of how humanity might live in a future society. Political ideologies are both descriptive and prescriptive. Judgement is, however, largely predicated on a concept of human nature. Ideological portraits are dependent upon human nature not only to describe what is wrong with society now (as the concept of alienation is employed in Marxism), but how those wrongs should be put right. Human nature, then, is an evaluative tool by which rival ideologies are either welcomed or spurned.

The dimensions of human nature

The concept of human nature is simply one piece in the jigsaw that helps to establish the overall pattern of an ideology. Concepts of history or some wider metaphysic also play a fundamental role in constructing this ideological matrix. The centrality of the concept of human nature to this process, though, is incontestable. But human nature itself is what is commonly referred to as an essentially contested concept. What is at stake here is the authenticity of the epistemology through which human nature is defined. In other words, there is often basic disagreement about what constitutes human nature – and such is the stuff of politics. Are human beings essentially sinful, as the Bible tells us or are they basically innocent, as someone like Rousseau would have us believe? Whatever the answer, there appear to be two procedures for laying claim to what amounts to a supposedly truthful account of human nature. Either human nature is taken to be a construct of one's social context, or it is held to possess certain transcendent, universal qualities. That is, either human nature is regarded as a product of the environment of which it is a part, or it is seen as something which is given about humanity. It is either contextual or universal.

Locating the essence of human nature is an immensely difficult if not impossible task. And even if it is possible to identify the transcendent component(s) of human nature (i.e., that which is sometimes referred to as the essence of human nature), it does not automatically follow that human nature can yield a prescription about how society ought to be organized. As Raymond Plant has argued, 'in so far as the theory of human nature is factual in content it cannot yield any conclusion about the morally desirable form of human organisation'.[3] The dilemma is created by the is/ought or fact/value distinction, and to say that 'facts' about human nature prescribe moral outcomes is to commit what is known in philosophical jargon as the 'naturalistic fallacy'. Conversely, in so far as a conception of human nature is not factual but evaluative then it may be said to be capable of sustaining moral arguments about social and political reform. But that still leaves the unanswered question: in what will that conception of human nature be grounded?

The dilemma, however, may not be as absolute as it first appears, since the dichotomy of contextual and universal elements of human nature is seldom hard and fast in political ideology. Conservatism, for example, is commonly held to be indebted to a contextualist conception of human nature, with its emphasis on the individual's gradual acquisition of culture and language as a major element that forges personal identity. Despite this perception that an individual's context is vital to an understanding of what goes to compose that person, the conservative may equally accentuate the influence of a universal component like original sin or the cogency of emotions over the limited capacity of humankind's power of reason.[4] Likewise, liberalism is often considered to exhibit a universalist conception of human nature. Reason or rationality is the hallmark of humanity, according to the liberal; but even here due credit is given to the character-forming basis of circumstance.[5] Indeed, if it were not for the ability of the environment to impress an identity on individuals' minds then the whole liberal impulse of the Enlightenment would have been an irrelevant exercise in the triumph of reason over faith and superstition.

Common misconceptions

Conceptions of human nature, then, often combine both contextualist and universalist arguments, and anarchism (as will be demonstrated below) is no exception. Unfortunately, this fact is not always recognized by those who reflect upon the nature of anarchism. The discipline of political ideology is central to the study of politics and has spawned a growing number of commentaries in recent years. But most of these texts rest on a fundamental error concerning the anarchist conception of human nature. They point, quite rightly, to the fact that anarchists operate a contextualist conception of human nature, but fail to detect the givenness or universality that anarchists ascribe to human nature. This leads some commentators to suggest that anarchism has little to say about human nature that has not already been said by the black sheep of the Enlightenment, Rousseau. Barbara Goodwin, for instance, argues that along with Rousseau some anarchists picture 'the individual as a *tabula rasa* (blank sheet) at birth, innocent of evil and only corrupted later, by invidious social institutions'.[6] An almost identical argument emerges in the work of Ian Adams. In his book, *Political Ideology Today*, Adams argues that anarchism rests 'upon certain basic assumptions about human nature and its relation to society', one of which is: 'Humanity is essentially good, but is corrupted by government'.[7] Alternatively, anarchists are said to espouse an overly optimistic assessment of human nature. Thus Andrew Heywood contends that the core of anarchism is founded on

> an unashamed optimism, a belief in the natural goodness, or at least potential goodness, of humankind. Social order arises naturally and spontaneously; it does not require the machinery of 'law and order'. This is why anarchist conclusions have been reached by political thinkers who possess an essentially optimistic view of human nature.[8]

The prominence that is attributed to an optimistic account of human nature, allegedly espoused by anarchism, is not only, as April Carter has noted, 'an over-simplification',[9] but 'a perennial half-truth that deserves to be critically examined'.[10] Sadly, this confusion is perpetuated by sympathetic and more knowledgeable analysts of the ideology. George Woodcock has sometimes concluded, erroneously in my opinion, that certain anarchists, such as Proudhon and Kropotkin, propound an optimistic conception of human nature.[11] Elsewhere, however, Woodcock appears to be cognizant of the general caution that anarchists tend to adopt when discussing human nature.[12] Clarity is still found wanting in Marshall's mammoth-sized successor to Woodcock's erstwhile standard reference to the movement and its ideas. In his *Demanding the Impossible*, Peter Marshall vacillates between two contradictory positions. On the one hand, he states that anarchists: 'are unashamedly optimistic. Many base their optimism on the existence of self-regulation in nature, on the spontaneous harmony of interests in society, and on the potential goodwill of humanity'.[13] On the other, he contends that few 'anarchists believe in natural goodness'. On the contrary, 'it could be argued that the anarchists have not only a realistic, but even a pessimistic view of human nature'.[14] While implying that the conception of human nature that anarchists employ contains an assumption that there is something given or innate about human nature, Marshall simultaneously argues that whatever it is that is innate in human nature, most anarchists do not think that it is natural goodness.

Redressing the balance: anarchism and human nature

It is one of the tasks of this chapter to clarify these clouded assessments by offering a detailed analysis of the anarchist conception of human nature. Anarchism is neither inspired by 'an unashamed utopianism', at least not in the manner that Heywood believes, nor is it the ideological narrative of those working with 'an essentially optimistic view of human nature'.[15] Although anarchists certainly rely on environmental factors to establish the groundwork for their belief that human nature is capable of providing a strong enough basis for anarchy to be a realistic alternative to State-led exploitation and oppression, this is only one side of the coin. Concomitant to the contextual element of the anarchists' conception of human nature there is a given or inherent constituent that is incontrovertibly characterized as badness. Anarchists are proprietors of a double-barrelled conception of human nature. Human nature is composed of both sociability and egoism (which corresponds rather loosely to what Heywood and others term goodness and badness). The point that these interpreters seem to miss is that in elucidating a vision of the good life (a process at the heart of all ideologies), anarchists have advanced a series of proposals that are tinged with an air of realism and prudence that is fuelled by what is, at times, a particularly honest if not pessimistic account of the darker aspects of human nature.

Judgements that point to excessive optimism about human nature are not without warranty, but are grossly exaggerated. Kropotkin is rightly identified as the most optimistic of the classical anarchists. As George Woodcock has remarked, one is struck by 'the particular benignity of Kropotkin's view of human nature', especially when compared alongside Bakunin who exhibits a measure of realism that Kropotkin's stricter scientific basis seems unwilling to yield.[16] Kropotkin's concept of mutual aid may have fuelled his undoubted optimism, but this has to be taken in context. The other leading anarchists of the nineteenth century, Proudhon and Bakunin, both highlight the baser elements of human nature. Proudhon in particular does not recoil from admitting that humankind knows how to do 'evil with all the characteristics of a nature deliberately maleficient, and all the more wicked because, when it so wishes, it knows how to do good gratuitously also and is capable of self-sacrifice'.[17] Indeed, it is this recognition of humanity's capacity for evil that constitutes one of the points of division between anarchists and Marxists. The rationale behind the anarchist objection to Marxism is, to put it very simply, that Marxist-Leninists have misunderstood human nature. There is, anarchists caution, a lust for power in humankind that will jeopardize the very outcome of the revolutionary process itself. As Bakunin advised: 'No one should be entrusted with power, inasmuch as anyone invested with authority must, through the force of an immutable social law, become an oppressor and exploiter of society'.[18] History seems to have vindicated the anarchists' account. Anarchists, as Miller has observed, are cognizant 'of the imperfections of human nature'.[19] As Bakunin commented, with the best will in the world, one simply has to recognize the corrupting effects of power on all human beings. 'Take', Bakunin suggests, 'the most sincere democrat and put him on the throne; if he does not step down promptly, he will surely become a scoundrel.'[20] Likewise, Proudhon contends: 'Give power to a Saint Vincent de Paul and he will be a Guizot or a Talleyrand'.[21] Once incumbent, the occupier of power will simply abuse the privilege bestowed by that position. The notion of a will to power establishes itself as a central plank in the anarchist conception of human nature, with even Kropotkin acknowledging its existence, despite Woodcock's judgement, in order to explain the rise of the modern State.[22]

Anarchism and history

The true nature of this insistence on an innate capacity for wrongdoing or a lust for power in human nature cannot be properly appreciated unless it is balanced against the contextualist understanding of human nature that permeates many anarchist writings on the subject. Anarchists draw attention to the inherent will to power in human nature, of that there is no doubt; but they do so in conjunction with the belief that this is simply one potentiality of human nature. Egoism is counterbalanced by sociability. It is this which helps explain, for instance, the anarchist philosophy of history, expounded principally by Proudhon but followed by Bakunin and Kropotkin.[23] According to Proudhon, history is characterized by two competing, permanent tendencies: authority and liberty. Each and every society is governed by the relationship of authority and liberty.

> *Authority and liberty are as old as the human race; they are born with us, and live on in each of us. Let us note but one thing, which few readers would notice otherwise: these two principles form a couple, so to speak, whose two terms, though indissolubly linked together, are nevertheless irreducible one to the other, and remain, despite all our efforts, perpetually at odds.*[24]

History, then, is to be seen as a series of developments in either direction, towards a burgeoning of authority or a flowering of liberty. As history unfurls its consequences upon the human race, this is, for anarchists, confirmation of their understanding that human nature may be subject to the influences of either egoism or sociability.

Such thinking again isolates the anarchists from the Marxists, for history becomes a matter of human will. This divergence in understanding on the nature of history was most famously expressed in the attack launched by Marx on Bakunin. Marx wrote, in his *Conspectus of Bakunin's 'Statism and Anarchy'*, that Bakunin 'understands absolutely nothing about the social revolution, only its political phrases. Its economic conditions do not exist for him . . . The *will*, and not the economic conditions, is the foundation of his social revolution'.[25] Of course, the essence of Marx's critique is correct but misplaced. Anarchists do not subscribe to the materialist conception of history for the very reason that their conception of human nature forbids it. The course of history cannot be mapped out according to the development of the relations and forces of production. As Proudhon wrote in his *Confessions of a Revolutionary*, in 1849, the philosophical method of studying history reveals 'that there is no inevitability in particular events and that these may vary infinitely according to the individual wills that cause them to happen'.[26] Following in the footsteps of his predecessors, Kropotkin announces that two opposed recurrent traditions have vied with each other for supremacy throughout the history of civilization: 'the Roman and the Popular; the imperial and the federalist; the authoritarian and the libertarian'.[27] Within anarchism there is an implicit relationship between human nature and historical progress, with the rise of the State corresponding to the rise of self-assertion or egoism, and the development of free communes, or medieval city-states in Kropotkin's historical analysis, corresponding to a growth in sociability. The struggle of historical forces, the battle between libertarianism and authoritarianism, is occasioned by a comparable contest within human nature.

Human nature and its environment

It is at this juncture that the interconnection of history and human nature becomes all important, for the anarchist analysis points to the significance of environmental factors in curtailing the expansion of egoism. Humankind has the capacity for both egoism and sociability, but these potentialities exist in what may be best described as a symbiotic relationship with the environment. Social, economic and political institutions, together with the evolution of social and political ideals, act in the manner of a gardener's trestle, shaping and bending human nature in one particular direction. There are innate components of human nature, the development of which is encouraged by the environmental context within which individuals find themselves. Human nature is malleable, but not completely so. Just as the evolution of the modern State facilitated the intensification of egoism, so sociability continues to persist in the form of mutual aid. Human nature provides the sustenance for the development of history just as history releases the possibility of its own fulfilment. In other words, social circumstances may inaugurate the consummation of a historical trend. Human nature acts as a catalyst establishing a basis for the victory of one trend over another. In this sense a political or social movement may act as an environmental trigger liberating both the forces of history and the potentialities of human nature. The one feeds off the other as they chart their progress through the course of social evolution.

Anarchists can never be accused of historical determinism. At the same time, however, the interplay between their conceptions of human nature and history illustrates why it is imperative to ensure the right kind of environmental context for the flourishing of mutual aid and sociability. Ideas alone are insufficient to bring about historical change or insure against an outbreak of egoism in human nature. Anarchism is very definitely a philosophy of praxis; and one of the best ways to stimulate the ascent of sociability over egoism is through appropriate social praxis. This reflects the fact that anarchists are much beholden to materialism, because it is this which inspires the contextualist dimension of their conception of human nature.[28] Adopting this contextualist line of reasoning, Bakunin argues that humans are what their environment makes of them. No one, he opines, 'will seriously dispute this opinion, that every child, youth, adult, and even the most mature man [sic], is wholly the product of the environment that nourished and raised him – an inevitable, involuntary, and consequently irresponsible product'.[29] Bakunin's writings are notorious for their inconsistencies and Bakunin's contextualism, which reads like materialistic determinism, rubs hard against his submission that power is attractive to people. As Bakunin himself admits, every person 'carries within himself the germs of this lust for power'.[30] Moreover, as he wrote in his *A Circular Letter to My Friends in Italy*, humankind's 'nature is so constituted that, given the possibility of doing evil, that is, of feeding his vanity, his ambition, and his cupidity at the expense of someone else, he surely will make full use of such an opportunity'.[31]

Despite Bakunin's inconsistencies, both materialism and contextualism remain a fundamental part of anarchist ideological thinking. Indeed, one may say that anarchists have to adhere to these concepts if only because the feasibility of anarchism demands it. Without the accent on contextualism, the anarchist tale of a better society to come would have to be dismissed as complete nonsense or utopian. Contextualism is imperative not only in the anarchists' critique of Marxist-Leninist revolutionary strategy, but in the belief that a fresh social environment is capable of fostering a new social morality and consolidating the victory of mutual aid. Given the right circumstances, human nature can be transformed from that which corresponds to the climate of economic liberalism to that which maintains the establishment of an anarchist-communist society.

The anarchist conception of human nature, then, reflects that of other ideological conceptions. It is indebted to a contextualist *and* a universalist reading. More importantly, it comprises both egoism and sociability. A simple enough thesis one might admit, but it has largely gone unnoticed in academic analysis. However, the double-barrelled character of the anarchists' conception of human nature may seem confusing and somewhat paradoxical. The paradox is overcome by simply accepting that anarchism is ambivalent or indeed inconsistent about the issue of human nature. Anarchists do concede that human nature has intrinsic properties and these include both sociability and egoism, propensities which may be said to lead to good and evil. The former (contextualist and sociable) reading reflects their shared heritage with socialism and accounts for their belief in the ultimate attainability of a peaceful, harmonious society that is devoid of the oppressive structures that demarcate capitalist society. The latter (universalist and egoist) reading is indicative of what they have in common with liberalism. It explains why anarchists observe with a measure of accuracy the corrupting effects of power and why they counsel against the Marxist concept of the dictatorship of the proletariat or a workers' State.

It is this broader understanding of the anarchist conception of human nature that reveals one of the greatest strengths of anarchism.[32] The duality of their thinking on human nature may illuminate a central tension within the ideology (but then most, if not all, political ideologies are subject to similar tensions), but most importantly it signals, as John Clark has perceived, one of the anarchists' towering strengths:

> It is the belief that power corrupts, and that people become irresponsible in their exercise of it, that forms the basis for much of their criticism of political authority and centralised power. Power must be dispersed they say, not so much because everyone is always good, but because when power is concentrated some people tend to become extremely evil.[33]

Lessons for the future: 1. Against the New Right

As the second millennium draws to a close there are encouraging signs for anarchism ahead. There are many opportunities to be gained from strengthening already existing bonds with new social movements like ecologism and feminism. Both ideologies have done much to break through barriers, once regarded as insurmountable, in human relationships within human society and with the natural world. Feminism's evaluation of the personal as political has done much to illustrate the nature of women's oppression and has encouraged a fundamental rethink on what it is to be male and female. Equally important, though, are the consequences of the feminist analysis of 'patriarchy' for everyday life. Politics is no longer confined to the public arena of States, governments and political parties. Feminism's great achievement has been to redraw the boundaries of the public imagination in terms of the pervasiveness of political relationships, which cross the threshold and extend into many areas of family and personal life. Arguably the first and most fundamental form of human oppression, feminism's dissection of female oppression has done much by way of illustrating how a superficial dependence upon class politics and a utopian faith in the magical powers of Marxist revolution are not in themselves sufficient to guarantee the liberation of all humankind. Similarly, ecologism has not only revealed the arrogance of the anthropo-centrism of mainstream ideologies, but has forced many people to re-consider the nature of their own being in light of an increasingly relevant and persuasive philosophy of ecocentrism that highlights the inter-relatedness and interdependence of all organisms that inhabit the Earth. Relationships between human beings and between humanity and the planet are now being reconsidered in imaginative and auspicious ways. The possibilities for a cross-fertilization of ideas between anarchism and these new social movements are both fascinating and extensive. However, this is not my area of concern here; rather, I seek to draw attention to some recent developments, both in practice and theory, that anarchism would do well to avoid. Two that will be examined here, albeit very briefly, are the rise of the New Right in Britain and a proffered courtship with existentialism.

History has vindicated the anarchist assessment of human nature on more than one occasion. Anarchists like to think that the history of the Soviet Union justified their concern about establishing a dictatorship of the proletariat. Investing power in a revolutionary élite or vanguard party not only flouted the principle of commensurability between means and ends (authoritarian vs. libertarian), but also confirmed their suspicions that power is an addictive drug which if not checked will jeopardize the smooth functioning of any society. The argument has been most cogently expressed by Bakunin. There is no real difference, he believes, between a revolutionary dictatorship and the State. Both govern by a minority in the name of the majority. And both consolidate 'the political and economic privileges of the governing minority and the political and economic slavery of the masses'.[34] Dictatorship, he notes, has only one objective: to perpetuate itself. 'Anyone who doubts this is not at all familiar with human nature.'[35] Thus Bakunin enunciates a conviction that lies at the heart of anarchist thinking:

> the only way to render any political power harmless, to pacify it and subdue it, is to destroy it. The philosophers did not understand that there can be no guarantee against political power except its complete abolition. Words, promises, and vows mean nothing in politics, as an arena of mutually contending forces and facts, for the simple reason that any political power, as long as it remains a real power, by its very nature and under the threat of self-

destruction must inexorably and at all costs strive for the realisation of its objectives, regardless of or even against the will of the authorities and princes wielding it.[36]

Just as anarchists have been persuaded against supporting Marxist-Leninist revolutionary strategy because of its lack of understanding of human nature, then so they should not be deluded by the rhetoric of the New Right.[37] One of the leading proponents of the New Right in Britain was the long-serving Prime Minister, Margaret Thatcher. During the 1980s her commitment to rolling back the frontiers of the State, which at first glance may appear to share some common ground with anarchist objectives, simply disguised the now well-known strategy that a minimal or free market economic State demands and depends upon a highly centralized and exceedingly powerful political State to support it. Notions of maximum individual liberty within a minimal State have to be tempered upon realization that the minimal State is only minimal in certain areas: notably, economic regulation of the free market. As local democracy degenerates under an increasingly powerful stranglehold exerted by central government, it would appear that the New Right is oblivious to its own teachings on human nature.

It has become customary now for the New Right to describe itself as having more in common with nineteenth-century Liberalism or the Manchester school of economics than traditional Conservatism.[38] This is generally true, and as such the New Right operates with a conception of human nature that is underpinned by assumptions about humanity's selfishness, competitiveness, acquisitiveness and hedonistic nature. This view of the bourgeois individual dovetailed perfectly into the demands of capitalist society, and proved fundamental to the Thatcherite school of the New Right. Hence their libertarian guru, Keith Joseph, argued that human nature is so constituted that it is natural

> *to pursue private rather than public ends. This is a simple matter of observation. The duty of government is to accommodate themselves [sic] to this immutable fact about human nature . . . Men [sic] have a natural right to their ambitions because it was not for the purpose of abolishing competitiveness that they submitted to government; it was for the purpose of regulating competitiveness and preventing it from taking violent, fraudulent or anti-social forms.*[39]

By its own admission, humankind is ambitious and competitive: it is power hungry, and will swallow up any opportunity for power that presents itself.

This may make sound sense, in their eyes, for a minimal State, but for anarchists it is a recipe for no State at all. The New Right has proved more than capable of putting its philosophy into practice in terms of free-market policies, but it has chosen to ignore the consequences of the power-seeking and ambitious disposition of humankind. It is not that the New Right is incognisant of this dimension of human nature; rather, such thinking serves to corroborate their belief that society is a hierarchical command structure in which those most able to assume positions of power and responsibility will do so. The complicating factor is that not all of human life is subsumed under private activities. As a programme for political rule, the inherent danger in all this is that once incumbent in positions of power, the office holder will use that office for private rather than public ends. In other words, the New Right philosophy engenders the very real possibility of an abuse of power and office. Having created an ethos of selfish egoism throughout the 1980s, the erosion of political accountability in the creation of a culture of government-appointed quangos and deregulated industries has suddenly come home to roost with a vengeance in the mid-1990s.[40] Anarchists can learn from this experience. Suppositions about power, ambition and egoism in human nature teach that power should be decentralized and devolved wherever it cannot be eliminated altogether. Anarchists have noted and should continue to take note of Acton's caveat that 'Power tends to corrupt and absolute power corrupts absolutely'.[41] The experience of the New Right has been a painful one, but if nothing else it has taught us the dangers of unaccountability and the centralization of power. Human nature has much to say about political practice.

Lessons for the future: 2. Against existentialism

Another important development that has occurred recently is the suggestion that anarchism should discard any dependency on human nature in favour of a marriage with existentialism. This is the position adopted by Marshall in his essay, 'Human nature and anarchism'.[42] In purporting to reject human nature, he writes

> *that we should abandon the use of the term 'human nature' since it implies that there is a fixed essence within us which requires certain conditions to express itself, or some inherent force which directs us outside the influence of history or culture.*[43]

At face value this may seem like an apostasy of nineteenth-century conceptions of human nature in favour of twentieth-century existentialism. However, Marshall stops short of migrating into a fully-fledged existentialism. Instead, he opts for what he terms a 'soft determinism'. Whilst Marshall acknowledges that 'there are causes which influence us', he qualifies this admission by suggesting that 'all causes [are] incomplete and open-ended. Such causes dispose but do not determine.'[44] Furthermore, as for the search for an unmistakeable identity or essence of human nature, whether it be goodness or badness, we should leave well alone. 'We have', he acknowledges, *innate tendencies for both types of behaviour; it is our circumstances which encourage or check them. While our present authoritarian and hierarchical society encourages egoism, competition and aggression, there is good reason to think that a free society without authority and coercion would encourage our benevolent and sympathetic tendencies.*[45]

Seemingly, Marshall wants to divorce himself from any dependence upon a concept of human nature but is forced to concede that human nature does exist and that its identity is largely (because the environment can only dispose and not determine) a matter of environmental factors. It is patently obvious that, existentialist overtones aside, Marshall remains securely rooted in the nineteenth-century anarchist tradition. His own personal views bear a remarkably striking resemblance to those of the social anarchists in general and Kropotkin in particular. For whatever reason though, Marshall is unable to recognize the similarity of his own views and the assumptions that underpin the social anarchists' conception of human nature in his voluminous tome on the history of anarchism.

One contemporary anarchist writer who is more consistent in her belief that anarchism should abandon human nature is L. Susan Brown. In her article 'Anarchism, existentialism and human nature: a critique', Brown argues that anarchists should jettison the outdated nineteenth-century model of human nature in favour of modern existentialist considerations.[46] Brown's intention is to 'argue against any inherent nature to humanity at all, and propose that we are that which we make of ourselves'.[47] The evidence of her article indicates that it is perfectly possible to tender the argument that we are what we make ourselves to be, whilst maintaining a conception of human nature in which there is something given or innate. Initially, Brown's idea might sound like an attractive proposition. But the problem is that, in rejecting the concept of human nature, existentialism discards not only that which embodies an essence or innateness that is common to all humankind, it also jettisons the argument that political circumstances or the social environment have to be altered if anarchy is to flourish. Existentialism is opposed to both dimensions of the anarchist conception of human nature: the universal and the contextual; and it is the latter which demands social change for the better of humanity. Of course, it is important to stress that to repudiate any notion of human nature is in itself a theory or conception of human nature; however, the point is that existentialism seems entirely at odds with the activist nature of anarchism. As Mark Leier has noted, if we believe with existentialism that individuals 'can always choose to be free, why should we bother to try to change anything except our own minds?'[48] Anarchists stand to gain little if anything from entering into a partnership with existentialism. With its notion of metaphysical freedom, existentialism is in no better position than anarchism to conclude that history will evolve in the direction of greater freedom rather than increased authoritarianism. As Brown admits, there is nothing to prevent individuals from choosing fascism over anarchy.[49]

Conclusion

Even if anarchists refrain from embracing existentialism, they may find themselves in a similar position in that they cannot predict with any certainty the outcome of social or historical evolution or revolution. As Peter Marshall has highlighted,

> [there] is no pre-ordained pattern to history, no iron law of capitalist development, no straight railroad which we have to follow. Although it is always made on prior circumstances, history is what we make it; and the future, as the past, can be either authoritarian or libertarian depending on our choices and actions.[50]

History is autonomous; it may move in either direction – such is the consequence of accepting the twin basis of egoism and sociability in human nature, and such is the consequence of importing the existentialist belief that humans are what they make of themselves. Revolution is a matter of will rather than economic or social circumstances. But the advantage of possessing a conception of human nature is that the morality that accompanies forms of social organization resides in something more solid than anything existentialism has to offer. Whether we like it or not, human nature is vitally important as a critical tool in expressing a judgement about society and its dispensation of justice. In this respect, human nature emulates the capacities of human rights. Anarchism's belief that freedom and sociability are fundamental to human nature helps it to undermine the dehumanizing and authoritarian consequences of State power. At the same time, anarchism's cognisance of the effects of egoism engenders a permanent vigilance against new forms of oppression and abuses of power. History has taught anarchists that they should be prepared to grasp any opportunity that presents itself for moving in the direction of a freer society, whilst paying attention to human nature and avoiding any repetition of past mistakes in the twenty-first century. To that effect, anarchists will have to suffer a while longer the individualist ethos that looks set to close the door on the twentieth century, whilst working hard to bring about the success of a society inspired by communalist, participationist and non-hierarchical goals.

Notes

1 Marshall (1992), p.630.

2 Berry (1986), p.x.

3 Plant (1991), p.70.

4 A point made by Burke (1982), p.183.

5 See, for example, Smart (1983), pp.36–52.

6 Goodwin (1992), p.10. Rousseau's argument is developed in *A Discourse on Inequality*, commonly referred to as his Second Discourse.

7 Adams (1993), p.172.

8 Heywood (1992), p.198. Andrew Gamble is another who misjudges the anarchists' conception of human nature. See Gamble (1981), pp.109–10.

9 Carter (1971), p.16.

10 Clark (1984), p.121.

11 Woodcock (1972), p.172.

12 Woodcock (1975), p.19.

13 Marshall (1992), p.664.

14 Ibid, p.643.

15 Heywood (1992).

16 Woodcock (1975), p.206. Concurring with the tenor of Woodcock's judgement, Marshall talks of Kropotkin's 'optimistic frame of mind which at times could be almost fatalistic in its confidence in progress'. See Marshall (1992), p.309.

17 Proudhon (1972), p.410.

18 Maximoff (1964), p.249.

19 Miller (1984), p.93.

20 Dolgoff (1973), p.91.

21 Quoted in Guérin (1970), p.22. Saint Vincent de Paul was the founder of many Roman Catholic women's congregations in seventeenth-century France to aid the poor and needy. Guizot was the leader of the conservative constitutional monarchists during the July Monarchy of 1830–48 in France. Talleyrand was a senior French statesman renowned in political circles for his ability to survive. He held high office during the French Revolution, under Napoleon, at the restoration of the Bourbon monarchy, and under King Louis-Philippe.

22 A point that is recognized by Marshall (1992), p.324; and Crowder (1991), p.140.

23 A point acknowledged by Kelly (1982), p.121.

24 Proudhon (1979), p.6.

25 This essay is contained in Marx (1974), pp.334–5.

26 Proudhon's remarks can be found in Edwards (1970), p.237.

27 Kropotkin (1987), p.59.

28 See, for example, Bakunin's *The Knouto-Germanic Empire and the Social Revolution*, in Maximoff (1964), p.65.

29 Ibid., p.153.

30 *Protestation of the Alliance*, in ibid., p.248.

31 Ibid., p.249.

32 A fact perceived by Kropotkin (1995), p.110.

33 Clark (1984), p.129. Emphasis in the original.

34 Bakunin (1990), p.137.

35 Ibid., p.178. Cf. also ibid., p.179.

36 Ibid., p.150.

37 The author is aware of the divisions within the New Right and that there may be fundamental differences between them. For the purposes of this chapter, the New Right is referred to as that movement which took control of the British Conservative Party in the second half of the 1970s.

38 The Manchester school refers to an economic school of thought in England from 1820 to 1850. It was inspired by the political-economic philosophy of *laissez-faire*, and used arguments centred on free trade to reform measures such as the Corn Laws.

39 Joseph and Sumption (1979), pp.100–1.

40 The word quango refers to quasi autonomous non-governmental organizations. Figures released by the UK government in 1993 gave a total number of quangos of 1389. Research by the

University of Essex in the first half of 1994 concluded that a more accurate figure is close to 7000. Despite differences of categorization, quangos cause widespread resentment because of their unaccountable and unelected nature. Consequently, many critics from all political hues have condemned the use of quangos by recent UK governments to subvert and undermine the processes of local democracy.

41 This familiar quotation is drawn from a letter which Acton wrote to Bishop Mandell Creighton, 5 April 1887. Acton was a Liberal historian and moralist who espoused a philosophy of resistance against the evils of the State. He was elected to Parliament in 1859, became a close associate of the Liberal Prime Minister Gladstone, and was raised to the peerage in 1869.

42 See Marshall (1989), pp.127–49.

43 Ibid., p.138.

44 Ibid., p.141.

45 Ibid., p.142.

46 Brown (1988), pp.49–60.

47 Ibid., p.54

48 Leier (1993), p.37.

49 Brown (1988), p.54.

50 Marshall (1989) p.144.

CHAPTER 3

Neither State Nor Market

An Anarchist Perspective on Social Welfare

Steve Millett

In this chapter I outline briefly the development of the Welfare State in Britain, stressing the importance of social control in its evolution. I then look at the evidence regarding the issue of who benefits from the State provision of welfare. I suggest that welfare can only be considered as a function of empowerment, and conclude that not only are participatory alternatives separate from the State a necessity, but that these alternatives offer a possible starting-point for the creation of a Stateless society.

The absorption of all social functions by the State necessarily favoured the development of an unbridled, narrow-minded individualism. In proportion as the obligations towards the State grew in numbers the citizens were evidently relieved from their obligations towards each other.

Peter Kropotkin

The ever-growing power of a soulless political bureaucracy which supervises and safeguards the life of man from the cradle to the grave is putting ever greater obstacles in the way of the solidaric co-operation of human beings and crushing out every possibility of new development.

Rudolf Rocker

Introduction

The twentieth century has been the epoch of the interventionist State. It impinges upon, through monitoring and regulation, most aspects of people's lives. To a large extent this intrusion is justified because people think that the alternative would be worse – they believe the State to be in many respects beneficent. This is particularly true of the State-provision of welfare, and the Welfare State is commonly seen as the crowning achievement of the post-war social democratic consensus.[1] While there was never one clear motive underlying the creation of the various pillars of the Welfare State, its 'progressive' nature – promoting social cohesion, offsetting the worst inequities of capitalism – was part of the rhetoric of Tawney, Titmus, Crosland[2] and others who saw the State as a means of promoting social justice, and the Welfare State as setting Britain on the road to socialism. If not everybody shared the more radical views of the Left, the Welfare State has always had considerable popular support, and many people believe that public expenditure on the social services has produced some form of equality in welfare. Where the Welfare State has been questioned, it has been mainly from the Right, concerned to cut public spending, and to increase the ability of the wealthy to spend their money as they will. However, on closer examination, the Welfare State offers less to those concerned with issues of equality, empowerment and social justice than might at first appear to be the case. State-provided welfare can instead be seen as another tool in the hands of the powerful, a tool which, while perhaps successful as a means of social control, contributes less to issues of equity and justice than many people imagine.

Origins and history

The foundations of the Welfare State

The foundations for today's Welfare State were laid over three hundred years ago when the establishment and consolidation of the nation-state in the late fifteenth and sixteenth centuries brought about increasing legislation aimed at social control. The breakdown of the mutual aid communities of the Middle Ages[3] and rapid population growth threw up new and more worrying problems for the fledgling governments of the sixteenth and seventeenth centuries; as the number of beggars and vagrants rose, concerns about social unrest merged with a moral imperative to stamp out idleness. At first it may seem unreasonable to go back three hundred or so years to begin an investigation of the Welfare State, which is usually assumed to have emerged from the collective experience of the Second World War. In fact, there is a long history of State intervention in welfare provision in Britain, beginning with the first coherent English Poor Law of 1572. The evolution of State welfare policy in Britain from the Tudor period has led one writer to conclude that 'it is not a total anachronism to call [the welfare apparatus], as it had developed by 1700, a welfare state'.[4]

The early Poor Law legislation authorized local parishes to raise revenue for the relief of the poor, while banning most forms of begging and codifying punishments, usually whipping, for vagrancy. In addition, workhouses began to be erected, in greater number after 1610 when their building was made compulsory in every county for 'the keeping, correcting and setting to work . . . of rogues, vagabonds, sturdy beggars, and other idle and disorderly persons'.[5] That the legislators' concern was with issues of morality and public order is clear; while in the late sixteenth century, Parliament began to take an increasingly lenient view of the actions of the élite, legalizing usury, for example, it passed an increasing number of Acts aimed at controlling the manners and social behaviour of the 'lower orders'. 'All this suggests that the machinery of the poor law was not designed as an economic regulator, but as a moral, social and political one'.[6]

It was at this time that the differentiation between the respectable or labouring poor, those unable to find work through no fault of their own, and the idle or dangerous poor developed. The preoccupation with this latter group often led to a degree of paranoia about the threat to stability and order by vagrants, a fear that resulted more from social stigma and the involvement of vagrants in petty crime than in any real threat of riot or rebellion.[7] The social division was exacerbated by the funding of poor relief through local rates which created categories of 'payers' and 'receivers', although the vagaries of the economy meant that the boundary between the two groups was fluid, and many who were payers one day could easily find they were receivers the next.

The development of the contemporary Welfare State

The Tudor and Stuart Poor Laws were eminently suited to small rural communities, and formed the basis for poor relief until the coming of industrialism and the creation of an urban proletariat destroyed the traditional structures of the village community. The demands of capitalism for a controllable pool of human resources found voice in the new class of industrialists and businessmen who were brought to power by the Reform Act of 1832. To them 'The old system of local parish relief was seen as mollycoddling the labourer, sheltering him from the bracing winds of competition and costing the ratepayer dearly to boot'.[8]

The Poor Law Amendment Act of 1834 ushered in a more explicitly punitive regime, centred around the infamous workhouse; but the rapid expansion of the industrial cities created problems of public health and rising crime that forced government intervention with the Public Health Act of 1848, the Police Act of 1856 and, at the turn of the century, an ever increasing body of welfare legislation in the areas of health, education and employment.

By the 1890s, with the precedent having been set by the earlier Acts, increasing pressure from working-class organizations[9] combined with fears about national degeneration had coalesced into various demands for government action. Bismarck had already demonstrated the possibility of integrating the working-class movement within the capitalist system through welfare reforms. But for many, a *fin de siècle* national uncertainty, precipitated by the appalling health of Boer War recruits and Britain's failing economic performance in the face of competition from Germany and the USA, sparked the urge to reform what was seen as an essentially decadent social system.[10]

This drive for increasing State intervention led the Liberal governments of the early twentieth century to pass a series of laws covering many aspects of social welfare: workers' injury compensation; State education and school meals;[11] old age pensions; limitations on the hours children could work; health and unemployment insurance. The extent of these reforms was such that, by 1911, Britain certainly had an embryonic State welfare system. The *reasons* for the creation of this system are less clear, but it has become apparent that it had less to do with philanthropy than has been suggested in the past. On the contrary, recent research has suggested that:

> *The desire to retain as much as possible of the existing capitalist economic system, at a time when it was under increasing pressure from within and without, seems to have been the most important motive in the origins of the Liberal reforms.*[12]

In adapting to the changing nature of capitalism, and consequently increasing the number and degree of State intervention, the governments of the late nineteenth and early twentieth centuries began a new series of assaults on institutions that they perceived as disorderly and not toeing the central line. Education Boards were abolished to be replaced by Local Education Authorities, while the local boards of governors or public assistance centres that attempted more liberal and humane regimes were taken over by central government.[13] The Liberal reforms remained the keystones of State welfare provision until the Second World War, during which all aspects of public life came under the control of the national government.[14] It was this high degree of central control, and the election of a Labour government at the end of the war, that precipitated the next phase in the evolution of the Welfare State.

The post-war Welfare State

It is not accidental that the Welfare State as we know it today came about under the aegis of the Left. Initially there were both pro- and anti-State strands in the Socialist movement, but it was the Statism of the Fabians and Social Democrats that gained the ascendancy. 'Both social democratic reformers and socialist revolutionaries wanted to supplant the anarchy of the market with the rationality of bureaucracy.'[15] Socialism became associated with social management and the struggle for *self*-management became peripheral.[16] Instead, the belief that socialism could be brought about by the rational management of the nation's resources – underpinned by the strategy of mass nationalization of industry – became the dominant idea of the Left in Britain and engendered a belief in the necessity of strong central political control. Although there remained a tension between the different wings of the labour movement until the Second World War, most of the energy of the anti-Statist wing, as exhibited in the syndicalist and Guild Socialist movements of the pre-First World War period, was spent by the 1940s. Labour's manifesto was, by 1945, primarily Fabian Socialism.[17] This signalled the triumph of the expert – scientific, economic and technical as well as political. The technological advances of the war and the bureaucratic structures created under the national government allowed the prospect of a degree of control of society that had previously been undreamed of. Keynesian demand-management seemed to offer a means of controlling the economy and, for the socialists, keeping the capitalists at bay. According to Anthony Crosland, the State could no longer be seen as simply the executive committee of the capitalist class – it was now the (social) State that called the tune.[18] With the post-war boom and the resurgence of an interventionist United States, the possibility of a social–capitalism providing for all arose – a consumer society where the need to promote demand led to a welfare system directed towards supporting consumption. 'The Welfare State had furnished the prerequisites for the regeneration of capitalism, in which it could appear in a new and benevolent guise: no longer the stern taskmaster, but the bringer of all good things.'[19]

Welfare, then, became more all-encompassing, as the State increasingly took on the role of needs-satisfier. Welfare was still administered from on high, and the Welfare State was a strictly top-down institution, but the elements of social control became less clear, even as the working-class districts were bulldozed to make way for an 'expert's' idea of adequate living requirements. The State could, apparently, provide for all. The penalty for this was the unfreedom of the totally administered society; but, as Marcuse points out, '*Geist* and knowledge are no telling arguments against the satisfaction of needs'.[20]

As the post-war boom came to an end, the extravagant claims made of the Welfare State became open to question. The increasing demands put on the social democratic State appeared to be destabilizing it economically, ironically for the same reasons (needs-satisfaction) that initially promised to legitimize it.[21] But while the Welfare State bordered on crisis, the crisis management that was instituted to rescue social democracy, by Labour in the 1970s and continuing under the Conservatives, aimed not at abolishing the Welfare State, but at paring down the offer of needs-satisfaction to certain, more valued members of society. Consequently, the element of social control evident in all forms of social welfare became more apparent, as attempts to cut public spending failed while the State supported increasing wealth-generation aimed at the better-off sections of society (while targeting the less well-off under the guise of a series of moral crusades). This has been particularly evident in the use of benefits as a means to penalize single mothers and reassert the primacy of the role of men as economic providers. The divisiveness of a system that separates welfare providers (in the form of taxpayers) from those in need has become increasingly clear as wealth has become more concentrated: the middle classes have become more entrenched, and the welfare system itself is increasingly viewed as economically unsustainable.

While the element of social control has become increasingly obvious, so has the failure of the Welfare State to live up to the dreams of its creators. It is to this question – of the efficacy of the State as provider of welfare – that I turn to next.

The efficacy of the Welfare State

The Welfare State in Britain is often held up as the primary achievement of the post-war Social Democratic consensus, a move away from the barbarity of naked capitalism that defined the 1930s. Given the reverence accorded the Welfare State, even asking pertinent questions – Exactly how efficacious is the Welfare State?; Has it promoted equality?; Has it affected the distribution of wealth? – can be difficult; and when the questions are asked, finding clear answers is not easy, although there has been significant work done in this area over the last twenty or so years.

One of the difficulties in answering these questions is that of not comparing like with like. The post-war world was in many respects different to the pre-war one, in ways that have already been mentioned. Capitalism was reconstituted as consumerism; industries were nationalized; governments intervened in the economy; State bureaucracies grew; and a technical and professional élite was created, commanding high incomes as well as high prestige. There was undoubtedly an increase in the amount of wealth in the economy, but it is less clear that its distribution was anything to do with the emerging Welfare State. For example, although the bottom 80 per cent of the population increased their share of the wealth by two-and-a-half times between 1924–40 and 1951–6, it is difficult to argue that this was due to the redistributive effects of the Welfare State. Indeed, after this, the figures change very little over the next twenty years, a period when it would be expected that the post-war Welfare State would begin to seriously challenge the distribution of wealth.[22] Le Grand suggests that in Britain in 1980 the share of the national income received by the bottom half of the population had not changed since 1949.[23] In other words, if the standard of living of the poor increased, it was because the cake was bigger, not because they received a greater share of it. The gap between rich and poor did not decrease, and people tended to stay in their place in the social hierarchy, as Lois Bryson puts it '[i]t was as if people were standing on a slowly-moving escalator'.[24] While it would be reasonable to expect some redistributive effects of State-provided welfare, it appears that these were not from the rich to the poor.

Although there seems little doubt of a continuing and significant redistribution of wealth away from the very wealthiest portion of the population to the less wealthy majority of the population, the bottom portions of the population have been relatively unaffected . . . the thrust of wealth redistribution has been from the very wealthiest to the merely wealthy or affluent sections of the population.[25]

It was still the case in 1984 that the richest 10 per cent of the population owned 53 per cent of the marketable wealth, while the poorest 50 per cent owned only 6 per cent.[26]

It is likely that the position of the worst-off in Britain has worsened in the last fifteen or so years – in fact, much evidence is brought forward to show the failure of the Right's claims that a 'trickle down' effect will eventually make everyone better-off. But this criticism is still couched in terms that suggest simply increasing spending on State welfare, without necessarily questioning the nature of the provision of welfare. While it is a tragedy that the number of homeless families increased to over 93,000 and the number of people below Supplementary Benefit level began to approach three million between 1979 and 1985, the most striking statistic is that in 1979, *before* the Conservative government and after thirty years of the Welfare State there were still 56,750 homeless families and 2,090,000 people below Supplementary Benefit level.[27]

In her book *Welfare and the State: Who Benefits?* Lois Bryson carries out an overview of some of the research that has been done into the distribution of State welfare. Looking at a variety of studies that cover not only Britain, but Continental Europe, Scandinavia and Australasia, it is clear that in most areas of State Welfare *the better-off benefit more than the less well-off.* This is particularly true in health and other services, and most markedly in education, described as 'the public provision whose benefits are most systematically related to income'.[28] In health, reports from a variety of sources have consistently shown that in Britain the poor suffer more than the better-off. There are

marked differences in mortality rates between the occupational classes, both sexes and at all ages. At birth and in the first month of life, twice as many babies of unskilled manual parents die as do babies of professional class parents.[29]

In terms of healthcare it has been suggested that the top socio-economic group (professionals) receive up to 40 per cent more NHS expenditure *per ill person* than the bottom group (manual workers).[30] This inequality continues in the field of housing where, even though public provision of housing assists the less well-off, issues of taxation effectively mean the system is biased in favour of not only owner-occupiers, but the wealthiest owner-occupiers.

Le Grand (1982) suggests that this disparity in service use is because of the following:

1. The better-off have more time to utilize services;

2. They are more able to take advantage of extant services (particularly education);

3. They are more likely to be able to get services provided for them and keep those services in the face of cut-backs.

This last point is particularly significant given the attacks on State-provided welfare carried out by governments over the last fifteen or so years. Not only do the poor get comparatively little from the Welfare State, in times of retrenchment they have to struggle to keep what little they have. Bryson reveals that sociology has a name for this process – the Matthew Principle, after the Gospel of Matthew: 'For whosoever hath, to him shall be given, and he shall have more abundance: but whosoever hath not, from him shall be taken away even that he hath'.[31]

Bryson looks not only at service provision, but also at fiscal and occupational assistance. Although she notes that the actual effects of different measures vary from country to country and time to time, she concludes that 'Investigation of the intricacies of taxation systems largely confirms that fiscal welfare, like occupational welfare and most social welfare, conforms to the Matthew Principle. Essentially all three welfare systems entrench the current social hierarchy.'[32] It appears, therefore, that claims that the Welfare State has supported social justice and redistribution of wealth are open to question.[33] There is little evidence to support the widely-held view that the solution to welfare problems can be conceived within the framework of State intervention. Rather, the State consistently acts to maintain existing hierarchies, leaving the poor, as ever, at the bottom of the ladder. This suggests that a genuine attempt to re-organize social welfare may have to be constructed outside of the State; and it is to alternatives to State-provided welfare that I turn next.

Welfare and anarchy

Against the State – Right or Left?
I have so far suggested that the essence of the State provision of welfare is social control, and that the Welfare State fails to achieve what it promises in terms of promoting equality and redistributing wealth. If we accept that State-provided social welfare is an illusion, what are the alternatives? One, commonly put forward by the Right, or the 'Free Marketers', is that the winding down (or, for Libertarians or Anarcho-Capitalists, the abolition) of the State should allow free play of the market mechanism, where every-thing is available to those who have the wealth, with no government

intervention (or even no government). There are numerous reasons for thinking that this state of affairs would be unlikely to provide a satisfactory means of maintaining any form of welfare, since it would in effect simply exacerbate the existing market system, that is, rationing by price.[34] In addition, there is little reason to think that the unrestrained profit motive would create an ecologically sound social and economic system, and present levels of environmental degradation would continue unabated, or more likely worsen, with predictable effects on health.[35]

Another alternative sees the winding down and minimizing of State interests in welfare as accompanied by an increase in user-participation and worker democracy – in other words, a reclaiming of control from the State, often termed 'empowerment'. The issue of empowerment has attracted the attention of many who are sceptical that the solution to the problem of social welfare lies in throwing more money at it. Feminists in particular, but also Greens and others on the Left who are not in awe of the State, have suggested that welfare provision could be dramatically improved by radically altering its priorities, concentrating not on costs and central planning but on *participation*.

> *Participation means involvement of actual and potential users and other citizens in the development, organisation and actual running of services. The corollary of this . . . is a decentralisation and localisation of services. To be a reality participation must be local – at the level of the health centre, the local school, the housing estate, the social services area office, the old people's home.*[36]

In a similar vein, Brian Abel-Smith, one of the first critics of the middle-class bias of welfare distribution, offered this suggestion of the way forward:

> *We would re-build hospitals on modern lines – outpatients' departments or health centres, with a few beds tucked away in the corners. We would close the mental deficiency colonies and build new villas with small wards. . . . We would pull down most of the institutions for old people and provide them with suitable housing. . . . We would provide a full range of occupations at home and elsewhere for the disabled, the aged and the sick.*[37]

This is the first step in the process of releasing welfare from the strait-jacket of social control, and placing it in the hands of the recipient. Strategies for participation already exist – and have existed for many years – though they suffer from trying to function under capitalism and therefore often having to rely on the State for resources. However, there are numerous examples of co-operatives in food distribution, in housing, in manufacturing and service provision; there have been many self-build housing schemes; credit unions and community businesses; neighbourhood councils; tenant action groups; self-help groups and self-help centres; participatory practices in healthcare at general practice and hospital level; experiments in libertarian education; women's refuges and women-only health centres.[38] In addition to all these more formal experiments, there is, of course, the reality that the majority of caring in society is done outside of the State – usually by women. In many cases (if not most) the carers are underpaid if not unpaid, and the resources available to them are limited. Nevertheless, often the sort of environment generated by these formal and informal welfare arrangements is beneficial in itself; it is not a poor relation of an expensive State-provided alternative. This applies in particular to healthcare, where the old, the mentally ill, and the terminally sick are often considerably happier in the community or in their families than removed to an institution and dependent on the opinions and actions of 'experts'. It is also likely that, as well as the benefits accruing to the person who is being cared for, the breakdown of the institutions helps those who work in them, for as Colin Ward notes, 'the servants of the institution are as much its victims as the inmates'.[39]

This participatory and decentralist approach is one that appeals to anarchists, who for the last hundred or so years have articulated a critique of the increasing power of the State from just such a perspective. However, although this approach would be one that anarchists would favour, and it is likely it would be a considerable improvement on the centralized, expert-biased systems we have at the moment, there are reasons to be sceptical about the continuing interest of the State that many commentators, even those in favour of decentralization, still favour.

The case against the State

The first point to raise is that the State is not static – its present position has been attained through the swallowing up of local initiatives and the strengthening of the positions of the élite.[40] There seems to be little evidence that any form of State can escape this dynamic of destructiveness. Even a defender of the Welfare State, looking favourably at Sweden in the 1970s, is forced to note cuts in the number of local government units in the interests of 'administrative efficiency', a concomitant decrease in the opportunities for direct participation in local government, and the growth of an '"Establishment", a new élite enjoying high positions, income and status deriving from their authority in the power blocs they represent'.[41]

However, anarchists criticize the State as much for what it represents as for what it is. The State is singled out for particular attack because it is the exemplar of the top-down organization, based on power relationships, hierarchies and institutionalized violence. And it is the existence of power relationships and the systems of domination that they support, that anarchists have consistently attacked, their ultimate aim being the creation of a society – an 'anarchy' – in which such relationships have been abolished.[42] These power relationships are not embodied solely in the State but permeate the rest of society. In seeing the State as not something unique but rather as the supreme manifestation of a system of power relations, anarchists have recognized that the only way to dismantle the State is to construct other relationships[43] – or, conversely, that there can be no 'free' society with the State since its existence justifies the existence of other power relationships in society. So for anarchists, ideas of participation and decentralization, however relevant or significant they might be, are insufficient in themselves; rather, they are the key elements in describing *alternatives* to the State.

Any definition of society should include an ability to take care of the welfare of its members, not just those members who have a privileged place in the social hierarchy. Welfare should be an intrinsic part of any society, therefore, not simply a functional extra. This requires that society is organized first and foremost to provide welfare. What anarchism calls for is the re-absorption of the provision of welfare into the daily lives of the citizens of the community. Welfare thus becomes not simply a function – something provided by a system or the workers in a system – but part of the everyday life of the community and the citizens. As such, it also becomes a way for individuals to develop themselves. It is a learning process, a process of growth which allows us to accept the old, the young, the sick, the dying in society, not cast them into institutions out of sight of the relatively able-bodied and young. It is also a learning process in that we develop knowledge about our own welfare needs, and ways of satisfying them, rather than having to defer to experts and institutions. Direct action in social welfare is the central element of any future liberatory and ecological society, and the central tenet of any movement wishing to create such a society:

> [Direct Action] is the means whereby each individual awakens to the hidden powers within herself and himself, to a new sense of self-confidence and self-competence; it is the means whereby individuals take control of society directly. . . . Direct action, in short, is not a 'tactic' that can be adopted or discarded in terms of its 'effectiveness' or 'popularity'; it is a moral principle, an ideal, indeed, a sensibility. It should imbue every aspect of our lives and behaviour and outlook.[44]

It is this perspective that Statism undermines, in creating the psychological as well as material conditions for the dominion of some and subservience of others, and that is why the existence of the State is incompatible with a welfare society.

Social welfare and the anarchist alternative

Despite this assertion, that the existence of the State is incompatible with a welfare society, it is reasonable to question whether such a Stateless society would indeed be able to provide adequately for the welfare of its members. There are some issues which would appear to suggest the necessity of some form of State body, such as:

1. The scale of the welfare problem;

2. The need for large-scale co-ordination of services;

3. The need for some form of professionalism and expertise.

However, these areas can also be seen as part of the anarchist alternative. Although the welfare problem is huge, it is in many respects the result of the current economic system, and no amount of State welfare is going to alleviate the problems as long as this system exists. This is particularly true of the already mentioned disparities in welfare that exist in class-divided societies, and the potentially apocalyptic effect that capitalism has on the environment. In addition, if State welfare provision is equivalent in most cases to social control and if social control is the antithesis of genuine welfare, then, although the idea of massive State aid is seductive, it must in the long-term be seen as counter-productive: as simply increasing dependency and forcing people to accept welfare on someone else's terms. Many issues of welfare can be resolved not at the level of the State, but at the level of the individual or the community. The enormous scale of human welfare need can instead be seen as an aggregation of smaller needs, best served at a much more localized level.

Anarchists are not against organization or co-ordination, but suggest alternatives that do not require a State – commonly a confederation of (rural and urban) communes. These communes would allow the possibility of maximum control by the population over their environment, while a confederation of communes would deal with issues over a wider geographical area.[45] Assuming that these mutual-aid communities would function to provide, as essential, basic subsistence at the very least, the issue of minimum standards of provision becomes less of an issue – particularly if all members of the community or other functional group have equal access to the means of welfare. Where resource-differences still existed, they could be dealt with through the confederated co-ordinating bodies.

Professionalism, expertise and technology[46] are areas that are very difficult to imagine outside of the framework provided by capitalism and the State, and a scepticism towards these areas as they are presently conceived suggests to many people an atavistic position that anarchists do not generally hold. Anarchism has frequently been perceived as harking back to a 'golden', pre-industrial age, and there are elements of this in the approach of some anarchists; but in most cases this criticism is unfair. It is true that anarchists have looked for historical examples to demonstrate the possibility of their suggested alternatives, and the evidence has often shown that certain alternative, more 'anarchistic', ways of organization are not in any way against 'human nature', but that they have flourished at certain times in most cultures. The co-option of the tools of reason by the agents of capitalism has resulted in a growing degree of hostility to the course of the development of science and technology – not surprising given the arrogance of the scientific establishment; the consistent application of science to produce better ways of killing more people; and, overall, the increasing separation of science and technology away from ordinary people and into the hands of an élite that can, directly or otherwise, use them for control and profit.

Despite this, it is important to recognize that in criticizing the use or application of something, a particular discovery, a method, a type of work – it is not always necessary to extend the criticism to the discovery, method or whatever, *in itself*. Admittedly, the dividing line is not always clear, as scientific and technological advances rarely proceed with issues of ethics as a central concern. However, in many ways science and technology, as the tools of reason and in an ethical and ecological context, are the best way humanity has to solve many of the problems it faces. While prevention is better than cure, and many illnesses that afflict us could well be eliminated if we lived in a more ecologically harmonious way, this would not dispense with the need for some medical care. Informal arrangements and various forms of 'alternative' medicine would no doubt be used extensively, but it would not necessarily be the case that all forms of conventional medicine would have to be discarded. It is also possible that informal arrangements may not always be the best way to deal with people's problems – they may sometimes prefer healers, counsellors or advisors that they are not familiar with. This suggests that there may still be the need for specialists in certain fields, and for certain people to have high levels of technical expertise.[47] This in turn suggests the need for institutions to train and examine these people. And, since the liberation of learning does not automatically mean the abolition of institutions of academic and practical expertise, but a reordering of these along non-hierarchical, non-authoritarian lines, these institutions (which could be organized along the lines of guilds or syndicates)[48] would not require experts to be deferred to, nor the entrenchment of bureaucracies, since there could be various countervailing structures to offset this tendency.[49] Of course, there may not be a need for many specialists of this sort, but the aim of anarchism is to offer a realistic alternative to capitalism and the State, and people are not going to suddenly become indestructible, perfectly balanced, or totally reasonable!

Here to there
The idea that we can only break down the State by constructing other relationships gives a crucial importance to welfare initiatives, because they are the means by which the prevailing hierarchies can be challenged on the basis of principles of mutual aid and cooperation. Certainly the radical feminist tradition considers that one reason for separatist women-only welfare provision is 'to develop a new relationship between welfare providers and clients based on shared knowledge and power within non-

hierarchical, democratic welfare structures, which could again challenge conventional, hierarchical welfare institutions'.[50] In the past, experiments and projects such as those mentioned briefly above have often been undermined by a lack of political vision. Where these groups come together in the face of a specific problem – as is often the case with community activism – their primary function is to attempt to obtain something from the constituted authorities. They consequently disperse when these aims are met (or not), and rarely attempt to radically alter the structure of service provision in the community. Attempts at more long-term projects may, on the other hand, lack a radical social critique, which can undermine their ability to liaise with other projects to create a genuine countervailing power. In both cases the groups need to be aware not only of the potential for change, but of the libertarian tradition of which they are a part.[51] A more widespread, over-arching social and political agenda would help begin this process, as has been suggested by some Canadian activists:

> It is important for the various citizens' organizations to acquire a comprehensive vision of society and for them to tie their specific struggles to this. A food coop, a housing coop, an ecology group, etc. . . . could form a new social network, thereby laying the foundations of a new society. The multiplication of citizens' initiatives opting for a collective mode of operation is an indispensable objective if we are to ensure that the working classes take their neighbourhood, their city, into their own hands.[52]

This approach would offer the possibility of developing new modes of action and theory within the context of a genuine attempt to negate State power. The difficulties involved in this kind of activity are enormous, not least in the provision of adequate resources, but with State-provided welfare increasingly seen as a burden on tax payers, the receivers of welfare may, in the long term, have little choice anyway. It should, though, given the limitations of the Statist option, be an alternative accepted with more than just resignation; rather, it could be the means of beginning to create a genuine non-Statist welfare-community, free of dependence on politicians, bureaucrats and experts. To quote Kropotkin again:

> Either the State for ever, crushing individual and local life, taking over in all fields of human activity . . . Or the destruction of States, and new life starting again in thousands of centres on the principle of the lively initiative of the individual and groups and that of free agreement. The choice lies with you![53]

Conclusion

It is ironic for anarchists that the failure of the Left to eliminate capitalism has at the same time led to the growth of the State; autonomy and empowerment are achieved no more through a bureaucrat's pen than through the 'unseen hand' of market forces. As long as welfare is the preserve of the State, it will be used as a form of social control; and, as Kropotkin eloquently described in the quote at the beginning of this chapter, handing over our welfare to the State undermines our innate social capacities and allows the pretence that we are atomic individuals, dependent on no-one – 'self-made', as the phrase has it. This is a myth – it is obviously a myth as regards the Welfare State since it is the wealthy that benefit the most from the State provision of welfare. Somewhere in this mythology of dependence and independence something essentially human – our capacity for caring and co-operation – is lost. The failure of the State to provide social welfare should not be seen as undermining the idea of social welfare itself, but of invalidating the role of the State; welfare is inextricably linked to empowerment, which is why State-provided welfare is always going to have minimal success. At the same time we should be under no illusions as to what the effects on the poor will be of the paring down of what State provision there is in the name of the market: without a viable alternative, the market simply means sink or swim, and to sink means poverty, destitution, homelessness, even death. The attempt to free welfare from the State cannot be left to the free marketeers of the Right. The need for a democratic and participatory alternative to the Welfare State has never been more urgent.

Notes

1. This chapter is written from an Anglocentric perspective. The uniqueness of the British experience does not detract from the overall point that I make since all Western Welfare States have developed along similar paths; see Pierson (1991), Chapter 4 for an overview of this development. Although no specific mention is made of either the Third World or the former Eastern Bloc countries, the underlying principle – that welfare problems (including poverty, hunger and overpopulation) result from disempowerment – remains the same. See for example Lappé and Collins (1988).

2. See George and Wilding, (1985), Chapter 4.

3. Kropotkin (1993).

4. Slack (1988), p.206.

5. Quoted in Slack (1988), p.128.

6. Ibid., p.130. Oxley (1974) suggests that the main purpose of the old Poor Law was 'to solve the problem of unemployment and its consequential evils by setting the able-bodied poor to work', p.102.

7. Slack (1988), p.105.

8. Hadley and Hatch (1981), p.8.

9. It has been suggested that during the nineteenth century a significant portion of the unorganized working class were hostile to the idea of welfare reforms perceiving, not unreasonably, State interference in social issues as another form of policing (Hay, 1975, pp.26–7).

10. See for example, Sydney Webb and the National Efficiency Movement, and Joseph Chamberlain and Tariff Reform and Imperial Preference (Newton and Porter, 1988).

11. A significant element in the history of social welfare and social control is compulsory State education. Anarchists have long seen the liberation of learning as vital to the development of a libertarian

society and have not only criticized authoritarian educational forms, but have also acted to create alternative, libertarian educational environments. Consequently, this is a very large subject area and because of limited space, I have avoided mentioning specifically the growth of State education. I would direct readers to John Shotton's *No Master High or Low: Libertarian Education & Schooling 1890–1990* (1993) which, as well as being an excellent resource, offers evidence to support my thesis regarding the connection between State welfare and social control.

12. Hay (1975), p.62.

13. Digby (1989); Hadley and Hatch (1981).

14. Hadley and Hatch (1981), p.12.

15. Kerans, Drover and Williams (1988), p.38.

16. Hadley and Hatch (1981), p.13.

17. Ibid., p.15.

18. George and Wilding (1985), p.78.

19. Blackwell and Seabrook (1985), p.82.

20. Marcuse (1972), p.53. *Geist* is best translated as [human] *spirit*.

21. This apparent 'contradiction' has been analysed by several neo-Marxists (see Pierson (1991)).

22. Figures from Rubinstein (1986), p.41.

23. Le Grand (1982), p.41.

24. Bryson (1992), p.9.

25. Rubinstein (1986), p.97.

26. Wilson (1989), p.18.

27. Figures from Walker (1987), pp.24–5.

28. Bryson (1992), p.128.

29. *Inequalities in Health*, DHSS (1980), c.i. Wilson (1989), p.14.

30. Le Grand (1982), p.126.

31. Bryson (1992), p.134.

32. Ibid., p.154.

33. Other criticisms have been levelled at the Welfare State which, although important, I am unable to include for reasons of space. It has been attacked by feminists and anti-racists for the way it discriminates against women and ethnic minorities (Pierson, 1991, Chapter 3), while many Greens have criticized the consumer-oriented approach of the Welfare State, with its reliance on economic growth and large-scale technology, the promotion of an individualistic ethos, and its gross anthropocentrism (George and Wilding, 1994, Chapter 7). Also significant is the degree to which the economies, and hence the Welfare States, of the wealthier nations are supported by the exploitation of the less developed areas of the world.

34. Fotopoulos (1993), p.45.

35. For a brief introduction to this perspective, and a discussion of both left and right anti-Statist views of sustainable development, see Albrecht (1994).

36. George and Wilding (1985), p.143.

37. Brian Abel-Smith (1958) quoted in Ward (1973), p.124.

38. There is a considerable amount of published work on the sort of experiments mentioned here. As an introduction to the area, and for some examples, see Hadley and Hatch (1981), Ward (1973), Dale and Foster (1986), Hain (1976), and Shotton (1993).

39. Ward (1973), p.123.

40. This has been described as the Dialectic of Statism: 'the fact that the institutionalisation of the privileges of bureaucrats who control the State apparatus will create such powerful interests that it will eventually corrode the organs of self-management, rather than the other way around' (Fotopoulos, 1993, p.29).

41. Furniss and Tilton (1977), p.150.

42. John Clark comments: 'The most convincing anarchist theories, while accepting the noncoercive, nongovernmental, and, of course, nonstatist nature of anarchy, deduce further characteristics of a society that has abolished domination. Examples often mentioned by anarchists include economic,

social, racial, sexual, and generational equality, mutual aid, cooperation, and communalism' (Clark, 1984, p.14).

43. The most succinct statement of this position is the much-used quote of Gustav Landauer: 'The State is not something that can be destroyed by a revolution, but is a condition, a certain relationship between human beings; we destroy it by contracting other relationships, by behaving differently to one another' quoted in Marshall (1992) p.411, from Lunn (1973).

44. Bookchin (1980), p.48.

45. This is a significant part of the anarchist approach to social organization, and even a cursory overview of the subject would require more space than is available. Examples can be found in Ward (1973), Kropotkin (1995), Bookchin (1992), and Purchase (1994).

46. Murray Bookchin has argued for the liberatory potential of 'appropriate' technology since the 1960s, e.g. Bookchin (1974). For a more critical view of technology, see Zerzan and Carnes (1988).

47. Since anarchists have been critical of illegitimate authority, they have often considered what authority is legitimate. Recognizing the important difference between *authoritative* and *authoritarian*, they have generally concluded that it is legitimate to defer to someone's superior knowledge or experience in specific circumstances, but this should not entail revering that person, or suspending the critical faculty. See Bakunin (1990), pp.32–3; Godwin (1976), pp.237–48.

48. A *guild* is an organization of a particular craft or profession which flourished in Europe in the Middle Ages. They have often been seen as 'agents of social solidarity and economic morality' (Black, 1984, p.8) in the face of the development of capitalism, and inspired the Guild Socialist movement that developed in Britain at the turn of the century. *Syndicate* comes from the French for trade union, but specifically refers to the revolutionary

labour movement that flourished primarily in France and the Mediterranean countries in the late nineteenth and early twentieth centuries. For an introduction, see Miller (1984), Chapter 9.

49. The anarchist insistence on attempting to eliminate power relations and hierarchies has led to various suggestions for alternative means of decision-making – most commonly cited is the direct democracy of the Athenian model; Murray Bookchin is the most recent exponent of this idea (Bookchin, 1986; 1992). Less specifically, but at least of equal importance, is the need for the widest possible dissemination of knowledge as a counter-balance to the creation of opaque spheres of expertise. Bakunin was acutely aware of the potential for a scientific or technical élite to wield power; to counter this, he suggested that 'it is necessary to dissolve the special social organisation of the *savants* by general instruction, equal for all in all things, in order that the masses, ceasing to be flocks led and shorn by privileged priests, may take into their own hands the direction of their destinies' (Bakunin, 1973). Such an approach may seem unlikely to succeed in an era of increasing specialization and technical complexity; these factors do not have to be taken for granted, however, and the dissemination of knowledge could (and perhaps should) accompany a decrease in such complexity.

50. Dale and Foster (1986), p.156.

51. This point is not new. In 1976 in Britain, during a surge in community activism that had begun in the 1960s, it was argued that if they were to develop a new ideology, community activists needed to be aware that they were linked to the radical libertarian tradition of Kropotkin, Proudhon, and the Diggers (Hebditch, 1976, p.64).

52. From the journal *Le Q-lotté*, in Roussopoulos, (1982), p.233.

53. Kropotkin (1987), p.60.

CHAPTER 4

In Defence of Radical Direct Action

Reflections on Civil Disobedience, Sabotage and Nonviolence[1]

Lindsay Hart

This chapter examines the political activity of 'direct action'. Using both academic and personal sources it illustrates how certain meanings of direct action have been prioritized in academic and mass media discourses. These meanings are challenged and a core notion of direct action is proposed which enables a clearer understanding of this phenomenon to be made. Ideas of violence and nonviolence are examined, and accepted notions of the legitimacy of specific tactics and requirements of direct action are challenged. An argument for a more radical concept of direct action is made that includes the justification of sabotage and the countering of the idea that activists are obliged to accept the legal consequences of their disobedience. The use of direct action is situated within the New Social Movements (NSMs), and the example of direct actions used in the environmental movement is used to show the tensions between direct action and anarchist principles.

Introduction

'Direct action' has had a strong impact on the political landscape in the last twenty years. On one level the democratization of a wide range of countries through civil resistance, as has occurred, for example, in Eastern Europe, the Philippines, and South Africa, has demonstrated that such resistance can lead to national political revolution.[2] On another level, the high-profile direct action activities of such groups as Greenpeace, Chipko Andolan, Chico Mendes' rubber tappers and Earth First! have shown that specific problems, in these cases to do with environmental and development issues, can be challenged and changed (to some degree) by the use of direct action tactics.[3] Within the context of anarchism, direct action has a long tradition. Over the last thirty years anarchists have been involved in many of the so-called New Social Movements (NSMs), such as

Feminism, Environmentalism, Peace and Animal Liberation. The direct action that has developed within these movements has often had a distinctly anarchist flavour, with decentralist and non-hierarchical organizational structures and direct democratic decision-making forming part of the way that many campaigns have been conducted.

The direct action that has been engaged in by the above NSMs has challenged the ideas and the institutionalized norms of State and society regarding participation in the political process. Such norms have sometimes been reasserted in a draconian fashion: for example, the introduction of the Criminal Justice Act in Britain in 1994 severely limits the character of legal protest.

Illegal tactics have been used as part of direct action strategies performed within the above NSMs. Civil disobedience, for example, has been used widely in most of these movements. Although anarchists theoretically have no special problem with the illegality of these tactics due to their rejection of the State, I believe that they do have a responsibility to argue for the justifiability of their law-breaking. While convincing more people of the value of anarchism's tenets is a necessary task for anarchists, to attempt to do this while justifying one's law-breaking can often leave one trying to argue complex ideas within the opinion spaces of Sound Bite City! Tactically it is frequently far better to argue for the justification of one's present actions within the present political context than to argue for the dissolution of the whole of the theoretical underpinnings of the modern world.

Having said this, justifying one's law-breaking is not an easy matter in itself. Common among activists is the inability to adequately and clearly do just that. It is not obvious to many people why breaking the law is justifiable, even for the 'good' ends that it is undoubtedly and frequently used for. Despite this I believe that a radical stance must be made on the issue of justified law-breaking that is in accord with an anarchist political position. This will be my focus in the second part of the chapter, using the environmental movement as a particular example.

Constructing direct action

Notions of direct action are contested in a number of arenas of social and political life. Academia, the State, the mass media, activists, and the public all mould and manipulate notions of the character and legitimacy of direct action. Terrorist bombing campaigns and letter writing have both been identified as forms of direct action, but the inclusion of such extremes of political activity within one term is obviously not a recipe for clarity, either for describing such phenomena or attempting to argue for or against their legitimacy. It is therefore necessary to clarify what direct action is and to understand what political activities form the core of such an idea.

I will take the core notion of direct action as being the idea that a person or group of people act to achieve a particular social or political goal without primarily mediating that action through the formal processes and structures of the State and economic relations. Thus workers who strike unofficially, homeless people who squat in empty properties, campaigners who perform civil disobedient acts, and people who organize co-ops can all be said to have performed direct actions. Such a notion does not exclude the fact that violence may be a part of some direct actions. Therefore it is also necessary to distinguish between direct action and nonviolent direct action (NVDA). These are issues that I comment on further below.

To refine the characterization of direct action, it is important to distinguish between two main groups: protest and non-protest direct action. Co-ops are an example of non-protest direct action and civil disobedience is an example of protest direct action. Furthermore, within the category of protest direct action it is necessary to distinguish between protests such as fasting that are legal, and protests such as blockading a road that are illegal. My focus in this chapter is on illegal protest direct action.

Violence and direct action

The importance of examining assumptions regarding violence and nonviolence cannot be over-emphasized in the discussion of direct action and its relevance to anarchism. Unfortunately I do not have the space here to go into detail about the issues involved. I will, however, map out some of the points that I regard as being significant in any subsequent debate.

The notion that violence is predicated on the use of physical force is untenable as Galtung and Harris have both shown.[4] Instead, the criterion of harm, either caused through intention, negligence or recklessness, would seem to offer the most useful way of describing acts of violence. In addition, harm does not have to be only physical but can also be psychological, and there are good arguments for the idea that violence can also be structural.[5] It is evident from history that the greatest direct violence has been perpetrated by established authorities and not by those who have sought revolutionary aims. Moreover, although anarchists are often regarded as some of the worst perpetrators of political violence, the evidence does not support such a view. As Marshall states:

> In fact, anarchists have contributed far less to the sum of human violence than nationalists, monarchists, republicans, socialists, fascists, and conservatives, not to mention the Mafia, organised crime, and banditry. They have never organised indiscriminate slaughter that is war or practised genocide as governments have. They have never coolly contemplated the complete nuclear annihilation of the earth as nuclear scientists, generals and presidents have. They have never adopted a deliberate policy of terror in power as Robespierre, Stalin, or Pol Pot did.[6]

Academics and direct action: a case of indirect understanding.

Academic work on direct action has been strongly influenced by and mostly focused on the civil disobedience campaigns that have occurred mainly in Northern countries during this century, such as the anti-war protests against the conflict in Vietnam, the campaigns against nuclear weapons in 1960s and 1980s, and Civil Rights' struggles in the USA and elsewhere since the 1950s. The exception to this Northern bias has been the focus on the Gandhi-inspired *satyagraha* campaigns in India and beyond.

However, there is a conflict among perpetrators and theorists of direct action, which stems from the problem of defining exactly what constitutes violence or not in direct action activities. The issues here concern individual and collective choices, personal and institutional violence, violence against people or property, violence as defence or offence, and so on. I will deal with these as they come up in the following discussion.

The tactic of direct action that I primarily want to focus upon here is that of 'ecotage'.[7] I would define ecotage as:

> *An act that deliberately contravenes a law; aims to stop, frustrate, or slow down some process or act that the actor believes will harm or damage the environment; is an act of protest; and damages or destroys property of those who are the focus of the protest.*

Ecotage involves such acts as tree-spiking, damaging machinery and pulling up survey stakes.[8] There is, however, no evidence so far that intentional harm has been caused by such activities despite the mistaken views of some prominent writers in the field.[9] The incident that has formed the basis for much of the rhetoric defining ecotage as intentionally harmful took place in 1987, at a mill in Cloverdale, California, when a saw operator was injured by flying fragments of the bandsaw he was using when it hit a nail in a log. Foreman (1991) who provides the only comprehensive account of the incident, has stated that no evidence has ever been presented that implicates an Earth First! activist or other environmentalist; the prime suspect of the local Sheriff's office was a Republican who owned land next to the logging site; the spiked tree was not an old-growth redwood tree but a second-growth one (environmentalists usually campaign against the cutting of old-growth forests); the spiked tree was spiked after it had been felled (the whole purpose of spiking a tree from an environmentalist's point of view is to *prevent* felling); subsequently, the incident was revealed to be an issue of mill safety and not dangerous tree-spiking through evidence given by the *victim himself.*[10]

Ecotage has, however, even been equated with terrorism in some circles. Any reasonable critical analysis of the concept of terrorism indicates that its essential aspect is that it aims to engender fear through the intentional killing, maiming or serious injury of people. Such actions are therefore obviously distinct from the activities of eco-saboteurs who merely damage property. To deliberately equate the two types of activity is therefore delusive and undermines considered debate on these subjects.[11] As Roselle, an environmental activist, states, 'To use the word 'terrorism' for monkeywrenching [ecotage] is to totally cheapen the real meaning of what terrorism is all about and what people do when they are really desperate'.[12] He goes on to argue, in relation to the heated debate about tree-spiking that has taken place in the USA, that if eco-saboteurs were terrorists they would be 'spiking' the people responsible for environmental destruction and not the trees.

The misrepresentation of ecotage as terrorism in academic texts reveals a belief in the absolute sanctity of property similar to that which pervades the legal institutions of the State. However, value systems are not absolute. Instead actions (such as the destruction of property for political ends) must be considered in relation to their immediate and wider context. I argue later on that sabotage in some cases is a legitimate tactic.

The State's response

The belief in the judicial system in Britain as the fair arbiter of justice has, over the last few years, been significantly undermined. This has been due to exposure of a number of underhand methods that have been used to undermine the effectiveness and legitimacy of protests and to adversely affect the morale of protesters by the police and prosecution system. Some of the methods used against those engaged in environmental direct action have included: arrests that are made where no charges are made later; trivial cases being brought to court which are very often dismissed immediately or are overturned on appeal;[13] the imposition of excessively restrictive bail conditions;[14] and the ignoring of illegal actions performed by people other than those involved in the protest. In addition, members of other protest groups have suffered the imposition of sentences disproportionate to the offence.[15]

It would be difficult not to conclude that the first three methods (arrest with no charge, trivial cases, excessive bail conditions) are cynical attempts to frighten, inconvenience, and exclude from further protest those activists who are arrested and/or charged with an offence; that the penultimate example demonstrates that all are not equal before the law and therefore cannot have recourse to it or protection by it; and that the last example is an effort to create a notion of deterrence based on the excessive severity of potential consequences. These situations illustrate the fact that protesters are seen to be guilty of transgressing a political rather than a necessarily legal order, and punitive action of various sorts can legitimately be imposed on them outside any formal process of justice.

Some academics' views of the position of the police in environmental protest is naïve.[16] They follow the orthodox model that the police are neutral observers who are present to uphold the law impartially. Evidence from my own personal experience and others who have studied this issue demonstrates that the orthodox model is simplistic and untrue:

> *A loose alliance of activists had gathered together from all over the world to protest at the 50th anniversary of the World Bank's inauguration in September 1994 in Madrid. One of those actions was a banner-demonstration beside the road that led to the conference centre where the World Bank's AGM was to be held. I was part of a group of people holding a very long banner which read 'Fifty years is enough!' This banner was to be carried across the road to blockade the passage of those who were going to the conference centre. At a predetermined signal, we all marched across the road and blocked the dual carriageway. The Spanish police were quick to react: a large contingency of jump-suited officers were after all only fifty yards away. They had been taken by surprise and rushed across to where we blocked the road. Their tactics were very direct and violent. The officer that approached me attempted a forearm punch to my face, which fortunately I saw coming and pulled away from. He then proceeded to push me back to the pavement and at the same time to kick my shins, which were the visible part of my legs below the banner. I just stared at this officer and demanded that he look at me if he was going to injure my legs. I couldn't tell whether he knew what I said because I spoke in English, but I repeated that demand a number of times while he kicked my legs. At no time until the very end of our encounter did he look me in the eye. Although my legs hurt a lot, I felt powerful in this situation. Other people suffered similar unprovoked violence. Responses to it varied, such as shouts and screams of outrage, but no-one fought back physically. When we had been pushed back onto the pavement and the situation had been assessed to be under control by the officer in charge, the officer who'd kicked me looked at me and I repeated my demand. He said something in Spanish, but it had no force to it. Within a minute or two he had been told to return to his vehicle by the commanding officer. I will never know how my reaction to his violence affected this man. I just know that in that particular situation it was not the person wielding the fist and boot that was the one who felt powerful.*

The media's response

The construction of the notion of direct action is primarily mediated through the discourses of the mass media. The views of politicians, the police, the judiciary, the activists and sometimes even the general public are reported via newspapers, television and radio. The mass media, however, are not merely reporters of news but obviously interpret, modify, edit, and construct discourses that can be as much political actions in themselves as the actions and words that they report on.[17]

The mass media have constructed notions of direct action in a number of ways. For example, John Vidal in the *Guardian* has been openly supportive through his investigative reportage of direct actions, most recently in the case of the campaign against the Newbury bypass. Other journalists, such as Greg Swift of the *Daily Mail*, have tried to dismiss the arguments made by those involved in direct action at road protests by characterizing them as 'dole scroungers' and as constantly high on drink and drugs, and by revealing the 'squalor' of the protest camps. Others such as John Harlow of the *Sunday Times* have reported unsubstantiated allegations of 'terrorist' activities.[18] Harlow's (3/7/94) article is particularly lurid, claiming that 'extremists' have infiltrated the 'genuine' environmental movement and are intent on using any methods, including harming people, to achieve their aims.

Although there is a tendency for the institutionalized media to give negative coverage to Earth First! and other direct action groups, this is not necessarily a fixed outcome. It is also by means of the mass media that these issues have achieved such a high profile in the UK in recent years. It is also true that in some cases all publicity can be good publicity. For instance, a Gallup survey in 1995 showed that those members of the public who *approve* of blockading traffic rose by 70 per cent over the period 1984–1995.

The unreliability of the mainstream media has however also galvanized many people into taking another form of direct action through the production of 'underground' news-sheets, papers, magazines and videos.[19] Such publications, of course, do have their own agendas and some have their own sensationalistic style of reportage such as the *Class War* paper, but most provide an alternative source of information about direct action campaigns and ideas that contrasts favourably with the viewpoints of the mostly right-wing press.

Forms of protest

Three styles of nonviolent direct action that are common to many campaigns and which are currently being used within the environmental movement are: 'bearing witness', 'obstruction' and 'mass movement'.[20]

'Bearing witness': symbolism, media and self-evident wrongs

Bearing witness as a form of direct action has a long history as part of the Quaker tradition. It has a strong spiritual element regarding the importance of observing injustice wherever it occurs and is used to dramatic effect by groups such as Greenpeace. As Wapner states:

> *When Greenpeace confronts whalers on the high seas or blocks railway cars carrying toxic substances or plugs up industrial discharge pipes, it is attesting to what it believes is ecological injustice. Greenpeace is trying to create an image of ecological abuse which can be broadcast through the media to the widest possible audience. The idea is to invite the public to bear witness, to enable people throughout the world to know about ecological dangers and try to pique their sense of outrage.*[21]

The positive reaction to such acts of 'bearing witness' by Greenpeace has been substantial, with the issues involved receiving extensive media attention and some government and industry response. Moreover the high profile of these actions and the explicit adherence to an ethos of nonviolence have increased the acceptability of direct action in the public's mind.[22]

However, bearing witness, although it has its political uses, must be regarded by anarchists as limited, due to the fact that it relies disproportionately for its effectiveness on the mass media to communicate the message that the individual or small group of activists are bearing witness to. It is quite likely that media reports of actions may not be favourable to the aims of the group involved.[23] Furthermore, merely showing a wider public the (supposedly) self-evident wrong through bearing witness to it may be a necessary part of a campaign for change, but it is only really effective as part of a broader whole. There is also a problem that some organizations who practise this tactic rely on a small group of 'élite' activists to 'witness' the injustice on behalf of everyone else.

Obstruction: bulldozers, tree-houses and D-locks

Obstruction, like bearing witness, has a worthy tradition. The core idea of this type of direct action is to thwart or obstruct those involved in the action or process that is objected to. The tactics used may include various types of civil disobedience such as blockades and the occupation of buildings. In the environmental movement the actions of Earth First! against the felling of old-growth forests in the USA and the building of roads in the UK, for example, have involved this type of direct action.[24]

The roads protests of the 1990s in the UK have also seen a series of increasingly innovative tactics being used by groups such as Earth First! These have included locking oneself to heavy machinery with strong bicycle D-locks, cementing oneself into rooms of condemned houses, building houses in trees on proposed road routes, and sitting down in front of and inside bulldozers. Arguably, these forms of direct action have been instrumental in the cancellation of many development projects due to changing public opinion. Again there is the risk that such activities may only be carried out by an 'élite' group of activists, with the possibility that other, less glamorous activities become devalued in the eyes of the activists and the wider public.

Direct action by mass movements: people, power and participation

The style of direct action in the above two examples is performed by a relatively small number of people. Mass movements, however, ideally involve such large numbers of people that the law, policy or activity objected to is overturned or stopped by the weight of numbers involved. Such campaigns as the Civil Rights movements in the USA, Gandhi's campaign of national liberation in India, and the anti-Poll Tax campaign in Britain are all are examples of mass movements that have primarily used direct action as a means to political and social change.

Mass movements of direct action with regard to environmental issues have so far only occurred in countries where the issue has been one of immediate survival rather than one of longer-term ethical or political beliefs. For example, the Chipko and Narmada Bachao Andolans in India and the Forest People's alliance in Amazonia have campaigned against deforestation and dam construction using nonviolent direct action despite facing extensive repression and violence themselves.[25] These campaigns have met with some success in changing environmental policy both within the countries themselves and within transnational funding organizations such as the World Bank and IMF.

Nonviolence

In the current debate about nonviolence and violence within groups involved in direct action, the rhetorical contest between the 'fluffies' and the 'spikies' mirrors those which have occurred in most of the social change movements this century. The debate as to the most effective and the most ethical means to achieve one's goals draws on a wide range of sources: from Mahatma Gandhi and Martin Luther King to Marxism and anarchism. The concept of nonviolence, however, like that of violence, is often misunderstood in academic literature, mass media rhetoric and activist argument alike. The influence of Gandhi's ideas are perhaps most prominent in debates on nonviolence and will therefore be the focus of a brief look at nonviolence theory.

Gandhi has probably done more for the notion of nonviolence than any other person, and his actions and writings are often referred to as a sort of benchmark for the concept. Gandhi's concept of nonviolent action or *satyagraha* is often misrepresented and equated with passive resistance, whereas it is far more sophisticated than this.[26] *Satyagraha* has three main elements: *ahimsa* (nonviolence); truth seeking; and self-suffering. Bondurant (1967) gives a detailed account of the interplay of these elements in Gandhi's overall concept of political action.[27] It is enough here, however, to illustrate the complexity of Gandhi's ideas and the tensions inherent within them by looking at his views on violence and nonviolence:

> *While all violence [for Gandhi] was 'bad and must be condemned in the abstract', it was important to distinguish its various forms and contexts. Defensive violence was morally superior to the offensive kind. . . . Spontaneous violence was superior to premeditated violence. . . . The violence of long-suppressed groups lacking the capacity for concerted action was more 'understandable' than that of those with the opportunity to participate in political life and develop organisational strength. . . . [F]or Gandhi*

nonviolence was infinitely superior to violence, but the latter was infinitely superior to cowardice. . . . Gandhi also argued that violence had at least some deterrent effect and was likely to reduce the incidence of violence, whereas cowards only fed the voracious appetites of bullies. Where there was 'only a choice between cowardice and violence', he would advise violence.[28]

I accept the interpretation of ahimsa *namely that it is not merely a negative state of harmlessness but it is a positive state of love, of doing good even to the evil-doer. But it does not mean helping the evil-doer to continue the wrong or tolerating it by passive acquiescence. On the contrary, love, the active state of* ahimsa, *requires you to resist the wrong-doer by dissociating yourself from him [sic] even though it may offend him or injure him physically.*[29]

Violence in the above account is not an absolute, and it is clear from other sources such as liberal jurisprudence that different types and intensities of violence are and should be treated differently. Familiar examples of the acceptance of justifiable violence are when it occurs in the course of self-defence and when it is perpetrated in the course of a 'just' war. Gandhi's view of violence is not much different from this more general view, in that some violence may be necessary in certain situations.

Probably the most significant difference, however, between Gandhi's views on violence and most other people's is that he developed and used a concept of *nonviolence* that was radically different to previous conceptions. Gandhi's nonviolence demanded fearlessness, was an active not a passive concept, and meant that a person should commit their whole mind, body and spirit to the course of the nonviolent act. Such a stance demands a lot of the people involved, but the use of nonviolence, ideally and through careful training, could lead to positive social change.

Gandhi's view of nonviolence, however, although radical, was not absolute. Other values such as justice, truth and courage had to be reconciled with nonviolence. This view reveals the internal contradictions within Gandhi's thought on this subject. He was, however, not a philosopher but a social activist, who embraced many anarchist principles and practices.[30] Although some of the ideas in Gandhian nonviolence are problematic, such as the notions of 'self' and 'voluntary suffering' (which I comment on below), and that nonviolence does not mean that nobody ever gets hurt, many of his ideas and of others like him are valuable in attempts to create a radical direct action for contemporary struggles.

Nonviolence can have a startling effect on those who are faced with its strength. I will recount here an experience that I had while being involved in the campaign against the extension of the M65 motorway in Lancashire in 1994. One of the tactics that is used against tree fellers to prevent them felling trees is to physically intervene between the feller and the tree. Cinder Path Wood, a small but beautiful group of trees was set to be felled. Due to the protesters' presence, however, the felling gangs had to use surprise tactics to attempt to achieve their goal of clearing the wood. One particular morning, the protesters at the M65 were caught unawares by the early arrival of the chainsaw gangs and had to run to intervene. The main body of the fellers stayed in their pick-up, but one feller refused to be intimidated by the protesters' presence and proceeded to unload his chainsaw and march toward the wood. I ran to intervene as he started the engine of the chainsaw ready to begin his work. I managed to place myself between him and the wood and said something like 'You're not going in there', while I stood about one metre from him. What he did next shocked me: he thrust the running chainsaw blade (the motor was running but the blade was not yet revolving) up between my legs to within a few centimetres of my groin. We were both staring hard at each other. I repeated my statement. Eventually he removed the chainsaw blade and left. I was extremely stressed by what had happened and fellow protesters asked whether I was all right and what I had said. He had not harmed me physically but had threatened harm that would have been very serious. Yet my nonviolence – in word and in action – had worked. This tree feller talked to me some weeks later. He had given up his job with the contractors and often came to share conversation around the protesters' camp fires. He asked me how I had stood defiant but seemingly calm against his threat of violence. I replied that I didn't really know, except that I believed in what we were doing and that I had nothing against him personally. He seemed affected by the experience. I knew I certainly had been.

Reconstructing direct action

Direct action protest during the last twenty years has (re)developed in many ways. Although traditional methods of protest, such as marches, rallies and pickets have continued to be used, sometimes to great effect, it is the emergence of a variety of imaginative and striking tactics that has kept environmental and social issues in the public's eye. Environmental issues in the UK have been given a high profile both locally and nationally by the innovative tactics of such groups as Earth First!; Reclaim the Streets (which literally occupies a road and reclaims its space for people); the Citizen's Recovery of Indigenous People's Stolen Property Organisation 'CRISP-O' (which removes rainforest wood products from shops without paying for them and takes these to the police to challenge their legal status); and Critical Mass (which reclaims roads for cyclists in a mobile 'reclaim the streets' protest).

It is evident from the above groups' actions that the strategies and tactics of direct action are a continually evolving form of political action. Sharp's (1973) study of nonviolent actions lists nearly 200 types, and the examples given above add to this total. From a radical perspective, however, it is important to distinguish between protest and resistance. Protest is mostly a specific act of dissent directed at a specific issue and contains an implicit acknowledgement of an external authority to which the protest is made. Resistance, however, is a more inclusive concept that entails a broad-based opposition to established authority.

Civil disobedience

In a similar way, the tactic of civil disobedience can be seen as theoretically problematical for anarchists since it demands that the legitimacy of the State be acknowledged. A person, however, can perform an *act* of civil disobedience (and be justified in doing so) while maintaining a long-term *aim* for the overthrow of the State. To argue otherwise would be to deny either that Gandhi engaged in civil disobedient acts or that he was a revolutionary; both of which suggestions are equally nonsensical.

An anarchist perspective of civil disobedience goes further than one which merely calls for the powers that be to respond to direct action in a positive way, so that the direct action can ultimately cease. Instead, anarchists believe that political activism goes beyond the instrumentalism of the State and established channels, and that the purpose of direct action is to create organizational and social structures which can and do exist outside of and beyond the State.

Closely associated with the tradition of civil disobedience is the principle of accepting punishment appropriate to the 'crime', particularly with regard to illegal activities. In the following section I will discuss this principle and some of the complexities involved with its acceptance or not by anarchists.

Resisting the punishment

It is often asserted that being 'willing to accept the punishment' for breaking a law in the course of civil disobedience (or sabotage) is a significant part of the argument for the legitimacy of such illegal political action. The basis for the above concept concerns the obligations that citizens owe to the State. It has been shown by Buttle and others that such obligations are not absolute and therefore there cannot be an absolute obligation to accept the *legal* consequences of one's *illegal* acts.[31] Despite this, I think anarchists do have obligations to *civil* society. One of these obligations is to justify to those who are directly affected and to the wider public arena that one's actions are not intended to undermine civil society but to make improvements to the level of justice or the moral status of society itself. Therefore it is important that anarchists, like all others who would break laws in such cases, justify their illegal actions through clear statements of intent.

Many writers and activists, however, argue that the *goal* of the civil disobedient, whether it is to address people's sense of justice or moral beliefs, or to stir public opinion, requires that one should be willing to accept the punishment. Gandhi based his argument for this on the fact that suffering, voluntarily entered into, can 'open the eyes' of people to the grievance in question.

Now accepting one's punishment is certainly one (rather too obvious) way of suffering voluntarily, but it seems to me not to be the only or even the most important one. The voluntary suffering that is entailed by engaging in the very *act* of civil disobedience is often ignored but can be an adequate level of suffering to 'open the eyes' of the public and form the basis for the achievement of the civil disobedient's goals.

The Gandhian notion of voluntary suffering has also been criticized from a feminist perspective. The concept of voluntary suffering assumes:

that its value lies in its being sought – resulting in an extra, shocking and visible impact. For women, however, physical and emotional suffering is rarely sought, it is already much more a part of mere existence. Moreover should we not be cautious of men telling us that suffering is a good thing? Would Gandhi have accepted that from the British or Martin Luther King from the whites? No, the point is that it is we alone who can decide how much we are prepared to pay in each case for the cause in question.[32]

Voluntary suffering in this view is not something which *must* be sought to achieve the civil disobedient's goals. It can, instead, be seen to be a *sometimes* useful *tactic* in achieving those aims.

The above-stated goals of the civil disobedient are not the only ones that might be sought in engaging in such action. Both non-cooperation and physical obstruction are strategies that could render impossible the implementation of a State's law or policy.[33] An example of the former is the refusal to pay the Poll Tax and of the latter the tactics used in current road protests. Such objectives are more radical than the others mentioned above, and as Buttle says:

The success or failure of these strategies are not dependent on the acceptance of punishment and indeed such a strategy could very well be adversely affected if civil disobedients allow themselves to be arrested and therefore removed from the obstruction site.[34]

Resisting the punishment can also be motivated by the fact that the legal process can and has been used for political ends either by the State or its agents.[35] Therefore if there is evidence that one will not or is very unlikely to get a fair trial then, even if one agrees to the submission to the penalty on other grounds, it might be necessary on political grounds to resist the punishment. As Schochet argues,

The penalty need not be regarded as simply the application of a sanction and the legal consequence of breaking the law, but can be looked upon as a law or policy in its own right that is unjustifiable and can or should be violated on much the same grounds that the initial law was broken. So conceived, resistance becomes a further instance of civil disobedience.[36]

Sabotage

The damage or destruction of property has a particularly severe moral stigma attached to it in modern society. Arguments against it are embedded in beliefs about rights, violence and civility. The idea of the sanctity of property rights that has developed in modern consumer society has led to an acceptance of using violence towards people to protect things. Sabotage as a particular kind of attack on property receives a similar if not greater moral condemnation than 'criminal' theft or damage.

History is, however, resonant with cases of the use of sabotage in particular cultural and social contexts and for specific political or economic aims: the Luddite destruction of machines that threatened traditional livelihoods in the early nineteenth century is perhaps the most celebrated and often misunderstood example. Similarly, many campaigns for economic and political changes in society have involved elements of sabotage activity.[37] Both the animal liberation and environmental movements have witnessed the development of sabotage as a means to achieve movement objectives. The rationale behind using such strategies has been to make the groups involved in animal exploitation and environmental degradation incur financial penalties that undermine their ability to continue with their activities. If exploitation and degradation cost too much, those involved will be forced to stop doing it.

There is evidence to suggest that such a strategy has had some effect in achieving stated objectives. For instance, in the late 1980s the Animal Liberation Front (ALF) in Britain was causing £6,000,000 worth of damage a year, and ecotage in the USA was costing the companies involved $20–25,000,000 per year.[38] It is argued that ideally the money used to repair the damage, to improve security and to pay increased insurance costs is money that does not go towards animal exploitation and environmental degradation.

There are a number of ways that people have justified the use of sabotage: it has been regarded as a derivative of the idea of self-defence; it is carried out in accordance with a 'higher moral law'; and it is done because the means justify the ends and good consequences result from such acts. In the discussion below I will be specifically looking at sabotage in the environmental movement (ecotage).

'Self'-defence

Common in radical environmental literature are notions of justifying illegal activity through an idea of an expanded sense of self-defence. The idea is well expressed by Manes:

If our selves belong to a larger self that encompasses the whole biological community in which we dwell, then an attack on the trees, the wolves, the rivers, is an attack upon all of us. Defence of place becomes a form of self-

defence, which in most ethical and legal systems would be ample grounds for spiking a tree or ruining a tyre.[39]

The rhetorical strength of this approach in justifying sabotage is perhaps its best element. Nearly everyone would agree that defending oneself against a life-threatening attack is justifiable even if that means harming the attacker. However, there are a number of theoretical problems in this area due to the fact that the defence of non-human third parties, such as a forest or river, through damaging machinery or spiking trees is not the same sort of defence as normal self-defence.

Higher laws?

Many activists within the radical environmental movement use the notion of a 'higher moral law' or of 'higher ecological laws' to ground their justification for civil disobedience or ecotage. Higher law theories are either based in theological or naturalistic ethical systems but here I only deal with non-theological higher law theories. There are a number of serious objections that are often made against higher law theories in general: first, the verifiability of what the higher laws are is always dependent on partial human knowledge and reason; second, there is no unbiased arbiter to decide in situations of dispute between higher laws and other values or laws. Thus, any use of higher law theories has to counter these objections. Few people within the environmental movement do this, relying on the fact that the higher laws are self-evident. Although there is certainly rhetorical power in the idea of higher laws, it is important to ground such notions in a more substantial elucidation of the theory.

Although the status of a set of clear ecological laws to ground higher law theory is problematic, List (1993) argues that scientific ecological knowledge *can* be used in an evidential capacity rather than as an ultimate law to inform ethical principles.[40]

Therefore, in concert with other principles such as 'the inherent worth of non-human nature' or 'the obligation not to cause suffering to non-human animals', scientific ecological insights and information can form a relevant higher ecological 'law' that can be used to justify illegal acts in certain situations.

Do ends justify the means?

A common approach in activist discourse is to assert that bad consequences will inevitably happen if illegal actions are not taken (or good consequences will happen if they are taken) to remedy the environmental crisis. Academics such as Cohen (1971), in the case of civil disobedience, and Martin (1990), in the case of ecotage, have also used a consequentialist theory to ground their arguments for justifications of illegal action.

According to Cohen and Martin, the success of the justification is dependent on the goals of the activists being in accord with that of the public at large, and a careful assessment is necessary of the conflicting factors that arise due to the controversial nature of the means that are used.[41] With respect to the environmental movement, it is clear that there is a shared sense of concern by the public about wildlife protection, pollution-prevention and resource-use. Therefore, according to Martin, these shared goals can form a basis for the justification of ecotage if other means to achieve them can be shown to have failed. Although Cohen's and Martin's arguments are useful in forming a more radical defence of illegal action, they both fail to appreciate that sometimes part of the disobedience that activists engage in is to challenge the accepted notions of justice and morality as well as the accepted means by which such aims are brought about. Therefore, the challenges to traditional moral notions of what beings are valuable and thus should be respected, as are expressed in such philosophies as 'Deep Ecology', can form a significant part of the reasons why the activists deem illegal action to be necessary.

Conclusion

In this chapter I have tried to show some of the issues involved in the discourses and practices of direct action and the possible relationship between this form of political action and anarchism. I have shown that contestations of legitimacy regarding direct action between various actors in society has confused the discussion of this type of political action. Despite this imprecise use of the term, I have argued that a core notion of direct action can be made. Challenging ideas about violence, nonviolence, protest and resistance, I have attempted to characterize direct action as a specific form of political action that can be justifiably used in a number of situations.

My defence of radical direct action has been necessarily partial and has assumed that illegal political action is justified. I want, however, to add a caveat to my discussion because it might be assumed as stated in a recent paper that 'anything goes' in movements such as the one to protect the environment.[42] I do not think this is a defensible position, and it is evident from most of the strategies and tactics used by the movements I have mentioned that one of the central beliefs is in an ethos of nonviolence towards people.

Having said this, it is nevertheless important not to fetishize the idea of nonviolence and to realize that violence that is limited and carefully directed at the source of the injustice may be justified *in extremis*. In the vast majority of situations, however, any planned use of violence is counter-productive, the State having both the material advantage in using violence to deal with such tactics and the propaganda advantage in contests of legitimacy. As Wells succinctly says, 'The group that has the political power will always have the edge over the revolutionaries when the issue of the justification of violence arises.'[43]

The mobilization of enough people committed to (and trained in) nonviolent direct action is probably a necessary condition for fundamental changes in the areas of society that are of concern to the groups I have mentioned.[44] A widespread use of NVDA is, however, unlikely to occur within the timespan relevant to the environmental crisis. This sense of urgency (which also has occurred in other social change contexts, such as the Suffragette movement and Civil Rights movement in the USA) poses a challenge to advocates of direct action and anarchism alike. If time is of the essence then pragmatic considerations will increasingly weigh heavier than those of consistency with principles in strategies of social change.

Notes

1. I would like to thank Mags Adams for her special contribution of continuous help and support in making sure that I finished this project; the editors for originally believing in my enthusiastic ideas and for being incredibly patient throughout; John Murray for sharing thoughts with me despite the circumstances, and all the other people who have helped me through a very difficult few months. Also Stuart Parkinson for his calming influence, Phil Benn for comments on police and protest and Ian Maxey for ideas on violence.

2. I am *not* assuming here that such democratization has resulted in social and economic change that has radically benefited those who are worst off in the countries listed. Time will tell, but the penetration into or further expansion of free market capitalism in these countries has potentially serious adverse environmental social consequences.

3. See Brown and May (1989) for the international history of Greenpeace; Guha (1989) and Shiva (1989) for differing views on the Chipko Andolan movement in India; Gross (1989) and Revkin (1990) for details of Chico Mendes, the Brazilian rubber tappers and Amazonian indigenous peoples' fight for survival; and Manes (1990), Foreman (1991) and UK EF! (1995–96) for radical Western environmental activists' use of direct action.

4. Galtung (1965); Harris (1980); see also Gerver (1968).

5. Galtung (1965); Harris (1980).

6. Marshall (1992), p.629.

7. 'Ecotage' is a shortened form of '*eco*logical sabo*tage*'. This type of action is also called 'monkeywrenching', 'ecodefense', or 'night work' in the USA and 'pixieing' in the UK (which is derived from the acronym of the group Earth Liberation Front (formerly Fairies) – ELF – thus 'elves' is the name of the people who partake in this type of action and 'pixieing' is what they practise).

8. Tree-spiking is the tactic of driving metal or ceramic spikes into trees to make them commercially useless. See Foreman and Haywood (1985).

9. See Dobson (1995) Martell (1994) and Des Jardins (1993). It should be noted here that Dobson in private correspondence has admitted that the statements in his books regarding harm caused by ecotage are not proven.

10. Foreman (1991), p.149.

11. Hargrove (1983) equates ecotage with terrorism by defining terrorism as 'the use of force as a political weapon to demoralise, intimidate, and subjugate'. This definition is to be found wanting when compared to more considered versions. See Sproat (1991), Primoratz (1990) and Wardlaw (1989).

12. Quoted in Manes (1990), p.177.

13. Three examples: a number of people were arrested and charged for the theft of 'timber of indeterminate value' at the M11 construction site in London. The court case involved three visits to the court and resulted in dismissal of the trial through the failure of the main prosecution witness to appear. The trial judge said, in dismissing the charge, that enough public money had been wasted on such a minor charge. Another case at the M11 involved the arrest of someone for the theft of a piece of string. A case at the M65 protest involved the charging of someone for criminal damage to a pair of trousers of a security guard. The trousers were damaged by accidental splashing of them by a protester who did not have a bucket in his tree and who needed to defecate. The security guard had refused to move a few steps away from under a tree when requested. The protester was found guilty at first but the decision was overturned on appeal.

14. Many bail conditions now being given by magistrates against anti-road protesters have meant that they are unable to travel to necessary places of work without having to break them.

15. For instance the sentence of 14 years (on appeal reduced to 11 years) given to Keith Mann, an animal rights activist, can be seen as being politically motivated. The trial judge was a farm-animal breeder and a hunter. Mann was found guilty of charges related to criminal damage valued at £6000, conspiracy to cause criminal damage, and possession of substances that could be made into explosives. In comparison, a recent conviction for manslaughter by dangerous driving resulted in an 18-month sentence.

16. Taylor (1995), p.341.

17. Fairclough (1989); Herman and Chomsky (1988).

18. *Daily Mail* 13 January 1996; *Sunday Times* 3 July 1994.

19. Examples of these are *Squall*, *Green Anarchist*, *Pod*, and the *Earth First! Action Update* which are all text-based media and *Undercurrents*, an 'underground' television news video.

20. See Sharp (1973) for an exhaustive examination of nonviolent tactics.

21. Wapner (1995), p.307.

22. While Greenpeace's effect on the public's view of the acceptability of taking direct action is difficult to ascertain, the 26 per cent increase between 1984 and 1995 of members of the public who agree that disobeying laws can be a justified form of protest must owe something to the high-profile actions of Greenpeace over this period.

23. Wapner (1995), p.307 for instance, totally ignores the influence that the media have on the issues they report (or don't report) in his defence of Greenpeace actions of bearing witness.

24. See Purkis (1996).

25. Guha (1989); Shiva (1989); Baviskar (1995); Revkin (1990); Gross (1989); Rich (1994), p.107–47.

26. Teichman and Evans (1991), p.101; Scruton (1982), p.346 among others. The term passive resistance is more properly used to describe the nonviolent code that Tolstoy advocated which influenced Gandhi's ideas.

27. See also Naess (1974).

28. Parekh (1988), pp.213–14.

29. Bondurant (1967), p.24.

30. See Marshall (1992), pp.422–7 for Gandhi as an anarchist.

31. Buttle (1985).

32. Feminism and Nonviolence Study Group (1983), p.36.

33. Buttle (1985), p.652.

34. Ibid.

35. Schochet (1972), p.189, outlines the political nature of the trial of Dr Spock and others in America for anti-Vietnam actions.

36. Ibid., p.193.

37. Thompson (1968), pp.604–28; see also Guha (1989) for evidence of sabotage as part of resistance against deforestation in India; Gross (1989), for sabotage action that has occurred as part of rubber tapper opposition to deforestation in Amazonia; Raeburn, (1973), for the use of property damage in the Suffragette movement.

38. Manes (1990), p.188; Henshaw (1989), p.133.

39. Manes (1990), p.177.

40. List (1993), p.14.

41. Cohen (1971), p.123; Martin (1990), p.299.

42. Welsh and McLeish (1996), p.31.

43. Wells (1970), p.34.

44. See Carter (1993).

Part II

Culture and Anarchy!

CHAPTER 5

'Anarchy in the UK'?

Anarchism and Popular Culture in 1990s' Britain

Jude Davies

This chapter offers a retrospective theoretical description of the Anarchy in the UK festival, which took place in London between 21–30 October 1994. Rather than analysing the events that took place in detail, I argue that the festival stands for an important trend in 1990's British anarchism: the appropriation of and intervention in mainstream popular culture. I seek to show the importance of the relays between anarchist political action and cultural production by first, considering anarchist notions of the relationship between culture and politics, second, by reviewing the theoretical debates over popular culture and politics among academics such as John Fiske, Jim McGuigan, John Storey, and Angela McRobbie, and finally by an analysis of some anarchist appropriations of the TV character Mr Blobby.

> *I mean surely the thing about popular culture is that it is just about one of the few things that the working class have in common, I mean, they might vote conservative or labour, or they might be anarchists or not, but at least they might all watch Victor Meldrew on a Saturday night and it[']s this sharing of ideas, however you might want to put it, that is the binding force and not groups and it is that which has to be exploited to put radical ideas across. [Popular Culture] not only combines the working class, it combines all of the classes [. . .] And it raises some questions, what exactly the working class is.*[1]

Introduction

Billed as 'Ten Days that Shook the World', the *Anarchy in the UK* festival was held at various sites in London between 21–30 October, 1994. In this chapter I offer a retrospective theoretical description of the festival, focusing on the ways in which it brought together anarchist politics and culture. My argument is that the festival stands for an important trend in

ANARCHY IN THE U.K.

LONDON
OCTOBER 21ST - 30TH 1994

TEN DAYS THAT SHOOK THE WORLD

The biggest ever anarchist festival, slap bang in the middle of London, with over 500 meetings at a hundred venues. All currents of anarchist thought, practice, culture, history and lifestyle will be there.

From DURRUTTI to DADA, RAVACHOL to ROTTEN, McCLAREN, to MALATESTA, SITUATIONISM to SYNDICALISM, PUNK to PAGANISM, STONEHENGE to SEX, ANIMAL LIBERATION to ANARCHA-FEMINISM, FOOTBALL to ANTI-FASCISM, DRUGs to DRUIDS, RIOTS to RAVES, EARTH FIRST to CLASS WAR .... This one's got the lot! If you don't do anything else for the rest of the millennium don't miss out on this!

PLUS ..... Anarchist film and video season, live music from those anarchist bands day and night, comedy club, poetry, raves, dancing and the best ten days social life you're ever likely to experience!! PLUS ... all night central political debate for ten days and those anarchist eye witnesses you always wanted to hear from Barcelona to Brixton.

PLUS worldwide participation and massive anarchist STREET MOBILISATION!!

Provisional programme out March 1st 1994 (S.A.E. + £1)
Special ten day cheap rate: Book before March 1st 1994 and £25 will get you in to all meetings otherwise all events pay on the door.

HELP, OFFERS OF SUPPORT, SPEAKERS, IDEAS, ORGANISERS, MONEY, PRINTING, PUBLICITY LEG WORK, BOOK/RECORD STALLS, BANDS and DEMANDS FOR FURTHER INFORMATION TO:

ANARCHY IN THE U.K. '94
P.O. BOX 96 BRISTOL BS99 1BW

Fig 5.1   *Anarchy in the UK* flyer, early 1994

63

1990s British anarchism: the appropriation of and intervention in main-stream popular culture.

Politics vs. culture

The flyer for Anarchy in the UK, distributed up to a year in advance and reproduced here (see Figure 5.1), promised: 'The biggest ever anarchist festival, slap bang in the middle of London, with over 500 meetings at a hundred venues. All currents of anarchist thought, practice, culture, history and lifestyle will be there.'[2] This breathless series of juxtapositions is continued in a listing that includes such pairings as 'From Durrutti to Dada, Ravachol to Rotten, . . . Stonehenge to Sex, . . . Football to Anti-Fascism, Drugs to Druids, Riots to Raves, Earth First to Class War', before adding, as a triumphant afterthought, 'PLUS worldwide participation and massive anarchist STREET MOBILISATION'.

As it turned out, the festival was remarkable for its diversity of ideological strands, including (in random order) Green, feminist, anti-fascist, animal liberation, syndicalist, libertarian, anti-roads, pagan, communist, and class war tendencies. This ideological diversity is characteristic of contemporary British anarchism. It is worthy of further critical investigation, especially in relation to the tensions between political coherence and single issue protests (roads, veal calves).[3]

Important as these overtly political debates are, I want here to focus on a related issue: the ways in which Anarchy in the UK brought together politics and culture. The festival programme listed workshops, an anarchist feminist programme, and other events under many other headings: rallies and demos, fun stuff, lesbian/gay, football, films and videos, pagans and magick, sexuality/culture/pornography, performance, eco-armageddon, pacifist/nonviolent anarchist events, counter-institutions/unmedia/community activism, music, raves, parties.

In fact, the scope and diversity promised by the flyer and the sixty-page festival programme were not fully realized. There was also criticism that some tensions were needlessly exacerbated by some of the organizational practices adopted by the festival's prime mover, Ian Bone, widely perceived as the man behind the anarchist tabloid/movement *Class War*. Having noted this, I want to approach a theoretical analysis of Anarchy in the UK, via a sense of what Bone, post-*Class War* was picking up on: the connections between anarchist politics and popular culture.

Anarchy in the UK featured political discussions and direct action (including an attempted levitation of Parliament), alongside cultural transgressions (typified by the *smutfest*, ad. line 'anarchy begins in your underpants'). The festival also gave rise to its own comic, which featured, among other things, a strip of the 'Levitation of Parliament' action before the event. In all this, Anarchy in the UK foregrounded long-standing questions about the relationship between (anarchist) politics and culture, and, arguably, played a part in reconstructing this relationship. The central issue raised here is that of the relays between politics and culture: did Anarchy in the UK turn politics into culture, or did it help to produce a usefully anarchistic conjuncture between the two?

The anarchist journal *Black Flag* ran an article attacking Anarchy in the UK for its culturalist turn. Meanwhile, Stewart Home wrote in the *Independent* that 'the Anarchy in the UK festival in London this week demonstrates that the vast majority of anarchists have little interest in throwing bricks and bottles at the police'.[4] Whether celebrated or opposed (the tone of Home's article gives little away), the festival was regarded by many on the anarchist left as merely cultural, not political. What Home calls with calculated irony its 'bohemianism' was viewed by others as a reactionary backsliding, a turning away from politics into culture.

In this chapter I reject both the anti-culturalist position and concomitant attempts to define an authentically anarchist separatist cultural tradition, whether it be conceived in terms of 'alternative', 'counter-cultural' or 'sub-cultural'. British anarchism needs to be and is being revitalized through strategies and interventions between politics and culture, and Anarchy in the UK, symbolically at least, stands for this revitalization. What this project of revivification necessitates is a break with certain anarchist traditions which have displayed an overwhelming suspicion of popular culture. These tendencies can be traced back to the European Enlightenment philosophy which stimulated the anarchist thought of such people as William Godwin and Percy Bysshe Shelley. Godwin and Shelley pushed the scepticism of the Enlightenment further than most, to develop critiques not only of Statism but of what came to be known as 'false consciousness'. Out of this tradition comes not only a denial of the legitimacy of authority based on law, custom, class, and power, but also a grave suspicion of the cultural formations which are seen as habituating people to these authorities. So far, all well and good. But what this has led to in the twentieth century is the belief that any anarchist cultural practice must be one of two kinds: on the one hand, the project of demystifying the mainstream, and on the other hand, the securing and maintenance of a separate, authentically anarchist alternative.

To begin to conceptualize the interventions I have been discussing, it is instructive to look at some comments on autonomy and authority by the nineteenth-century Russian anarchist activist and philosopher, Mikhail Bakunin. Bakunin's work is characterized by an extreme scepticism of what we might now call mainstream culture. However, a close reading of Bakunin offers some support for the position I have been recommending, which I term 'cultural omnivorousness', for reasons that will shortly become clear.

In *God and the State*, Bakunin sets out to distinguish what differentiates humans from animals, and hence to define the motive force of human history:

> *Yes, our very first ancestors, our Adams and our Eves, were, if not gorillas, very near relatives of gorillas, omnivorous, intelligent and ferocious beasts, endowed in a higher degree than the animals of any other species . . . with two precious faculties – the power to think and the desire to rebel.*[5]

Having drawn attention, bizarrely enough, to three supposed characteristics of human ancestors, in the rest of *God and the State* Bakunin only develops an account of two of them. For him, human history is determined by the combination of ferociousness and intelligence. These correspond to the two things that stand between animality and humanity, or at the birth of history and society: 'Man [. . .] has begun his distinctively human history and development by an act of disobedience and science – that is, by *rebellion* and *thought'*.[6] This is not the place for speculation on the strangeness of Bakunin's formulations, nor as to why omnivorousness is mentioned in the list of humanizing characteristics, and why, once mentioned, it is not further developed. However, it is significant that while omnivorousness disappears from the text, the category of 'culture' never appears. Bakunin's treatment of culture is reductive to say the least. The nearest his account comes to describing a cultural dimension is his notion of a mystifying conspiracy on the part of the ruling class. 'Is it not plain,' he asks, 'that all these governments are systematic poisoners, interested stupefiers of the popular masses?'.[7] This position has real value, and remains powerful in anarchist circles. The notion of culture as 'systematic poison' underlies a general feeling among many anarchists that the State or the mainstream has somehow appropriated working-class culture and turned it into something conservative and stupefying. But there is nothing intrinsically anarchistic about hostility to 'the media', and there is nothing innately leftist in thinking of mass communications and mass consumption as eroding 'authentic' consciousness or masking real social relations. Similar arguments can be found in a wide variety of contexts, allied to a huge range of political positions, including for example, the libertarian Right and the Christian Right. Versions of this grand scepticism can be found in the neo-Marxist cultural theory of Adorno and the Frankfurt School of Critical Theory, and in most non-feminist critiques of 'mass culture'. It is not necessary to be familiar with any or all of these to realize that a scepticism of mass culture by itself has no political affiliations.[8]

This grand scepticism of mass culture still has a wide currency in contemporary anarchism and Situationism. Stewart Home identifies it as practically a whole tradition, whose parameters are made clear in the title of his work, *The Assault on Culture: Utopian Currents from Lettrisme to Class War* (1988). Not that all Situationist critiques are similarly compromised, but in certain Situationist-inspired work 'the Spectacle' is accorded homogenizing and monolithic significance.[9] This scepticism can also be seen in the determination of practitioners. of mail art, or DIY culture, to remain outside the networks of commodity consumption for purely philosophical reasons. Both of these are exemplified in the otherwise highly suggestive *Radio Sermonettes* of the Moorish Orthodox Radio Crusade Collective. While this US Situationist-inspired group has rightly been influential, there is a tendency in some of their material to criticize capitalist modes of exchange not on the grounds of economic inequality or exploitation, but philosophy. According to the *Radio Sermonettes*, the first step to resolve the contradictions of capitalism lies in artistic practices. Capitalist 'immediatism' is overcome only by the free exchange of gifts among artists.[10] What is happening here, I think, is that undue emphasis is being placed on the processes of media culture and mass consumption, rather than capitalism and its power relations. Therefore, the overcoming of media alienation is perceived as the first step, or even the major step, in effecting wholesale social change. This position cannot be regarded as a Situationist deviation, since it signals an affiliation of anarchism with a wholesale rejection of industrial society, a position with appeal to many (though by no means all) groups associated with anarcho-primitivism, eco-anarchism, and others, with a history in Europe and in America as long as industrialization itself. While many activists are empowered by this argument, I reject it for reasons which will be explained below.

Let me make it clear that I do not mean to include in this critique the numbers of anarchist-affiliated and other cultural producers who shun mainstream modes of dissemination for practical reasons (for example, to avoid self-censorship, economic censorship, or prosecution). Some of these will figure later in my account of some of what I regard as the most vital elements of anarchist culture. Similarly, this is not to deny the value of work which analyses the mechanisms by which dominant ideologies are disseminated and contested ideas are marginalized or silenced.

Nuanced accounts of these operations such as Noam Chomsky's book *Necessary Illusions* and the video *Manufacturing Consent* are best read as contesting assumptions of a monolithic, universally alienating 'mass media'. What I am arguing against is a knee-jerk rejection of mainstream cultural production, and the attendant fetishization of an exclusionary, retrospective anarchist popular culture. For me, anarchist cultural production is at its most vital when it explicitly engages with, raids, subverts, and contests mainstream representations. I am not rejecting *per se* materialist accounts of media institutions, such as those by Chomsky and in *Test Card F* (see below). My point is that they need supplementing by a more complex notion of cultural mediation, including textual analysis of the ways in which identity is constructed in mainstream and 'subversive' texts.

The Institute of Social Disengineering's *Test Card F: Television. Mythinformation. and Social Control* (1994) is a materialist critique of broadcasting institutions, which focuses on current affairs and on the economic structures behind television production. Early on, *Test Card F* acknowledges the pluralist dissonance of contemporary television:

> *Even so, it is patently not the case, in Britain anyway, that we receive a constant barrage of undiluted corporate and State directives. It is relatively easy to read between the lines of explicit propaganda for particular capitalist enterprises or the government of the day. The messages of this medium are many and multi-layered. It is in rather more subtle methods that we find television's power to shape social reality and enforce social control.*[11]

Clearly this is an attempt to come to terms with the complexity of television culture. However, in the book as a whole this project remains grounded in monolithic notions of alienation and the maintenance of power. 'Individuals' and unalienated social relations are thought of as existing outside the media, i.e. outside culture. Thus a social class can be posited which needs liberating from the alienating effects of television media. This position is deeply flawed. Although class seems to be the operative term here, in fact economic relations of production are ignored, as are other determinants of identity such as gender, ethnicity, sexuality, age, geographical situation, and family relationships. The assumption is that all viewers are alienated by viewing, therefore all viewers are alienated in the same way and to the same extent.

This becomes explicit when at the end of *Test Card F* its writers seek to imagine a way of evading media alienation and social control. Here a Situationist discourse of desire is adopted, among an undifferentiated 'we':

> *Throw your telly out the window (open the window first). . . . We start by communicating on equal terms – without the mediation of technology, specialism and representation – with those who suffer the same alienated experience. We grow stronger as like-minded people work together seriously (and playfully) in common projects of self-determination that shatter established social relations.*[12]

Silent on issues such as gender, ethnicity, and sexuality, this passage implies that media alienation is *the same* for everyone ('those who suffer the same alienated experience'). Social relations are perceived as an effect of media representations, and can be magically transformed, without reference to economics or anything else, just so long as mediation is absent.

Test Card F typifies certain strands of anarchist cultural criticism. It stands squarely in two anarchist traditions: one going back to Bakunin's notion of culture as stupefying poison, and the other with roots in Situationist notions of the 'society of the Spectacle'. For both, at base a simplistic notion of the goodness of human nature is mapped on to a simplistic notion of institutional media alienation. 'State authority perverts human relations – get rid of the State and human relations will perfect themselves' becomes 'The mass media perverts human relations – throw the telly out the window and human relations will perfect themselves'.

The corollary of all these positions is a focus on a hermetically sealed alternative anarchist culture which needs protecting from the mainstream lest it be co-opted, sold out, or spectacularized. It seems to me that such cultural productions and critiques fail to challenge the capitalist economic structures and power relations within which they are embedded. Whatever its rhetorical attractions, the wholesale rejection of mainstream culture is debilitating. Instead, thinking back to the formulation earlier stolen from Bakunin, it is omnivorousness that I wish to use as a model for anarchistic cultural practice.

Although from the outside, mainstream culture might appear seamless and monolithic, from the inside it is unstable, dynamic, and even occasionally transgressive. Admittedly, the apparently transgressive moments in mainstream culture might often be a substitute for politics rather than a route into politicization. But this is not necessarily so. The crucial thing is to understand mediation as a two-way process. Capitalism may thrive on cultural anarchism (from Dada to Surrealism, punk to new wave), but this is no justification for a nostalgic view of anarchist popular culture on the folk model. Instead, potentially the most powerful anarchist cultural politics is one which gets messy and fucks with mainstream culture.

Cultural omnivorousness vs. cultural populism

Readers familiar with recent debates in cultural studies may have experienced a sense of *déjà vu* in the preceding section. The argument I have been making in the specific context of British anarchism has many points of contact with certain tendencies in the academic study of popular culture, and in particular with the positions dubbed by Jim McGuigan 'cultural populism'.[13] For example, my account of the relays between culture and politics obviously has something in common with the work of neo-Gramscian critics such as Dick Hebdige, Angela McRobbie, Paul Willis, and John Fiske. Essentially, these critics develop the work on hegemony (or dominance) of the Italian Marxist, Antonio Gramsci, who looked to traditional and emergent forms of popular culture as possible embodiments of resistance to ruling class authority and power.[14] These and other critics have therefore contested monolithic accounts of mass culture by reference to appropriations of mainstream culture by groups of consumers. However, major problems attend the use of these critical positions in considering an anarchist cultural politics. In this section, therefore, I will outline some of the problems in appropriating the neo-Gramscian tradition of cultural studies for an anarchist politics of cultural production, and suggest some necessary revisions.

First and most obviously, political activism remains beyond the interpretative horizon of most cultural populism. For many cultural populists, politics tends to be either entirely separate from culture or is subsumed within it. Thus, for example, John Fiske celebrates the practice of wearing ripped jeans as 'excorporation', i.e. 'the process by which the subordinate make their own culture out of the resources and commodities provided by the dominant system'.[15] Still more bizarrely, Fiske argues that certain acts of consumption amount to a kind of guerrilla warfare with 'the market system', such that 'Consumption is a tactical raid upon the system. . . . Shoplifting is not a guerilla raid just upon the store owners themselves, but upon the power-bloc in general.'[16]

For Fiske, even browsing is an anti-authoritarian gesture, in which First World consumers play out equivalent roles to Third World freedom fighters:

> They try on clothes, consume their stolen images in the store mirrors and in each other's eyes, turn the place of the boutique into their lunchtime space. . . . The boutique owners know these tactics but are helpless before them: one estimated that one in thirty browsers becomes a consumer. And no one can tell which is which. The US Army could not tell the Viet Cong from the innocent villager, for at a different time, in a different space, one became the other in a constant and unpredictable movement into and out of the order.[17]

What is perhaps most dangerous about Fiske's argument here is that the flip side of this celebration of individual autonomy is a drastic foreclosing of social relationships. Distinguishing only between 'the people' and 'the power bloc', Fiske's writing has no real grasp on power relations inflected by class, ethnicity, gender, sexuality, or anything else. As with certain Situationist positions discussed earlier, for Fiske, everyone is equally alienated by mass culture and is in theory equally able to develop strategies for resisting it.

The celebrative mode of cultural populism in general, and of Fiske in particular, is by no means unchallenged within British cultural studies. Against Fiske's version of cultural populism, Jim McGuigan reasserts the primacy of political economy. In his book *Cultural Populism* he outlines a critique of the work of Fiske *et al.* on the grounds of its exclusive concern with textuality, and its resulting failure to ground itself with respect to economic and material circumstances. McGuigan regards cultural populism as characterized by the purely hermeneutic, uncritical endorsement of popular taste and pleasure.

According to McGuigan, in the late 1980s the very useful neo-Gramscian hegemony theory, developed out of the Centre for Contemporary Cultural Studies at Birmingham, was deconstructed and re-formulated around an uncritical understanding of youth cultural consumption. As McGuigan points out, the tendency to celebrate the practice of consumers in picking and mixing 'their' meanings from the cultural artefacts they consume bears a marked similarity to economic liberalism's concept of 'consumer sovereignty'. Thus the textually 'subversive' activities of ripping jeans, browsing, etc. may fit neatly into the material processes of capitalist production and consumption. Either way, as McGuigan implies, on the part of the critic a purely textual analysis is incapable by itself of specifying a material politics.

Against cultural populism as constituted by Fiske, McGuigan asserts the need for a move away from a hermeneutics of consumption, and towards what he calls 'a materialist perspective [on] social relations': 'the problem goes deeper than the uncritical drift out of hegemony theory: it derives from the original schism between the hermeneutic mainstream of British cultural studies and the political economy of culture'.[18] Thus, for McGuigan, it is not just that cultural populists ignore material relations of production and power (which are, for him, determined by economic class): he argues that they are led to do this by an exclusive concentration on hermeneutics – the purely textual attention to the production of meaning.

The applicability of McGuigan's critique to the work of Fiske has been contested, and his bracketing together of Fiske with cultural populism in general is particularly open to question.[19] Similarly, McGuigan's argument does not exhaust feminist work in the tradition of the slogan 'the personal is political'. Nevertheless, I find it difficult to resist the power of McGuigan's case as a description of major *effects* of much writing in cultural studies, given that its primary site of consumption is in the resource-starved and increasingly consumerized system of higher education in Britain. However, his prescription, a move to 'a materialist perspective [on] socio-economic relations' is more questionable. An exclusively materialist analysis of public communication, institutional power, and socio-economic relations, as demanded by McGuigan, would collapse acts of consumption back into static material relations. This might enable academics to come to precise conclusions about specific phenomena via their situation in relations of production, but in so doing it closes off any sense of ambiguity, re-reading, and appropriation.

On the level of cultural theory, McGuigan's position therefore may be regarded as in some respects equivalent to that of the anarchists mentioned earlier who wish to compartmentalize politics safely away from culture (as well as bearing major similarities to the position of the Socialist Workers Party). McGuigan's book seems to evince a nostalgia for the unquestioned power of the academic theorist, and is locked into a project of pinning down singular definitions of cultural practices. In the past, such singular readings and totalizing logics of production led to gender-blind readings of male subcultural activities. As McRobbie points out, in the early work of Hebdige and Willis there was a concentration on practices which empowered working-class men, without considering the construction of the symbolic objects (frequently women) over whom these victories were won.[20]

But, *pace* McGuigan, there is no necessary link between taking seriously processes of consumption and a naïve assumption of empowered readers. In fact, the best way of contesting the pseudo-liberatory readings of critics such as Fiske is not a move wholesale into the materialist analysis of social relations, but a combination of materialist and textual analysis. In other words, culture exists as both commodities and texts, and demands analysis as such.

What I am arguing then is that the rejuvenated materialist analysis called for by McGuigan must be supplemented by a concern with hermeneutics, and in particular a more critical attention to consumption. Such attention highlights real weaknesses in many accounts by so-called cultural populists, who frequently only go so far as to demonstrate that certain readings of culture are *possible*.

Instead, I believe it is necessary to understand more clearly the precise conditions under which mediation occurs, by reference both to social power relations and to strategies of appropriation and re-appropriation. Fiske uncritically celebrates the textual ambiguity of culture, while McGuigan seeks to close off textuality, to re-embed cultural practices and artefacts in socio-economic contexts. What I am interested in doing is to theorize and to analyse anarchist cultural productions as texts, while also paying full attention to the social and economic relationships that are the material contexts of culture and politics. In some respects, this is to stake a claim also for anarchism as a third way, differentiated from both liberal humanism and Marxism.

Two things give this project any importance it may have. One is the importance of cultural constructions of identity in relation to politics. It seems obvious that if any political project is to succeed in delivering a revolutionary transformation of society, it must envisage a transformation of identity. The second is the existence of a well-theorized anarchist/DIY. culture, which demands to be read in relation not just to a tradition of anarchism, but also in relation to mainstream culture. It is exactly this culture which, although it existed before Anarchy in the UK, emerged at the festival to take centre stage in British anarchism. By way of illustrating some of the issues and strategies involved, in the next section I will trace the various mediations of one particular cultural phenomenon in mainstream and in anarchist culture.

Blobby, Blobby, Blobby

Mr Blobby is a monstrous but loveable character who is played by a man in a large pink costume. His appearances on the prime time BBC1 television show *Noel's House Party* ostensibly disrupted the power of Noel Edmonds, the host and ersatz lord of the manor. Blobby would enter from behind Edmonds, to cheers from the audience, going on to indulge in playful horseplay with Edmonds' 'guests'. As his popularity grew, Blobby appeared on a variety of television shows in which he sat on people, damaged sets, and generally behaved in a unpredictable but predictably disruptive manner. Unlike his most obvious predecessors on British television, hand puppets such as Rod Hull's Emu, who also acted disruptively and attacked hosts, Blobby acted obviously and (to many) hilariously beyond Edmonds' control.

As the product of a State-funded broadcasting system, copyrighted by millionaire Noel Edmonds, the material production of Mr Blobby is clearly defined. The consumption of Blobby, however, is more ambiguous, since he is a product who regularly attacks his creator. Seemingly, part of the fun of watching Blobby is to see controllers embarrassed, the mighty brought down, to see put at stake not only authority itself but the mechanisms by which television production is ordered and controlled. The continued popularity of Mr Blobby from his first appearances on *Noel's House Party* in 1993 implies a large mainstream audience for images of disorder and subversion: Blobby's indiscipline is his attraction.

This popularity attracted much coverage in the broadsheet press, where Blobby was explicitly connected with carnivalesque figures such as the Lord of Misrule. The tabloids, however, gave more coverage to 'real-life' Blobbies who had 'gone too far' and whose activities had had to be brought explicitly under the control of the State. These included cases of civil disorder, criminal damage to property, and also, reputedly, robbery. In all these stories, the mere putting on of the Blobby suit (hired for some special occasion) gave the person inside a sense of licensed (mis)behaviour. The ensuing court cases are readily seen as instances of the State policing the boundary between licensed disorder (carnivalesque) and unacceptable behaviour. At first sight, it seems that these are codified on a scale of increasing mediation: Blobby's behaviour on television is licensed by its highly mediated status – it is almost only 'pretending'; while to put on a Blobby suit and to push people around, smash up birthday parties etc. is unacceptable, too 'real', and will land you in court. The court cases then policed a boundary not simply between behaviours, but between reality and fantasy.

One effect of this, paradoxically, was to reinvest the mediated Mr Blobby with more subversive power than he originally had. By association with behaviour perceived as non-mediated, Blobby's act took on more vulgar and disreputable connotations. These were intensified by scandalous revelations about the personal life of the actor in the Blobby suit. As if in response to this, the scenarios for TV Blobby's appearance were changed. He was contextualized increasingly in relation to children, both as child-like and as children's entertainment. Symbolically, this stereotyped Blobby's disruptivity as a phase to be indulged to some extent but to be grown up from when the authority of civil society is accepted with adulthood. In a more sophisticated move, the narratives of Blobby's appearance were later developed in 1994–95 so as to emphasize his transferability. Instead of focusing on Blobby's subversion of authority figures, the media people who would at first have been his victims queued up to don the costume themselves. Thus the Blobby persona was presented as ever more available, but its subversive activities were curtailed. Perhaps, however, this proved less popular than his earlier routines. Certainly, at the time of writing it is possible to discern a shift back to Blobby's original disruptive presence on *Noel's House Party*, while Edmonds, genuinely or not, often appears annoyed.

The shifts in Blobby's persona just described imply that final judgements of Blobby as 'genuinely' disruptive or merely a licensed fool must be nuanced. However, placed in the context of 'trash TV', Blobby can be seen along with *Eurotrash, Beavis and Butthead*, and perhaps *The Word*, as ultimately presenting a spectacle of subversion. Along with precursors such as *The Tube*, Spike Milligan's *Q* series, and perhaps even *Monty Python's Flying Circus*, what all of these have in common is the staging of a takeover of authority by those unable or unconcerned to legitimate themselves. Spectacles of non–control or amateurishness in *Eurotrash*, missed cues, 'accidental' swearing on *The Tube*, the poor standard of drawing of *Beavis and Butthead*, *The Word's* general tackiness, and the lack of a gusset in Blobby's costume (often displayed as he falls over backwards) – all signal an empowerment of the disempowered, but signal is all they do.

In fact, Blobby helped to reinstitute the patriarchal order in a variety of ways. At the height of Blobbymania over Christmas 1993, Mr Blobby held the number one spot in the UK singles chart, relegating the boy group Take That into second place. The video, shown several times on *Top of the Pops* and elsewhere, featured a pastiche of subcultural images and behaviour. Blobby was shown smashing up musical equipment, taking over the scenarios for familiar pop videos, and dancing with Mrs Blobby and Blobby offspring, the latter sporting multicoloured mohican hairstyles. Thus Blobby not only symbolically domesticated the dangerous elements of popular music, but reasserted the power of the father and the hegemony of the nuclear family. In this case it is clear that the collapse of authority is merely spectacular, and Blobby's subversiveness is used in the service of patriarchal hegemony.

But why was it important to stabilize Blobby via reference to the heterosexual nuclear family? Because of course in some respects Blobby's gendered identity is itself unstable. Essentially, Blobby is a man with long eyelashes, large yellow spots, and no penis. The latter becomes unproblematic if Blobby is read, as in the quality press, as a priapic Lord of Misrule: he needs no penis because symbolically he is all penis. However, taken together, these three characteristics place Blobby in the tradition of drag, an identification reinforced by the name of the fictional village in which he is supposed to live, 'Crinkley Bottom'. Drag can be done as transgressive; for example it might uncover a 'perverse' underside to heterosexuality, and/or it might be read as staging the social construction (and hence instability) of gender. [21] In terms of gender though, Blobby's drag is wholly reactionary.

Mr Blobby's long eyelashes and the mysterious gap where his legs join his body reproduce the anti-feminist logic of drag: femininity as spectacle. His obvious lack of penis, meanwhile, forestalls the problematization of masculinity that, arguably, drag sometimes stages. Thus Mr Blobby's drag reproduces males as having a centred and authentic subjectivity while femininity is something constructed, to be put on and taken off at will. His yellow spots are perhaps more ambiguous. No doubt, like his long eyelashes, they were intended to signify that he was child-friendly. However, many viewers read them as signs of disease, spots in the sense of lesions.[22] This reinforces a patriarchal appropriation of the female body as not only spectacular but also as ill.

These textual analyses have shown that in his role as subversive, TV's Mr Blobby stages or spectacularizes transgression, while from a perspective of gender, he works ultimately to reinforce hegemonic power. The subversiveness then of the mainstream Blobby is only apparent. But I want to close this section by looking at two more Mr Blobbies, which are mediations of the large and pink one by the anarchist left.

The fifth issue of *You What*, an A3-size underground newspaper, was distributed free in London during the winter of 1994–95.[23] Eschewing high quality production values, the front cover was composed of a photographic reproduction of a youngish male, barefoot, dressed only in a loincloth, holding a large knife. The head of this figure is the head of Mr Blobby, a headpiece or mask complete with oversized bow tie, but without the long eyelashes of the original. This unnerving image revitalizes some of the subversive tendencies that the mainstream Blobby invokes only to domesticate. The knife obviously plays an important part here, in recoding disorder as threatening and violent. What the image closes down though, is the drag connotations of the mainstream Blobby. Without the large eyelashes gender is firmly fixed by reference to male youth leisure. This perhaps cements the image in the context of barbarism, emphasizing the wild carnivalesque elements of anarchy and excluding its transformative dimensions. Although there are some elements of disruption here, the image remains bounded within patriarchal constructions of male youth: a portrait of the anarchist as lager lout.

The Blobby reproduced here (see Figure 5.2) reconstructs the mainstream Blobby in still more complex ways. This is a flyer advertising a 'sexhibition' by the Manchester-based Homocult group which formed part of the 'Anarchy in the UK' festival.[24] Immediately, it is apparent that this is a mediation of Mr Blobby that appropriates the transgressiveness associated with the original (which is, as we have seen, originally merely spectacular), and recontextualizes it via reference to a supposedly 'disgusting', yet vital and hedonistic sexuality. In this sense, the image revitalizes the subversive meanings invoked only to be repressed by the mainstream Blobby.

Blobby's spots give the image a more complex set of meanings. Here the association of disease is obviously moved from femininity to homosexuality. This has both symbolic and more literal meanings. Symbolically, the association of homosexuality with disease reinforces Homocult's presentation of Queer as dangerous and perverse. More literally, the image can be read as a Queer response to representations of AIDS in contemporary Department of Health television ads. These concentrated on normalizing AIDS as differentiated from sexuality (and hence implicitly heterosexual). In the television commercials a series of 'ordinary' people with regional accents gave voice-over narratives which invariably ended in the revelation that they were HIV-positive. The Homocult Blobby throws back this de-homosexualization of AIDS, reiterating through the association of homosexuality with disease that it is gay men who constitute the majority of the HIV-positive population. This may be considered an important political statement, as a foundation for demands for gay-specific healthcare, etc. Ordinarily, what such statements risk is the perpetuation of dominant heterosexual discourses of homosexuality as the other of healthy identity. The Homocult Blobby not only evades this but goes one better. By its juxtaposition of hedonism, signs of disease (spots), and mainstream discourses of homosexuality ('buggered', 'disgusting'), the flyer problematizes the rhetoric and reality of disease. More than ever, AIDS is revealed as a counterpart to mainstream discourses of homosexuality as disgusting/as disease. In this sense, Homocult have arguably produced an anarchist representation of AIDS.

It would be a mistake, however, to view the Homocult Blobby purely as an example of a subcultural strand of anarchism. What is important about the Homocult Blobby is not that it unmasks the mainstream Blobby as reactionary in gender terms and as a bogus subversive (though it does both of these). Rather, it re-produces Blobby as politically and culturally subversive. In simple terms, anyone having seen the flyer would never see the TV Blobby in the same way again. Words on the flyer such as 'buggered', and 'disgusting' must be understood as operating in two discourses, both mainstream and subcultural. In the same way, the Homocult flyer itself mediates between mainstream and revolutionary positions.[25] Of themselves, neither the Homocult nor the mainstream Mr Blobby put at stake hegemonic (i.e. dominant) masculinity and heterosexuality. Instead, the Homocult Blobby enables its viewers to see

Fig 5.2   Homocult Sexhibition flyer, October 1994

the fractures and instabilities within dominant positions, and also perhaps to enjoy their destabilization.

Anarchy in the UK

The difference between the *You What* Blobby and the Homocult Blobby can be illustrated by reference to a pair of cartoons on the contents page of *Anarchy in the UK – The Comic*, an A5 'zine published by Slab-O-Concrete and sold at the festival (see Figure 5.3). These set up a binary definition of anarchism. In the first frame, the earnest young man emblematizes anarchism as a strategic utopian project with the aim of creating a peaceful, ordered, non-governmental, and non-violent society. He is invaded in the second frame by the clichéd anarchist bomber, who is explicitly related to comedy and fun by the punchlined 'moral' 'Don't lose your sense of humour in the struggle . . .'.

The binary set-up here derives both from internal tensions within the anarchist movement and from the relationship of anarchist self-representations to mainstream representations of anarchists. On the one hand, 'earnest-young-man' style anarchism is intellectually respectable, positive, not very threatening and not much fun. On the other hand, the bomber represents anarchism as scary, disruptive, violent and possibly fun – very much like the *You What* Blobby. However, the image of the anarchist bomber is also noted as a 'cliché' and a 'stereotype'; it is a mainstream image used to dehumanize and to stigmatize those whom it purports to represent. This reading is given weight later in the comic, in a piece by Donald Rooum which shows his famous anarchist stereotypes, the 'wildcat' and the 'egghead', and one interloper: the black-caped and -hatted 'Karl Yundt', 'a fictitious type'. A note explains:

> *Karl Yundt does not appear at all [in Rooum's Wildcat comics], because his attitude is not remotely connected with anarchism, despite his influence on ideas of 'anarchism' among the ill-informed. (He began as a character in* The Secret Agent *by Joseph Conrad.)*[26]

However, as the first cartoon implies, the anarchist bomber can represent an important element of anarchism, at base the notion that subversion and transgression are enjoyable, even liberating, in themselves. In Rooum's comics, the subversive and often violent wildcat fulfils this role. This raises something of a dilemma: on the one hand, to completely reject such portrayals as the bomber is to lay claim to a discourse of positive images that has as its ultimate horizon of achievement an equality within the status quo; on the other hand, as Rooum points out, to leave it uncontested is to accept a marginalizing and historically dubious representation.

The 'Disclaimer' cartoon in '*Anarchy in the UK – The Comic*' attempts to resolve this problem by humorously suggesting the importance of both images of anarchism, and hence reconstituting anarchism as including a

Fig 5.3   *Anarchy in the UK - The Comic* (Hove: Slab-O-Concrete, 1994)

series of binary oppositions: both political activism and violent struggle, serious reflection and playful disruption, 'politics' and 'culture'. Now to return to the anarchist Blobbies: the *You What* Blobby can be regarded as an updated, anarchist reimaging of the bomber stereotype: threatening, a little absurd, motivated by manic glee. The Homocult Blobby addresses the same tensions as the Disclaimer cartoon, while also at another level pointing up the instability of mainstream representation.

What the above has demonstrated, I hope, is that nothing is inherently and constantly subversive or marginal or liminal; equally nothing is inherently and constantly hegemonic, mainstream, or central: things only take on these meanings in relation to other things. This has been the implication of Homocult's work for years.[27] Although they come from the Situationist tradition of *détournement*, Homocult's strategies mark a decisive break with Situationism. In launching a double attack on dominant constructions of wealth and sexuality, Homocult reconnects a critique of representation with a sense of material economic relations. At the same time, Homocult and others have developed a specifically anarchist attitude to the cultural politics of representation. This firmly rejects leftist and liberal discourses of political correctness and positive images on the grounds that they can only secure equality within a culture and a society that require fundamental transformation. Homocult's Blobby gives the lie to liberal demands for positive images of people with AIDS as decent and respectable, while at the same time calling attention to the instability of mainstream representations.

Conclusion

In moving towards a conclusion, I would hope that, at a theoretical level, I have launched an argument which develops an anarchist cultural politics as triangulating liberal humanism (exemplified by John Fiske) and Marxism (exemplified by Jim McGuigan) by seeking to conceptualize hegemony and subversion as both textual and material. This argument has implied an anarchist cultural practice founded on a notion of cultural omnivorousness, i.e, a series of guerilla raids on the mainstream whose intention is not simply to seize certain signs and activities and make them its own, but also to bring to light the instability of hegemonic constructions of their meaning even when they are repossessed by the mainstream.

The Anarchy in the UK festival, with its actions, discussions, its anarchist football and its anarchist sex, both symbolized and enacted strategies of cultural omnivorousness. In this chapter I have not attempted to describe what actually happened in events organized by the festival. It is to be hoped both that such information is available elsewhere, and that those with more ability than myself will be able to present it without nostalgia. In any case, it should be apparent that I regard the importance of the festival as lying in the possibilities it held out rather than its realization. This could be summed up by the title 'Anarchy in the UK', appropriated from the Sex Pistols' first single. Stolen back from its use by consumer society (aka EMI), and freed from marginalization, the phrase reiterates anarchism as a politics, while at the same time retaining the original's sense of pure enjoyment – what my grandmother used to call, with precision, its 'devilment'.

Finally then, Anarchy in the UK can be seen as symbolizing a moment when the diverse resources of British anarchism came together to develop a pluralistic, dynamic critique of power relations, and to celebrate a pluralistic and dynamic anarchist culture. Whether or not the festival succeeded in achieving this is another matter. Nevertheless, it is only by acting upon this that the anarchist tradition will be able to challenge the power relations of the societies which produced it, and perhaps to realize that recurrent fantasy of leaving the twentieth century.

Notes

1. Anonymous contributor to discussion, *Popular Culture*, Glasgow Anarchist Summer School (1993), p.3.

2. Anarchy in the UK flyer. Kindly supplied by Jon Purkis. Thanks also to Peter Pavement.

3. One issue here is raised by the highlighting in the mainstream liberal media of a certain ideological poverty or confusion in single issue campaigns which, oddly enough, allows some sympathetic identification. See for example, Linda Grant, 'Just Say No / Ten Years of the New Protest', *Guardian Weekend* 3 June 1995, pp.12–18, 21–2.

4. Stewart Home, 'Organised Chaos', *Independent*, 25 October 1994, p.22. For a sustained articulation of Home's positions in the late 1980s, which are relevant to the culture/politics debate, see Home (1991).

5. Bakunin (1973), p.112 (emphasis in original).

6. Ibid., p.114.

7. Ibid., p.113.

8. This perspective was articulated by another speaker at the discussion of Popular Culture at the Glasgow Anarchist Summer School 1993, against the more fluid, 'culturalist' position of the speaker quoted at the head of this chapter. See Glasgow

Anarchist Summer School, 1993, *Popular Culture*, xerox, pp.3–4.

9. On Situationism, in addition to the Home volume, see Wollen (1993), Chapter 4 and Plant (1992), both of whom raise in different ways the politics/culture problem. Discussions of Situationist work which present it in the tradition of avant-garde art should be approached with extreme suspicion; a useful antidote to such work is Knabb (1981), which remains the best primary Situationist text in English.

10. See especially 'Involution', in The Moorish Orthodox Radio Crusade Collective *Radio Sermonettes* (1992).

11. *Test Card F* (1994), p.9.

12. Ibid., p.78.

13. See McGuigan (1992). As McGuigan points out, the phrase lacks a stable referent and his book is an attempt to wrest the term away from the writers he critiques. See further discussion below.

14. For a polemical account of this turn in British cultural studies, see McGuigan (1992). Among the large number of relevant books, the following are seminal: Hebdige (1979); McRobbie (1989); Willis (1978).

15. Fiske (1989), p.15.

16. Ibid., p.35.

17. Ibid., p.39.

18. McGuigan (1992), p.24.

19. On this, and for a swingeing criticism of what can be seen as McGuigan's academic and theoretical élitism, see Storey (1993), pp.181–202.

20. See 'Settling Accounts with Subcultures: A Feminist Critique' in McRobbie (1991), pp.16–34.

21. On cross-dressing as transgressive yet culturally central, see Garber (1992/1993).

22. My evidence for this is, admittedly, anecdotal. On three separate occasions when I have asked students and friends for readings of Blobby's spots, the first replies have cited disease.

23. Thanks to John Moore for drawing my attention to this image.

24. For an excellent and brief introduction to Homocult, see Mark Simpson 'Coming Over All Queer' in the cartoon story magazine *Deadline*, No. 60, March 1994.

25. It should be clear from this that the distinction between mainstream Blobby and subcultural or contestatory Blobby cannot be resolved simply by looking at relations of production.

26. *Anarchy in the UK – The Comic*, p.42.

27. See, for example, *Queer with Class: The First Book of Homocult* (1992).

CHAPTER 6

A Subversive Current?

Contemporary Anarchism Considered

Karen Goaman and Mo Dodson

This chapter looks at examples from contemporary anarchism to explore an important element in the anarchist tradition, namely its history of often symbolic and sometimes playful and humorous subversive action which breaks with orthodox politics. The chapter also looks at parallel changes in philosophy and theory since the 1960s – in radical communist theories and in post-structuralist perspectives – and considers these in relation to the contemporary anarchist interventions and texts discussed.

Introduction

This work is part of a subversive current of which the last has not yet been heard.

(Raoul Vaneigem, Situationist, writing of his book *The Revolution of Everyday Life*, 1963)

In spite of its shortcomings, the Situationist International has shown . . . it is . . . important to be something different from the attitudes and values of the society the revolutionary wants to destroy. . . . Such activity implies a radical break with politics . . . the task is to express (in a text or an action) a subversive relation to the world. However big or small, such an act is an attack against the old world.

(Jean Barrot and François Martin. *Eclipse and Re-emergence of the Communist Movement*, 1972)

It is now becoming accepted that demonstrations, marches, spectacles and shows don't lead anywhere. Waving banners, putting up posters, handing out leaflets, attacking the police are all activities which perpetuate a certain ritual – a ritual wherein the police are always cast in the role of invincible subjugators . . . there has to be a refusal of the old terrain of struggle – both in the workplace and in the streets . . . it will require a simultaneous movement towards the creation of new modes of life.

(Jacques Camatte. *Against Domestication*, 1973)

These quotes describe vital and important elements in the anarchist tradition and its history of subversive, often symbolic action: first, they express the idea of a subversive current which is part of a continuing tradition; second, they call for a break with orthodox politics and for symbolic action expressing a subversive relation to the world; and, third, they reject orthodox socialist means of opposition – party politics, demonstrations – and call for a move to new ways of living and acting.

This chapter explores these arguments in relation to contemporary anarchist activity. Our definition of anarchism is a broad one, incorporating many radical critiques of contemporary life – of State and government, capitalism, hierarchical systems, male domination and élitist Western culture. Anarchists, unlike orthodox socialists and Marxists, reject vanguardist leadership and any idea of seizing the power of rulers. For this reason anarchists have tended to find alternatives to accepted forms of parliamentary protest. This has resulted in a flourishing of alternative forms of expression, often cultural and symbolic, and always self-organized and produced.

This chapter will also look at parallel changes in philosophy and theory, and in particular at the post-structuralist rejection of Marxist theory and orthodox political action, and its subsequently rather 'anarchistic' approach to opposition. We will compare the views from two post-structuralist perspectives – Foucault's and Deleuze and Guattari's – with regard to resistance and opposition.

An unorthodox tradition

We'll consider first the idea of a move away from traditional forms of political opposition, towards more symbolic, playful, culturally expressed and 'localized' forms of opposition. Our argument is that this has been articulated, since the late 1960s, by two strands – one outside of academia (for example, by Barrot and Martin and Camatte) and one developed in an academic context (in post-structuralist writings). Yet this form of symbolic expression and radical critique has had a longer history in the anarchist tradition and in related 'avant-garde' movements such as Situationism. Since anarchists, as stated earlier, have always rejected both the traditional parliamentary process of opposition AND the Marxist idea of vanguardist movements to seize power, many anarchists and related avant-garde currents have tended to look for alternative ways of expressing and acting out opposition: from starting communes to Situationist-inspired activity and self-published texts.

After the radical protest events of 1968, particularly in France, the failure to sustain revolutionary momentum resulted in a radical rethinking of traditional ideas about political activity. This theorizing and rethinking were more evident outside of self-styled anarchist circles, possibly because anarchists tend not to look for hard and fast prescriptions about revolutionary activity and have always avoided the orthodox Marxist approach. This was particularly evident in France, presumably partly because of the more dramatic nature and outcome of events there in 1968. French writers such as those quoted at the start of this chapter – Barrot and Martin and Camatte – came from a radical communist background and not an anarchist one, and, although what they conceptualized as an appropriate direction for radical oppositional activity is notably anarchist, they were keen to distinguish their ideas from anarchism and to stick to a 'pure' version of the communist tradition (the word 'pure' here referring to a distinction from Marxist-Leninist/USSR-style communism). Their writing is a critical amalgam of anarchistic elements drawn from radical communism and the avant-garde tradition, especially Situationism.

Another French writer, Richard Gombin, held an academic post (at the Centre National de la Recherche Scientifique) where he wrote two books which theorized a new direction for radical activity.[1] In the first book, *Origins of Modern Leftism*, published in 1971, Gombin called this tradition 'leftism'; in the second book, *The Radical Tradition*, published in 1979, he renames this current, as the title suggests, the 'radical tradition'. However, the tradition that he outlines is recognizable as anarchism both in spirit and practice. He states that 'leftism disassociates [sic] itself from Marxism and all the varieties of 19th century socialism'.[2] Gombin also recognizes the overlap with both avant-garde currents – Dada, Surrealism, the Situationists – and utopian and millenarian traditions: he writes of the current which he somewhat misleadingly identifies as leftism:

> [it] has inherited from the dadaist and surrealist tradition a supreme contempt for the technological society, its greyness and boredom. From millenarianism and the 'horsemen' of the Apocalypse it has borrowed the aspiration towards a totally different world, a paradise which can and should be realized. It takes its fantastic constructions from utopia, but wants to integrate them into short-term projects; it refuses to banish the dream and boil down the real to what is currently achievable.[3]

Gombin echoes the assertion of Camatte in the opening quote to this article, in an expressed rejection of orthodox forms of struggle, writing that '[t]he struggle for a new world cannot use the reified instruments of the opposition movement inherited from the past'.[4] Gombin also looks to the importance of *subjectivity* and *play* in the current that he identifies.[5]

Gombin and the other French writers quoted at the start of the chapter each emerged independently out of a libertarian version of Marxism and/or communism, rather than anarchism. They all took an optimistic view following the events of 1968, seeing possibilities for future forms of opposition. Each described and theorized about this emerging current, and in all their texts, the elements of anarchism are recognizable. And yet none of them called this anarchistic current 'anarchism': Vaneigem, the

Situationist, would see the activity surrounding the Situationist International as an oppositional current inspired and informed by previous 'avant-garde' currents – Dada, Surrealism, Lettrism – as well as drawing on Marxism and anarchism; Barrot and Martin, and Camatte all have backgrounds in radical communism. None the less, we would identify these currents and milieus as broadly anarchist. One concern here is to look at some examples of ways these currents have continued through the last three decades of the twentieth century, and to reflect on their potential as we enter what Western systems have named the twenty-first century.

Post-structuralism and the radical tradition

Before moving on to some examples of symbolic, playful activity that present an anarchist alternative to orthodox political opposition, we will consider some developments that took place particularly within French academic life in the years after 1968.

France's most celebrated proponents of post–structuralist theory include a number of academics with previous connections to the radical milieu.[6] The development of post-structuralist theory is sometimes analysed in terms of a response to the failure of the revolutionary events of 1968. Terry Eagleton, for example, an academic specializing in literature and cultural studies, has argued that:

> Post-structuralism was a product of that blend of euphoria and disillusionment, liberation and dissipation, carnival and catastrophe, which was 1968. Unable to break the structures of State power, post-structuralism found it possible instead to subvert the structures of language. Nobody, at least, was likely to beat you over the head for doing so. The student movement was flushed off the streets and driven underground into discourse. Its enemies, as for the later Barthes [a post-structuralist], became coherent belief-systems of any kind – in particular all forms of political theory and organisation which sought to analyse, and act upon, the structures of society as a whole.[7]

The anarchistic and playful elements of Situationist approaches, which have been strongly influential in anarchist circles since the 1960s, suggest that changes in conceptions of radical activity were indeed already taking place. Also relevant is the fact that the focus and locus of radical activity were changing, coinciding with a new questioning of the dominance of Marxism in these areas.

Post-structuralist theory opposed the humanistic approaches popular in the 1960s. For example, the idea of alienation, a strong element in radical critiques, becomes redundant for post-structuralist theorists, since there is no concept of the human subject which stands outside of discourse systems, and thus there is no such thing as alienation because there is no essential subject or freedom from which the subject can be alienated. Could post-structuralism as a philosophical discourse have been attractive to academics because of its abstraction, which provides an escape from the realities of the world and of themselves? Alan Megill concludes in his study of Nietzsche, Heidegger, Foucault and Derrida that '[w]hen they ravel and unravel the myriad ironies of discourse, they are as distant from morality and suffering as the supreme rationalist'.[8]

Post-structuralist philosophy, in terms of its reconceptualization of modes of radical activity, goes in a distinctly anarchist direction in terms of form. In its rejection of 'grand narratives' (foundational theories such as Marxism), post-structuralists tend to look to the local, the particular, the sporadic, as a means of disrupting the normal order of things. It is sometimes argued that 'new social movements', such as ecological, feminist, gay, Black and ethnic movements, etc., with their particular set of views and claims, constitute a paradigm of 'postmodern' opposition. Certainly Deleuze and Guattari look to the emergence of these new social movements as throwing into question the global economy of the 'power coding machine and the nation states'.[9]

Post-structuralist writers also look to the radical potential of more abstract phenomena, such as Deleuze and Guattari's notion of desires, intensities and madness opposing capitalism; and of strategies of resistance via 'a-centred' (with no organizing centre) forms of resistance which they metaphorically term 'rhizomes' and 'nomadology'; Lyotard refers to a 'libidinal economy' and 'language games'; Baudrillard refers to a silence of passivity which the masses can adopt to resist contemporary 'hyperreality' (Baudrillard's term 'hyperreality' referring to a world of media signs in which the image is more real than the reality); and Foucault talks of refusing what we are, and makes an (oft quoted) allusion to 'bodies and pleasures' as countering the discourses of power/knowledge which determine the subject.

Post-structuralist strategies of resistance, with their ethos of resisting power/knowledge systems, sidestep orthodox forms of political activity and vanguardism. Orthodox socialism is rejected by post-structuralists as another example of the 'metanarratives' that they oppose, seeing it as a continuation of Enlightenment beliefs in rationality, science, progress and single theories to explain the world and to prescribe action within it. Sometimes this rejection is explicit, such as in Deleuze and Guattari's description of the traditional Marxist socialist model of revolutionary organization as an 'eternal impossibility'.[10] Other recognizably anarchistic elements of their critique are Guattari's awareness of the 'micro-fascisms' that exist in a social field, including gangs, and the 'Stalins of little groups'.[11]

Foucault, however, goes further in his sidestepping and rejection of orthodox forms. Implicit in Foucault's perspective is the idea that oppositional currents are merely part of the same order and find no ground outside of the discourses of 'power/knowledge' which determine us as human subjects. In Foucault's view, there can be no essential freedom that exists outside of the power relation, and therefore he suggests the idea of an 'agonism' – a term coined by Foucault to imply a relationship which is 'at the same time reciprocal incitation and struggle . . . a permanent provocation'.[12]

In other words, where there is power, there is resistance, but this resistance is part of the same order and not outside of it. The sociologists Laurie Taylor and Stanley Cohen describe it thus in their discussion of postmodern theory and its critique of metanarratives, writing that the 'collapse of metanarratives' implies that

> there is no single meaning system or metaphor that we can use to obtain a sense of the world from which we want to distance ourselves or against which we want to construct an alternative. . . . Any attempts to deconstruct the notion of alternative modes of transforming consciousness would depend not on the properties of the alternative but of the original. The task lies less in deconstructing the master destinations and metaphors of escape . . . than in looking at where you are coming from.[13]

Beyond post-structuralism

We want now to turn to a comparison between post-structuralism and the work of Barrot and Martin, Camatte and Gombin. All the latter theorists reject the authoritarian elements of Marxism and orthodox political organization, without recourse to post-structuralist abstractions and notions of language/power/knowledge as all-determining. Gombin is explicit in retaining the concept of alienation. For example, when he writes that his version of the emerging radical current

> aspires to build a life in which man [sic] is not a stranger to his fellows, where communication can be restored through a de-alienated use of language. The word will then be inseparable from the deed and will express human and universal truth, and not squalid everyday lies.[14]

Camatte's writing also refers to the notion of the 'alienation of being' (for example, in relation to the machine)[15] and he sees revolution as 'the reintegration of all that was separate, a coming together of future being, individuality and *Gemeinwesen*'.[16]

Gombin emphasizes the historical tradition of ideas in the 'utopia of liberation'[17]: while recognizing that the negation of order in any human society 'can never be anything but the expression of its era', Gombin also sees the 'radical tradition' as an 'alternative to authoritarian ideology [which] is as old as this ideology itself', an alternative which is 'playing out its role before history.'[18]

An important element in our own perspectives on anarchism and the possibility of radical activity is that there is a tradition of anti-authoritarian ideas, a rich oppositional current: from the thirteenth century Free Spirit (a heretical millenarian movement which stressed individual liberty); through the seventeenth century Ranters and Diggers (radicals in the English Revolution); William Blake; William Godwin; to the twentieth century avant-garde movements and anarchist currents. This is handed down through texts which, although they may not escape the determining systems and conditions in which the ideas are thought, acted upon and written about, are none the less expressions of a critique of authoritarian forms and hierarchical systems which can inform and influence further generations picking up on the same impulse. Barrot and Martin even imply that this impulse may be an essential part of ourselves which can be recovered and emerge at any time. They write that communist ideas 'do not come from nowhere; they always appear because the symptoms of a real human community exist emotionally in every one of us.'[19] This also illustrates Barrot and Martin's (humanist) belief in an essential self, an autonomous subject.

Theory into practice

Our look at some examples of contemporary anarchist activities will pick up mainly on two important elements which have emerged in this discussion. First, there is the existence, proclaimed by Gombin, of a rich tradition of anti-authoritarian ideas. We argue that this tradition, handed down orally and in texts, forms a counterweight to Foucault's negative notions about opposition: if this historical tradition is seen as a resource for inspiring an oppositional impulse, it might be seen as a potential force to challenge Foucault's conceptualization of power/resistance as part of the same order, playing out an agonistic struggle. We are aware that, from Foucault's perspective, these ideas handed down from the past are subject to the same determination by discourse/power/knowledge as contemporary phenomena. We do, however, dispute Foucault's notion (intrinsic to post-structuralism generally) of language/discourse as all determining. We are therefore positing the possibility of an area in ourselves which may become distorted by power systems but which is contactable and potentially recoverable. This is similar to the argument of Barrot and Martin expressed above, when they write of the symptoms of real human community existing emotionally in every one of us.

Second, the notion of opposition through symbolic, cultural, and, especially, playful activity is an element which could form common ground in terms of both post-structuralism and the reconstructed anti-authoritarian theorizing of Barrot and Martin, Camatte and Gombin.

In our discussion of some examples of anarchist interventions, there is evidence both of symbolic action and of the influence of a tradition of anti-authoritarian ideas. These are illustrations of a break with orthodox politics: as Barrot and Martin put it: 'the task is to express (in a text or an action) a subversive relation to the world . . . [h]owever big or small, such an act is an attack against the old world'.[20] The examples are fragmentary (space does not allow much contextualization) but they all illustrate symbolic activity which disrupts and subverts everyday life and challenges taken-for-granted issues.

The Artful Dodger

This is the title of the London-based Fare Dodgers' Liberation Front's paper. Issue No. 2 (July 1995) starts with the headline 'WE'RE STILL NOT PAYING!' and goes on to say:

> For millions of us, riding on the tube is mostly a means of getting to work. Often it is the most unpleasant part of the working day, and the bosses expect us to pay for it out of our own pockets! The bastards should be paying us! Every worker who's not completely resigned to their miserable lot knows that a spot of theft and sabotage help to brighten up the working day. So let's extend this into the miserable journey into work – let's refuse to pay their fares, and while we're about it, let's fuck up their advertising campaigns, their ticket barriers, their surveillance systems. . . . Let's use our imaginations![21]

The FDLF then make explicit their opposition to capitalism:

> For us, fighting for free transport is just one way of asserting our needs as human beings against the needs of a crazy system, capitalism, that puts profit before people: thousands sleeping on the streets, hospitals closing, people going hungry. . . . While we stand at bus stops in the rain, the rich drive past in cars worth more than our houses. Where does their wealth come from? It comes from us! We say 'stuff that, everything should be free!'

In *The Artful Dodger*, they document a 'tube party' held in May 1995. It attracted about thirty people and lasted for about one and a half circuits of the London Underground's Circle Line. Balloons and silly string were brought out, chocolate cake was distributed, and musical accompaniment was provided on two didgeridoos. Stickers were distributed along the whole length of the train. The response from other passengers was, they write, almost entirely positive.

The Artful Dodger, though cheaply and plainly presented in black print on A4 paper, makes engaging use of humour to put its message across, such as its suggestions for fare dodging: 'If you're a particularly small person you might prefer to crawl through the hole intended for luggage, but some might consider this undignified.' They call too for a 'Blatant Fare-Dodging Day' in which people, preferably in large groups, will shamelessly jump over the barriers or hold a gate open to let ten of their friends through. And they suggest that '[w]e might approach people buying tickets and try to persuade them not to be so silly'.

The writing and actions illustrate the spirit of anarchist symbolic activity. An orthodox approach to complaining about the price (or existence) of fares would be by writing letters to MPs and London Transport, petitioning, and demonstrating outside tube stations or London Transport's offices. The name Fare Dodgers' Liberation Front suggests a playfully satirical use of the names often used by orthodox nationalist movements. The approach of the FDLF uses ideas of pleasure, humour and play to engage people's attention and imagination by presenting their actions with enjoyable events. This kind of intervention potentially disrupts 'the boredom of everyday life' bringing to mundane situations (such as sitting on a tube train) a sense of play and pleasure that is normally absent, and, in so doing, offering a taste of an alternative reality.

Away With All Cars

Continuing with the transport theme, the pamphlet *Away With All Cars*[22] was produced in the early 1990s by Mr Social Control, a performance poet who has self-published various pamphlets. *Away With All Cars* explains where the title comes from with a quote from a newspaper report. It reads: 'Things got too much for (Yugoslavian) author Kudno Mojesic. He was arrested in the street outside his home attacking cars with an axe, yelling "Away with all cars they are the devil's work."' (*Sunday Mirror*, 11 January 1976). The back cover has a spoof car advertisement:

> *This luxury high performance pamphlet offers a unique combination of responsive handling and distinctive bodystyling. Its enhanced specifications include advanced antilock staples and its spacious yet economical pages are designed with all the passionate rhetoric and implacable logic that the discerning reader has come to expect from Mr Social Control.*

An example of Mr Social Control's rhetoric is where he reveals his critical connection to anarchism (a Situationist influence is also indicated by his critique of contemporary 'spectacular' society):

> *We hate cars because we are sick of living in a world where we have no control over anything we do. . . . We could be participating in the enjoyable. There is a distinction between watching a spectacle of life and really truly living. Unfortunately those anarchists (whoops, out of the closet now) who adopted this distinction as part of their opinions have often obscured practical political activities that tend to confirm their theories.*[23]

The title page of the pamphlet features a visual/textual reference to oppositional pamphlets of the past with its imitation of a hand-typeset and hand-printed panel (achieved by the paste-up of centred but wobbly lines of text) which reads, in old-fashioned language:

> *a sincere and zealous protestation of motorized carriages together with some suggestions towards the elimination of this discourge [sic] in the form of an open letter to all motorists being at once manifesto and manifestation of the outlawed Pedestrian Freedom Front.*

The name and logo of the publishing press also indicate the Situationist inspiration: Play Time for Ever Press is the name, and the logo says 'DON'T COMPETE: PLAY'. Here then is explicit evidence of the oppositional inspiration offered by past radical texts which, as we have suggested, embody a potential force cutting through the system which, in Foucault's view, we cannot be outside of.

Anti Clock-wise / No!

Anti Clock-wise and *No!* were two series of 'zines put out by one person, living in Liverpool. The 'zines were xeroxed and stapled pages – more the result of practical constraints rather than a deliberate striving for what *Bypass Zine* has called 'crap-xerox-chic'.[24] The title slogan in issues of *Anti Clock-wise* was always the same : 'Nihilists, one more effort if we are to be revolutionaries'.

There was a subscription list of about 200 for the two 'zines, and Rick, the one-person editorial team, sold them from time to time at suitable venues such as the Anarchist Book Fair in London. He produced them over a few years from the late 1980s to early 1990s. Looking at Issue 13 of *Anti Clock-wise*, this includes an editorial on the Gulf War; an article by Rick on animal rights expressing his reservations about the sabotage tactics and direct action carried out by the Animal Liberation Front; and rant from Rick about the way individuals have no say in the design or location of their homes. In it, he argues that

> Our whole lives are being dictated by finance, expediency and specialist ideology – as we know, ideology always serves the ruling class. We can make no demands on this society because this leads to reform which recuperates our anger and solves nowt. It is this society that has evaporated our spirit and desire for real life.

This issue also contains reviews of North American anarchist and Situationist papers. Noting the length and quality of anti-authoritarian papers there, Rick writes, 'there will never be a revolution in the States or Canada because everyone will be tied up in ploughing through all the text of their radical papers!'

Included is a review of a Situationist-inspired magazine called *Against Sleep and Nightmare*, produced by one man in Oakland, California. An article from one issue is included in *Anti Clock-wise* on 'The Theory of Spectacular Sex'. The text has a strongly detectable Situationist style, using the Marxist-derived Situationist analysis which offers a critique of commodity culture. The writer argues 'from religious ecstasy to S&M fantasies, it is not the "naturalness" of sensuality that has been lost but its wholeness'. The writer appears by implication to take on board something of Foucault's notion of there being no oppositional stand outside of the existing discourses, while offering the possibility of another direction: 'It is not possible to be outside of current systems of sensuality; it is only possible to be moving away from them.' And, using italics to stress his Situationist-style rhetoric, he writes, '*Every free expression today remains an expression of the negation of the current situation. The play of negations is necessary to move us beyond the misery of today.*' The article does not give any practical examples of what form these negations and runnings away might take.

Interestingly, a similar criticism was made of *Anti Clock-wise* in the libertarian journal *The Edinburgh Review*. In an editorial on 'Contemporary Marginalia': the editor writes of *Anti Clock-wise*. 'Its heart is in the right place, but rhetoric of this kind is essentially empty and useless, given that the how of such utopian projects is never broached. Instead, argument degenerates into slogans'.[25] This is a valid criticism, though it does not necessarily detract from the potential of these kinds of radical 'zines to make ripples and inspire oppositional impulses if they reach people open to questioning basic elements of the contemporary world.

SCUM Manifesto

A pamphlet which has become one of the longest surviving perennials of anarchist publishing is Valerie Solanas's *SCUM Manifesto*. The tract was first published in 1968 after Solanas had achieved notoriety for shooting and wounding the 'pop' artist Andy Warhol. *SCUM Manifesto* has had some influence outside of the anarchist milieu, for example, the band Manic Street Preachers made reference to some points from *SCUM* on their first album.[26]

The appeal of *SCUM Manifesto* lies in its sardonic humorous style and its radical critique of all aspects of society. SCUM stands for Society for Cutting Up Men, and part of Solanas's manifesto is the elimination of the male sex. A question that immediately arises is whether it would be acceptable for the same tract to be written by a man calling for the elimination of the female sex. This would probably provoke distaste and outrage in both women and men of any political persuasion. Solanas seems to get away with it BECAUSE she is a woman writing about men, and woman occupy a relatively subordinate position in a predominantly 'patriarchal' society; also, the writing style is over-the-top, and therefore invites the reader not to take the ideas too seriously.

It is possible of course that she was serious about the elimination of men: the act of shooting and wounding Andy Warhol suggests an extreme state of mind, and her anger and contempt against men and colluding women are clear even in the ironic and half-satirical style. Solanas herself is thought to be dead, so we will probably never know her intentions, if, indeed, she ever knew them herself.

There are, however, passages in which she writes about men in a way that is a brutal exaggeration and yet not devoid of all truth: some of us do recognize traces of her characterizations in some males we meet. For example, she writes:

> The male is completely egocentric, trapped inside himself, incapable of empathizing or identifying with others, of love, friendship, affection or tenderness. . . . Being an incomplete female, the male spends his life attempting to complete himself, to become female. He attempts to do this by constantly seeking out, fraternizing with and trying to live through and fuse with the female, and claiming as his own all female characteristics – emotional strength and independence, forcefulness, dynamism, decisiveness . . . etc. – and projecting onto women all male traits – vanity, frivolity, triviality, weakness, etc. . . . Women, in other words, don't have penis envy; men have pussy envy.[27]

Solanas writes that men are responsible for things that 'have made of the world a shitpile', for example, war, money, marriage and prostitution, mental illness, suppression of individuality, isolation, authority and government, philosophy, religion, prejudice, competition, formal education, social classes, prevention of friendship, 'Great Art' and 'Culture', boredom, suppression of knowledge;[28] even included in the range of things Solanas sees men as responsible for are 'Niceness, Politeness and "Dignity"'; she writes: 'Every man, deep down, knows he's a worthless piece of shit . . . the male tries to enforce a 'social code' that ensures a perfect blandness.[29]

Solanas's writing gives provocative potential insights, such as in her brief denigration of philosophy and religion, and Great Art and Culture. On religion she writes:

> The male's inability to relate to anybody or anything makes his life pointless and meaningless (the ultimate male insight is that life is absurd), so he invented philosophy and religion. Being empty, he looks outward, not only for guidance and control, but for salvation and for the meaning of life. Happiness being for him impossible on this earth, he invented Heaven.[30]

In her critical swipe at Great Art and Culture, she writes:

> Having stripped the world of conversation, friendship and love, the male offers us these paltry substitutes: 'Great Art' and 'Culture'. . . . The male 'artistic' aim being, not to communicate (having nothing inside him, he has nothing to say), but to disguise his animalism, he resorts to symbolism and obscurity ('deep stuff'). The vast majority of people, particularly the 'educated' ones, lacking faith in their own judgement, humble, respectful of authority ('Daddy knows best' is translated into adult language as 'Critic knows best', 'Writer knows best', 'Ph.D knows best'), are easily conned into believing that obscurity, ambiguity and boredom are marks of depth and brilliance.[31]

Her rant continues, showing a possible influence from Situationist writing of the 1960s and its critique of the 'society of the Spectacle' (though it is equally possible that she arrived at her view independently):

> *unable to create or relate, they (males) spectate. Absorbing 'culture' is a desperate, frantic attempt to groove in an ungroovy world, to escape the horror of a sterile mindless existence . . . [T]hey can pride themselves on their ability to appreciate the 'finer' things, to see a jewel where there is only a turd (they want to be admired for admiring) . . . they have to see beauty in turds because, so far as they can see, turds are all they'll ever have.*[32]

This last section illustrates Solanas's way of using insulting terms and colloquialisms in a humorous way. Here's some more from the final paragraph: 'The sick, irrational men . . . when they see SCUM barrelling down on them, will cling in terror to Big Mama with her Big Bouncy Boobies, but Boobies won't protect them against SCUM'.[33]

Her writing is aggressively derisive but the humour and the far-reaching radical critical analysis have probably helped to maintain the popularity of Solanas's rant amongst anarchists. The humour acts as a counterweight to the more ferocious elements of her argument about eliminating men. We suggest that her critique of males is misdirected and could be a more general critique of the contemporary system. Though Solanas is as vicious about women who collude with men as with men themselves, she appears to assume that men are by nature the problem, rather than seeing men (and women) as being overlaid or constructed by a wider system of social, cultural and historical forces. Solanas seems to fall into the same trap as many 'class struggle anarchists' who take the role of angry injured victims of the ruling class (in Solanas's case it is men, rather than the ruling class). It is to these class struggle anarchists that we now turn for our last example of symbolic and subversive activity.

Class War and 'class struggle anarchists'

The *Class War* paper, set out in the form of a popular tabloid paper (with the 'hospitalized copper' instead of the 'Page Three Girl'), is written in an essentially humorous and irreverent style – for example, several years ago, one article quipped that the Ayatollah Khomeini put the 'mental' back in 'fundamental'. The style can be enjoyable as a symbolic rhetorical statement of anger and injustice. The humour of the paper does, however, mask some of *Class War*'s apparently serious belief in a particular form of militant 'us and them' struggle in which the ruling class and its defenders, such as the police, are cast in the role of the enemy, who are to be attacked, perhaps in a mood of vengeance. Like Solanas's attitude, this ignores the extent to which it is the set of power relationships, and not just the people themselves, which creates these divisions. The class struggle approach perhaps confirms the very system it is attacking.

Foucault's notion of an 'agonistic struggle'[34] may have some relevance in this respect; certainly the way in which the popular tabloids love to write loathsome reports about *Class War* actions suggests a mutual taunting, as in a wrestling match, which the term 'agonisism' suggests. Camatte, one of the radical communist writers quoted earlier, offers insights into how to change the kind of reciprocal agonistic relationships identified by Foucault: Camatte is critical of the cycle of 'provocation–repression–subversion' in which leftists persist.[35] Citing the history of civilization as one of prejudice and enmity between different groups – in terms of class, gender, ethnicity, politics, religion – Camatte writes of the dangers of delegating 'all inhumanity to one part of the social whole, and all humanity to another'. He writes,

> *If human beings are to be destroyed, they must first be despoiled of their humanity. And so if, during the revolutionary struggle, people choose to proceed according to this view, are they not simply imitating the methods used by the capitalists, and thus furthering the destruction of human beings?*[36]

An attack on serious (high) culture

In a similar vein to Solanas's text, another critique of serious or high culture has, equally provocatively, been that provided more recently by Stewart Home. He has made a name for himself over the past ten years mainly by writing satires of pulp novels with mindless violence and sex, and by producing propaganda advocating his aim to demolish serious culture. He has had several novels and collections of short stories published, most of them showing a photograph of himself on the cover (he is a self-confessed active self-publicist). He has also written a history of the tradition of which he sees his interventions to be a part, entitled *The Assault on Culture: Utopian Currents from Lettrisme to Class War.*[37] Home has been mentioned in a number of anarchist contexts as being anti-anarchist, and certainly Home would not define himself as an anarchist, and would probably say that he is anti most things as this is part of his deliberately provocative stance. We would, however, regard his interventions as falling within our broad definitional framework of currents which are quite clearly related to anarchism.

One of the most engaging interventions he has mentioned (although he would probably regard it as insignificant alongside his more recent work) was an account of when he used to go to a club where performance poets would recite poetry. As a stance against the 'pretentiousness' of this kind of high culture, even though it was an avant-garde intervention, Home used to write poems about vegetables and read them out when it was his spot. At first he threw carrots and other vegetables out at the audience while reciting his poems about vegetables. The audience would throw them back, so he began taking in packets of frozen peas and throwing those out at the audience because he knew that peas would be too difficult to pick up again and throw back.

This humorous statement against high/serious culture demonstrates playful and symbolic elements which Home has carried through to his later work including: his (lone and self-publicized) three-year 'Art Strike', in which he publicized the fact that he was producing no cultural work; and his propaganda attacking examples of high culture such as the Turner prizewinner, artist Rachel Whitehead, and the composer Stockhausen. In his book *The Assault on Culture*, Home refers to the use of 'shock tactics' in the tradition of which he sees himself to be a part. He argues that:

> *Shock tactics are often employed to help maintain a sense of differentiation. If similar tactics are repeated too often they soon lose their impact. Icononoclasm has, by its very nature, a limited life-span. A movement such as* fluxus[38] *would be far more satisfactory if it had disbanded in 1966.*[39]

Some anarchists might argue, perhaps, that Home could 'take a leaf out of his own book' and change the direction of his own shock tactics and consistently provocational 'anti' stance.

These examples have been chosen as illustrations of a line of symbolic activity which has been sporadic but notably rich in anarchism and fringe and marginal currents allied to it. All of them break with orthodox forms of political opposition and express their messages and carry out action culturally and symbolically. While we would argue that, ultimately, some kind of widespread network, often called a 'movement', is needed to effect significant change in our world, our argument is that such currents of, as Barrot and Martin have expressed it, texts or actions expressing a subversive relation to the world are significant in themselves. Taking the metaphor of water, such texts or acts form ripples; other forms may appear as part of a general current, as eddies and waves, springs and streams, each of which may potentially challenge or redirect the mainstream and feed into, as Peter Marshall puts it, 'the river of anarchy'.[40]

Notes

1. Gombin (1975); Gombin (1979).

2. Gombin (1975) p.136.

3. Ibid., p.136.

4. Ibid., p.137.

5. Ibid., pp.136–7.

6. Jean-François Lyotard, author of *The Postmodern Condition*, was a member of the libertarian socialist group, *Socialisme ou Barbarie*, which included the influential writer Cornelius Castoriadis (and both the *Socialisme ou Barbarie* group and Castoriadis have been influential in anarchist circles). Jean Baudrillard was teaching with Henri Lefebvre at the University of Nanterre on a course attended by two Situationists, Guy

Debord and Raoul Vaneigem, in 1957–8, and Baudrillard has revealed how something of his initial attraction to Situationism has stayed with him (Baudrillard interviewed by J. Williamson, *Block 15*, 1989). Gilles Deleuze, together with Michel Foucault, was involved during the 1970s in political activity in defence of the rights of prisoners and against racist and sexist discrimination. (See 'Obituary for Gilles Deleuze' by David Macey, *Guardian*, 7 November, 1995.)

7. Eagleton (1983), p.142.

8. Megill (1985), p.352.

9. Deleuze and Guattari (1983), p.113.

10. Ibid., pp.109–10.

11. Ibid., p.97.

12. Foucault, M. 'Afterword on "The Subject and Power"' in Dreyfus and Rabinow (1982), pp.221–2.

13. Cohen and Taylor (1992), p.15.

14. Gombin (1975), p.137.

15. Camatte (1973), p.20.

16. Ibid., p.24. *Gemeinwesen* is a German word referring to the concept of 'community'.

17. Gombin (1979), p.8.

18. Ibid., p.9.

19. Barrot and Martin (1974), p.61.

20. Ibid., p.14.

21. *The Artful Dodger* No. 2 1995.

22. Mr Social Control (early 1990s).

23. Ibid., Point 7.3.

24. *Bypass Zine: Cross Currents in the Under-the-Counter Culture* No.1 (early 1990s), p.12.

25. *The Edinburgh Review* (1990) p.6.

26. Manic Street Preachers was a band which emerged in 1989. Their songs are noted for their expressions of angst and pain. They refer to Valerie Solanas in the lyrics and sleeve notes of a track on their first album (*Generation Terrorists*) taking up her points about males as incomplete female chromosomes and as emotionally deficient. The fact that they spell her name 'Solonas' on the sleeve suggests that they have read a version of the pamphlet published in the late 1980s, in which the name was printed 'Solonas'.

27. Solanas (undated, late 1980s), p.5.

28. Ibid., pp.3–15.

29. Ibid., p.3.

30. Ibid., p.13.

31. Ibid., p.17.

32. Ibid., p.17.

33. Ibid., p.24.

34. Cited in Dreyfus and Rabinow (1982), pp.221–2.

35. Camatte (1973), p.17.

36. Ibid., pp.14–15.

37. Home (1988).

38. Fluxus was an avant-garde group operating in the 1960s. Home makes the argument that, after the mid-1960s, the radical political edge of Fluxus gave way to a 'depoliticized aesthetic' (ibid., pp.56–9).

39. Ibid., p.104.

40. Marshall (1992), p.11.

CHAPTER 7

'It was easy, it was cheap, go and do it!'

Technology and Anarchy in the UK Music Industry[1]

Paul Rosen

This chapter argues that the independent record scene that developed out of punk rock in the late 1970s and early 1980s embodied anarchist principles, even though few of those involved would have called themselves anarchists. Advocates of independent records resisted the control of the mainstream music industry and in some cases actively sought to subvert it. They allied punk's 'access aesthetic', which challenged élitist conceptions of the 'artist' and aimed to break down the barrier between producers and consumers of music, to a do-it-yourself ethic that challenged the relations of production in the music industry. The chapter argues that change in the music industry is closely linked to technological change. Technology must therefore be a crucial element of anarchist cultural intervention, in music and elsewhere. The chapter highlights the limitations of existing anarchist approaches to technology, and suggests that anarchists need to treat technology as integrated with culture, rather than automatically equating it with hierarchical social structures.

Introduction

Let me try and define what I mean by anarchist. I mean, someone who doesn't believe in governments. Someone who believes in self-expression, self rule.

**Kate, the singer, in the film Breaking Glass,[2]
talking to the boss of her record label just after
signing a contract with him.**

This chapter is something of a hybrid. First, it's a personal excursion into my past, delving into the debris of my youth, much of which I spent listening to music by unknown bands,[3] going to their gigs, buying their records, playing in my own unknown bands and making our own records, as well as reading and writing about all this in various fanzines. Second, this chapter is an attempt to account for what I and others were doing then in terms that I've only come to understand later. Whilst a lot of people bandied the word 'anarchy' around in those days, especially followers of the band Crass and their associates, I certainly never recognized what I was doing at the time as anarchism in practice. In this chapter I'm going to attempt to make that link, and to draw in some aspects of social theory that I'd probably have cringed at fifteen years ago but that now occupy my time as much as music did then.[4]

I've made much use of B. George and Martha DeFoe's *International New Wave Discography, Volume II 1982/83*, and the *Zigzag* small labels catalogues mentioned in the text, to trace details about records, tapes and labels, although much of the result didn't end up in the chapter. *The Guinness Who's Who of Indie and New Wave* has been another useful source of information. I've also drawn considerably on the remains of my fanzine collection from around 1978–86; I'm sure I originally bought far more fanzines than I've kept, not realizing I'd regard them as research material in later years. Thankfully, I've probably kept all the independent records I ever bought. Writing this chapter has given me a welcome excuse to listen to many of them again, helping me recall the spirit of my topic.

My focus for the most part is going to be the flourishing independent record and cassette scenes that quickly followed the appearance of punk rock in the late 1970s, and survived into the early 1980s before dissipating. I also want to talk, though, about technology, as I feel this topic is central in bringing together independent music production with anarchism. Briefly, my argument is that anarchist writings tend to have a limited and often simplistic perception of technology. To achieve an anarchist society will require more than either eliminating technology, as some desire, or putting technology 'into the service of' anarchism, as might seem a better solution. It will, rather, require a transformation of the relations between technology and culture, something that I see as a major achievement of the musical cultures I'll be discussing.

Computers, the State and social interaction

To begin by looking at anarchist accounts of technology, a few years ago I spent an afternoon or two trawling through back issues of *Freedom* for references to technology. Predictably enough, I found a lack of consensus about the subject, or even about what 'technology' means. The various perspectives I found did tend, though, to take a negative view, and most focused on *information* technology. Computers in particular are, with good grounds, regarded by many anarchists as a symbol of the power of the State, facilitating the State's requirements in helping gather and retrieve information about its citizens, who can then be regulated with the help of this information.[5]

As well as facilitating the erosion of civil liberties by the State, information technology more broadly is mistrusted by anarchists because of the way it is perceived to undermine human social contact, something that can also be applied to technology in general. Denis Pym, for example, argues that microwave ovens 'undermine the conviviality of household meals and the sacredness of food'.[6] Andrew Hedgecock similarly regards the rise of video and computer games as contributing to children's growing inability to socialize,[7] while for Gregg Easterbrook this is an example of the way people in our culture are increasingly turning to computers rather than to other people for companionship.[8] These are important issues from an anarchist perspective because those who opt for the 'cosy myopia of manufactured fantasy will be unable to carry out an informed critique of the way we live'.[9] Technology is implicated, for these writers, both in the maintenance of a society which is antithetical to freedom and autonomy, and also in the construction of a psychology that is least conducive to these crucial elements of anarchism.

Technology in utopia

This outlook on technology isn't the only one open to anarchists. Murray Bookchin takes an almost completely opposite view to these writers, and to those who oppose technology outright on ecological grounds (see Edward Abbey's inspiring novel *The Monkey Wrench Gang*, for example).[10] Bookchin roots his approach in an understanding of ecology as something broader than simply 'the environment', and whilst he recognizes the role played by technology in the rise of industrial capitalism, he sees in certain new technological developments – such as automation, roboticization and flexibilization – a means of moving beyond such oppressive technology. Most specifically, he sees technological change as a potential means of alleviating the want and toil that characterize industrial capitalism for its workers. New machinery can, in his view, free people to pursue their own creativity.[11]

This view seems a little naïve given the nature of who controls the kinds of technology Bookchin discusses, and the way the development of this technology has been embedded in established economic practices – as Winner argues regarding computer technology.[12] Nevertheless, for Bookchin, ending the exploitation of people is crucial to ending the exploitation of 'nature', making technology of prime importance. This perception gives rise to the notion of a 'liberatory technology', centring around three questions:

> *What is the liberatory potential of modern technology, both materially and spiritually? What tendencies, if any, are reshaping the machine for use in an organic, human-oriented society? And finally, how can the new technology and*

resources be used in an ecological manner – that is, to promote the balance of nature, the full development of natural regions, and the creation of organic, humanistic communities?[13]

This approach clearly draws on the work of Lewis Mumford, especially on Mumford's distinction between 'two technologies [that] have recurrently existed side by side: one authoritarian, the other democratic, the first system-centred, immensely powerful, but inherently unstable, the other man-centred, relatively weak, but resourceful and durable'.[14] In these terms, anarchist studies of technology have tended to focus their attention on the authoritarian side of technology rather than on its democratic potential. This has consequently shaped the anarchist conception of 'technology' as something inherently authoritarian – rather than something which can also be democratic, or, in Bookchin's words, liberatory. The term 'technology' tends to be applied, and not just by anarchists, mainly to large-scale technologies. Eugene Schwartz, for example, refers specifically to '[t]he steel mill, the atomic reactor . . . an orbiting satellite . . . roads, communications and factories'.[15] He doesn't refer to any of the far more mundane artifacts of the kind that recent work in social studies of technology has focused on – for example, bicycles, light bulbs, stoves and fridges.[16] Such studies aim to explore the ways in which technology is interwoven with our everyday lives, rather than its more common portrayal as a rather sinister shadow that threatens us from a distance.

This difference between how we conceive large- and small-scale technologies is underlined in a chapter by Ron Sakolsky, who tells the story of WTRA/Zoom Black Magic Liberation Radio, a decentralized, open access, community-based radio station located in a Black housing estate in Springfield, Illinois.[17] Sakolsky sees this station as an example of 'anarchy on the airwaves', addressing in particular the way radio broadcasting regulations in America discriminate against community-based local radio. The station's transmitter is less than 10 watts, powerful enough to reach 70 per cent of its target audience in the local African-American community, and cheap enough for a poor community to afford. It is, however, illegal, since it falls short of the specified minimum transmitter capacity of 100 watts, which would be beyond the community's resources as well as unnecessary. Sakolsky treats this as a political issue, but not also as a technological issue, even though the relationship between politics and technology in this case raises important questions for anarchists: about the regulation of technology by the State, about the autonomy of local communities to organize themselves, and consequently about the scale and viability of community-centred technology.

Punk Rock, DIY music, and the 'access aesthetic'

For the rest of this chapter I want to look at another example that I regard as a democratic or liberatory use of technology. I'm going to narrate a story about the development of independent records and cassettes within the music culture that grew out of punk rock in the late 1970s and early 1980s, and to trace how this culture articulated concerns about autonomy and about breaking down boundaries between production and consumption – concerns that align it in my view with anarchism, although few of those involved explicitly called themselves anarchists. Technology has a central role in this story – in the production, reproduction and distribution of music – making it an exemplary illustration of how technological change and cultural change together can help further anarchist objectives and attempt to influence society more broadly.

I'm very conscious that this is a partial story, covering only a specific aspect of independent record production, and only my own particular version of this; others might remember it differently, or have stories of very different situations to tell. It is also only one example of independent record production in the history of the music industry, although it was more sustained than most and probably more influential.[18] Partial as it is, the story begins with punk rock, in particular the punk ethos of autonomy and individualism, of refusing to compromise with the establishment – of doing it yourself rather than accepting what's been offered to you by others. Many accounts now exist of the waves of people inspired by seeing the first punk bands – the Sex Pistols, the Clash, the Damned, etc. – to reject established rock music and form their own bands.[19] Hot on the heels of the bands came the fanzines, pioneered in Britain by Mark Perry (or Mark P. as he originally called himself to avoid being found out by the dole office) with *Sniffin' Glue* in the summer of 1976. *Sniffin' Glue* and other fanzines called on their readers to start their own fanzines and form their own bands, establishing what Jon Savage calls the 'access aesthetic'[20] – the notion that making and writing about music should be open to anyone (see Figure 7.1).

This period also saw the emergence of independent record labels such as Stiff and Chiswick that were initially linked to the pub rock scene which spawned forerunners and early stars of punk such as Elvis Costello, Nick Lowe, Dr Feelgood, and the bands that later became the Damned, the Clash and others. The major labels that controlled most of the music industry began scurrying for a piece of the punk action (and market share) following the Sex Pistols' high media profile from December 1976 onwards, and signed up almost all the most prominent punk bands during 1977, beginning with the Clash. At the same time, the number of independent labels was also beginning to grow. The Buzzcocks issued their 'Spiral Scratch' EP in February 1977 on their own New Hormones label, helping them sign with United Artists that summer. Between then and late

1978, dozens more independent labels began to release their first records, and the tide continued into the early 1980s.

The most prominent labels were set up by entrepreneurs of various kinds: Illegal, Deptford Fun City and Step Forward were all linked via Miles Copeland's Faulty Products umbrella; labels such as Rough Trade, Beggar's Banquet, Small Wonder and Good Vibrations were offshoots of independent record shops; Fast Products was set up specifically as a stepping stone for bands wanting to sign to the major labels; whilst others, including Cherry Red, had become key players in the independent scene by the early 1980s, as had Mute, originally the vehicle for proprietor Daniel Miller's own single as The Normal . . . and the list goes on.

From the bands' perspectives, independent labels served a variety of purposes, some contrasting sharply with the perspective of the entrepreneurial outfits. A few bands maintained a long career signed to an independent – the Fall (Step Forward, Rough Trade, Kamera, Beggar's Banquet) were a notable example for some time. Many others consciously used the larger independents as a stepping stone to a deal with the majors, for example, Stiff Little Fingers (from Rough Trade to Chrysalis), the Adverts (from Stiff to Anchor), Squeeze and the Police (from Deptford Fun City and Illegal, both to A&M), and the bands who signed initially to Fast: the Gang of Four (to EMI), the Mekons and the Human League (both to Virgin).

A further trend that developed, which I'm more interested in, saw many bands putting out records themselves, on labels which often released no other artist, or perhaps released only records by the proprietor's friends, or by bands from the local area. For many of these labels, this was an extension of the 'access aesthetic' promoted in fanzines – the idea that you didn't have to stop at forming your own band and writing your own fanzine, but could start your own record label as well.[21] The earliest example of this, as an explicit intention at least (and certainly in the independents' folklore), were the Desperate Bicycles, who stated on the sleeve of their second single, 'The Medium Was Tedium'/'Don't Back The Front' (Refill Records, 1977), that they 'formed in March 1977 specifically for the purpose of recording and releasing a single on their own label'. The sleevenotes go on: 'They'd really like to know why you haven't made your single yet. . . . So if you can understand, go and join a band. Now it's your turn.' Backing up a point made by fanzine writers, the Desperate Bicycles adopted as their slogan the phrase 'It was easy, it was cheap, go and do it'. Producing the first single, 'Smokescreen'/'Handlebars' (Refill Records, 1977) cost a total of £153 – in BBC Radio 1 DJ John Peel's words, an amount any band could afford if the bass player sold their motorbike and the rest of the band robbed a few telephone boxes.[22]

The example set by the Buzzcocks with 'Spiral Scratch' and the Desperate Bicycles with 'Smokescreen' was quickly taken up by other bands keen to put their own records out. *Zigzag* magazine's 1978 'Small Labels Catalogue'[23] listed 231 independent labels, including both the larger and the smaller ones, the specialist labels catering to specific tastes such as rock'n'roll and reggae as well as the newer labels inspired by punk. But it was this last category that caused the huge jump to over 800 labels by 1980,[24] although that figure had settled back down to a still high 322 by 1981.[25] It is the records from among this category, closely following the approach promoted by the Desperate Bicycles, that are the most interesting from an anarchist perspective. I want to look more closely at this approach as an example of anarchism in practice.

Rock contradictions: politics, autonomy and authenticity

My own perception of the development of 'do-it-yourself' (DIY) records centres around a few key players. First and foremost of these was Rough Trade, founded as a record shop in 1976, before expanding into distribution of independent records and setting up its own label in early 1978. Rough Trade was renowned as the most radical of the small labels – it was run as a workers' co-op, paying all shop and office workers equally. The rock commentator Greil Marcus pointed out in 1980 that the label was wondering how to bring musicians into this structure as well: 'as yet no one has figured out how to put musicians on that sort of payroll – something that had to be done soon, the Raincoats said with no little vehemence'.[26]

Nevertheless, Rough Trade was unique in even questioning the contradictory place of musicians in the record industry. This contradiction centres around the fact that the relations of production here, as in the culture industries more broadly,[27] are far more complex than elsewhere. The personnel of the music industry cannot be described straightforwardly as comprising simply the owners of capital plus the sellers of labour. In between record company management and the workforce on a pressing plant floor are the 'artists', people who are contracted to produce intellectual goods for record manufacturers and publishing houses, but who don't receive a wage. Rather, they receive an advance against future royalties, which must pay for musical equipment, recording costs and living expenses, and often for promotional activities too, such as touring expenses (not to mention drugs). If the artist's royalties don't match the value of the advance, they in effect owe the record company money; in any case, they only begin to earn money on record sales once their royalties have 'paid back' the advance.[28] As Frith shows,[29] the history of the music industry is marked by continual conflicts between record companies and artists over this relationship, notably concerning the question of artistic control, and this raises an issue that has strong resonances with the ethos of punk – the autonomy of musicians to control their own output.

This is also an issue close to anarchist concerns, and it raises further questions about anarchism and technology in relation to music. Debates

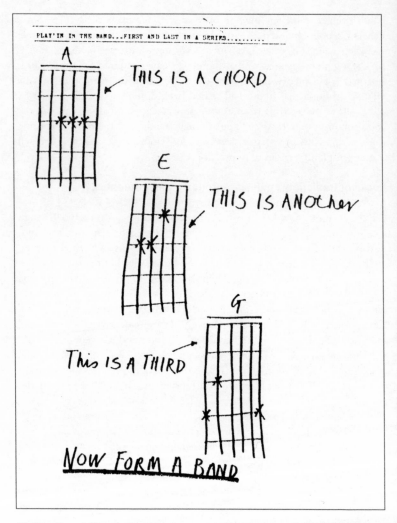

Fig 7.1   The rallying cry of punk's 'access aesthetic'. Whether it originated in the *Sideburns* fanzine or *Sniffin' Glue* is a matter of debate.

from the 1920s and 1930s among members of the Frankfurt School of 'critical theory'[30] seem highly pertinent in this respect, especially those between Walter Benjamin and Theodor Adorno. Influenced by the playwright Bertolt Brecht, Benjamin broke away from the élite 'high culture' perspective of Adorno, his mentor in the Frankfurt School, who watched the rise of that era's popular music with despair. In contrast, Benjamin embraced the emergence of popular culture, in particular the shift brought about by new technology from a world of unique works of 'auratic' art to one where mechanical reproduction made copies of a work available to all. For Benjamin this opened up the possibility of art becoming 'a vehicle of mass political communication',[31] and it contrasted with the aestheticization of politics that he saw happening under fascism. For Benjamin it was crucial that '[c]ommunism responds by politicizing art'.[32]

Rock music's place in these debates around high and mass culture is contradictory, as Frith shows.[33] Rock musicians tend to claim the 'authenticity' that's integral to high art, yet work within a mass culture medium. In many ways punk extended this contradiction, even though its claim to authenticity was pointed in a different direction to the one it aimed to supersede: it replaced the authentic artist with the authentic 'punk'. In terms of technology, punk's authenticity was also tied to a rejection of the growing sophistication of equipment used in rock. An authentic punk didn't need a 16-track studio or a thousand pound synthesizer to make the music of the streets. The access aesthetic aimed to break down that 'high art' élitist side of rock, with the emphasis on basic instruments – guitar, bass and drums – and recording equipment.

The small labels I've been discussing took this side of punk further, rejecting the sophistication of the whole industry 'package' as well as the sophistication of the equipment. By setting up an independent distribution network, labels like Rough Trade aimed to show that the glossy marketing-led approach of the major labels (with record packaging exemplified by the mid-1970s records of Pink Floyd, Yes and Led Zeppelin, and promotion that relied on record pluggers to woo radio stations and retailers) was unnecessary. With the support of a network of like-minded record shops, airplay from John Peel and coverage in the weekly music press and fanzines, it was possible to release a record with little capital, recorded cheaply by ordinary people. In this way the artistic control of musicians over their music was preserved (albeit at the expense of wider sales).

As a key promoter of this approach, Rough Trade became known, at the end of the 1970s and during the early 1980s, as an organization that supported bands wanting to maintain this kind of autonomy outside the mainstream record industry. If a band had released their own record, Rough Trade would probably help get it distributed. The company frequently made deals with bands to release subsequent records (for example, Swell Maps, following their first record on Rather Records, or Stiff Little Fingers, following their debut on Rigid Digits). They also developed an approach to contracts that avoided exploitation of the kind experienced elsewhere in the industry. Contracts were signed on a record by record basis rather than tying bands to a commitment based on either time or output, whilst all profits were divided 50/50 between the label and the band.

A crucial element of the independent scene at this time, then, was a concern to radically transform the relations of production: in particular, the relations between musicians and record companies, but also involving distributors, publishers, retailers and promoters. This fed back into the concern expressed in the access aesthetic to challenge the relation between producers (artists) and consumers (audience), a common theme in rock ideology.[34] It also exemplified Benjamin's argument about mechanical reproduction providing a means of politicizing art. Taking control of the means of production provided a platform for political expression – Crass are the obvious example of this, but others also existed, such as the anti-racist label People Unite, set up by reggae band Misty in Roots.

For many independent record makers, though, controlling their own output was a political end in itself, even if their music wasn't overtly political. In that sense, independent record production was intrinsically anarchistic in its approach to authority and control, while its approach to technology was close to Mumford's notion of democratic technics – people-centred, relatively weak but resourceful. In contrast, the major record companies operate more in line with authoritarian technics: while immensely powerful, they have repeatedly showed their inherent instability in the face of crises such as the oil shortages and falling record sales in the 1970s, or in the face of the punk explosion that followed. To counter such threats, the industry has had to develop predatory business strategies such as the horizontal integration of investment in the wider entertainments industry, and ruthless exploitation of innovations, both musical (e.g. punk itself) and technological (most notably with compact discs).

Independents, majors, and the DIY ethic

Given this wider industrial context, the more radical of the independent labels were constantly battling against more mainstream interests, which often included other small labels and punk bands. As mentioned above, the main objective of many bands was simply to get a record deal, no matter which company it was with, and several labels actively encouraged this, such as Fast. It has been argued that Rough Trade's record-by-record approach in fact made it vulnerable to being used as a stepping stone to the bigger labels. There was no contractual obligation to prevent Stiff Little Fingers from signing to Chrysalis, despite their chart success on Rough Trade (with the album 'Inflammable Material' in 1979), and the smaller label was thus deprived of the chance to benefit further from the band's success, which it had helped nurture. A commitment to autonomy can thus sometimes undermine itself.

These points are highlighted by the activities of another key figure in this scene who I've already mentioned, Mark Perry of *Sniffin' Glue* fanzine. As well as producing *Sniffin' Glue*, Perry also fronted a band, Alternative TV, and was involved as A&R man (i.e. talent scout) for the Step Forward label.

Perry was an important advocate of the DIY ethic, haranguing his readers and then his audience to get actively involved rather than remain just consumers. In 1977 he handed the fanzine over to Danny Baker (later of TV chat shows, washing powder advertisements and daytime pop radio) so he could concentrate more on his music. He was never satisfied with this, though, and deliberately challenged his mainstream punk following by producing more experimental music, both with ATV and subsequent bands.

Perry's support of independent record labels had a number of elements. At one level, there was a pragmatic sense that joining the rock'n'roll treadmill of signing with a major label was not good for a band's music. Perry has been famously quoted as saying that punk died when the Clash signed to CBS early in 1977:

> *I feel that there's no way that you can handle yourself properly in a big record company like CBS. I think it's still going on – bands are bringing out albums, and they're dissappointing [sic], they're just rubbish; big record companies don't do anything for the music really, they just sort of dampen it.*[35]

Also, though, Perry articulated a common suspicion of the music industry as a business, following personal experience of 'Polydor being all nice, and then turning round and saying "we hate your stuff really"'.[36] A similar view, typical of many small bands and independent record makers, is expressed in a fanzine interview with the band Take It:

> *C.N.: Nic, you seem disgusted by the music business?*
>
> *Nic: I hate music, I don't think it should be a business, it should just be for liesure [sic]. There's not such a thing as a professional musician.*
> *Igor: Well, I think that the music business is the most back-stabbing opportunist part of present economic society. Too much of the big fish eats little fish.*[37]

From such a perspective, the initial wave of punk bands proved a disappointment by signing to major labels with barely a second thought. Perry and others felt that had the Clash and other important bands signed to an independent label, the strength of the majors might have been diminished, influencing more of the bands that followed to stick with independents too. For Perry, the independent record scene

> *got waylaid by people like the Clash, people as strong as that, people with a strong following just bloody selling themselves short . . . and like the Buzzcocks, one record and that's your lot, what would have happened if they'd kept that going, you'd have the bands that have been influenced by the Buzzcocks like The Gang of Four perhaps not signing to EMI. I think it would have affected everything if the Clash hadn't signed to CBS.*[38]

As the first wave of punk became more established, then, there developed a strong tendency among some of those that followed to see independence as an end in itself, and not simply as a means to the end of getting a deal. This perspective certainly seemed to me at the time to predominate in the world I myself inhabited – a world of obscure bands, obscure fanzines, obscure gigs and regular trips to Rough Trade. By 1980 it had become something of a standing joke that every fanzine interview would include the question 'would you ever sign to a major label?' The following is a typical reply:

> *Biggles: No – full stop. No more questions.*
>
> *Nik: We're not interested. Well we just don't like the attitudes of the majors.*[39]

The logical conclusion of this perspective is expressed in a piece about Z Block Records, formed, like the Desperate Bicycles and their Refill label, with the aim of showing

> *by example how easy it is to release your own music on your own terms. . . . Our maxim was 'one band one label' as we believed, and still do, that the concept of decentralisation is of the utmost importance to the continuation and support of the spirit and survival of independence . . . [although now releasing records by other bands as well, w]e will only release music we personally find interesting by bands who we think won't use Z Block as a quick route to a contract with a major label. . . . We believe that the control of the production should always be in the hands of the producer. Bands have total control over their product.*[40]

The above-quoted article is accompanied by a detailed breakdown of costs of the various processes involved in producing Z Block's 'Is the War Over?' compilation LP (1979), along with addresses for the various companies used for recording, mastering (i.e. transferring the tape to a master disc), pressing, printing of labels and sleeves, and distribution of the final product. Such sharing of information was a key feature of both fanzines and independent record labels, with details provided on many a record sleeve (or in most cases on the folded A4 sheet that worked out far cheaper than a properly printed sleeve). If punk had begun with the aim of demystifying the process of performance and the distinction between artist and audience, these independent labels aimed to demystify the process of production: 'it was easy, it was cheap, go and do it'.

Records, cassettes and CDs
Within a few years, as with punk's access aesthetic, the coherence of the independence/autonomy/'do-it-yourself' ethic began to fragment. Many felt that the advances of punk had been reversed. In particular, 'the relationships between artists and consumers, the most important thing that

punk actually managed to alter, have regressed to the exploitative, dictatorial state of the early seventies'.[41] The same decline occurred with the DIY scene, with record shops becoming flooded with independent records of below-average quality (notwithstanding Mark Perry's view that 'anybody doing anything on their own is good, whether the product is good or not').[42] By 1981, it was already no longer guaranteed that a run of 1000 singles would sell out, as it had been a year or so earlier. Partly as a consequence of this, the most radical edge of the independent scene shifted, to a large extent, to producing independent cassettes. This bypassed the problem with records of laying out money on uncertain sales, and benefited from the immediacy and personal contact that a shift to mainly mail order sales provided. An added bonus with cassettes was that whilst they made it easier to distribute dross, this could be easily wiped over and the tape re-used.

The subculture that developed around both the remaining ideological independent record labels (as opposed to the more pragmatic or business-oriented ones) and the burgeoning cassette labels (*Zigzag's* 1981 'Cassette Book', an offshoot of its independent label catalogues, listed over 500 tapes) maintained the punk ethic of breaking down barriers and refusing to compromise. As with punk, though, the industry and the mainstream music press were quick to jump on the bandwagon – to 'sink their teeth in and begin to suck the idealism, ideas and vitality out', as *Zigzag* put it.[43] Around this time the most respected music papers, *Sounds* and *NME* – were running columns ('Cassette Pets' and 'Garageland', respectively) to help publicize small labels' products. *Sounds* even published an 'Obscurist' chart of cassettes and less well-known independent records. *NME*, however, disillusioned many of the more radical independent producers with its 1981 'C81' compilation cassette, produced in collaboration with Rough Trade. This release drew on the growing enthusiasm for cassettes being generated not just by the independent cassette labels but also by the appearance of the personal stereo. 'C81' gave no acknowledgement of the former, though, and was seen as being directed more at the consumer lifestyle market of the latter.

The same was true of Bow Wow Wow's first single, 'C30 C60 C90 Go', which along with the follow-up 'Flip Pack Pop' mini-album, available on cassette only, played with the topical issue of cassette piracy. Island Records tried to address the piracy issue also, by launching a series called '1+1', featuring an LP on one side, but leaving the other side blank for the buyer to record an album of their choice (illegally by implication). Despite their playfulness, these ventures helped re-establish the distance between producer and consumer, aiming to embed the *active* consumption of blank tapes (which allow consumers to choose what music they want to hear, and how and where they want to hear it) within a more *passive* consumption of deliberately marketed products. In this respect, the cassette innovation was only partial, since cassettes were an old format repackaged to support new playback technology, and consumers were assumed to be buying both records and cassettes. This trend towards passivizing music consumption was made more complete with the advent of compact discs. For CDs to be a complete success, consumers must upgrade their record collections rather than supplement them. It could be argued also that they must then slot themselves within one or more of the many musical taste identities being established through the re-releasing of huge amounts of the industry's back catalogue – of which early punk and independent records are just a small part – although the proliferation of (often independent) re-issue labels could be regarded as meeting the demands of a more active style of selective music consumption.

Leaving this issue aside, the decline of the early independent scene is perhaps symbolized by the return to recording of Scritti Politti in 1981/2, after a long absence following three singles that had epitomized the DIY ethic. Their first record, 'Skank Bloc Bologna', was released in November 1978 on the band's own St. Pancras label, and featured the ubiquitous folded-over A4 sheet detailing production costs. The second single, in 1979, consisting of a BBC session from the John Peel programme, was released jointly between St. Pancras and Rough Trade. The sleeve bemoaned the fact that their BBC contract prevented them from providing recording costs alongside manufacturing costs.

By 1982, though, the band – or rather their leader, Green Gartside – had revised their view of the value of independent records. Following a break caused by illness, the band contributed 'The Sweetest Girl' to the 'C81' tape, and then released the 'Songs to Remember' album on Rough Trade, to critical acclaim. The new Scritti Politti's less positive stance towards self-produced records was not welcomed by those still committed to the DIY ethic. One fanzine writer summed up Scritti's changing attitude, and the DIY response to it, as follows:

> Now I'm not going to knock the newfound white man's soul of Scritti and there's no denying that 'Faithless' was a good single, but reading between the lines it becomes almost like a confession, revealing Green to have betrayed all his old principles of independance [sic]. All the sweet music he can cram into three and a half minutes can't compensate for his disgusting attitude and the last I heard he was advising bands to sign for an established label rather than put out their own single. Is this the same person who wrote the sleeve note to 'Skank Bloc Bologna' encouraging people to put out their own records and advising on costs and facilities?[44]

From my own perspective too, this was a major downturn for DIY records and cassettes, marking the beginning of the end, although it didn't affect my activities at the time. I didn't begin to feel things were over for another year or so. If punk had died for Mark Perry when the Clash signed to CBS, for me the moment that killed the spirit of independence didn't come until I heard David Bowie's song 'Let's Dance' in 1983. Hearing Bowie sing the line 'put on your red shoes and dance the blues' seemed to me to symbolize the fact that we were once again being told to take our place in the audience; the fans could dance, but only professional musicians could *sing* the blues. As for making your own records, well, from Bowie's perspective that wasn't even an issue – something your manager would organize for you. Things were finally back where they'd been in the mid-1970s.

Moving forward: technology and resistance in the 1990s music industry

As I've already pointed out, my perspective here is very partial. I dropped out of the independent scene in 1984. For others, I'm sure, things seemed to be only just beginning. This was, after all, the period when the Creation label was releasing its first records, when New Order and the Smiths were just beginning to bring 'indie' music into the charts on independent labels, when the stars of 1990s 'Britpop' were beginning to form their first bands. It seems pertinent to ask whether what I've described here has had any bearing on the pop music culture of the 1990s, or whether musicians have now abandoned the latent anarchist tendencies of their forebears.

To begin with, these anarchist tendencies weren't unique to 'indie' music. In other popular music genres, too, there have been similar creative urges towards autonomy that I haven't discussed at much length. Most obviously, there was the explicitly anarchist strand of 'hardcore' punk centred around the band Crass, who supported others through their Crass record label. The legacy of this tendency is the continued presence in British pop music of artists such as Björk (formerly of the Sugarcubes) and Chumbawamba, both helped out by Crass early on in their careers. Whilst Björk's solo music tends towards a politics of the personal, Chumbawamba carry a blatantly anarchist (black) flag in all their work. Both artists are signed to the label One Little Indian, a spin-off from another band – Flux of Pink Indians – formerly involved with Crass.

The underground activities of the rave scene which emerged in the late 1980s also bear some resemblance to the ethos of the earlier independents, having baffled the mainstream music industry as much as punk had done ten years previously. Similarly, the soul band Soul II Soul is worth considering from an anarchist perspective, having begun as a workers' co-operative aiming to establish black-run businesses within 'a musical empire embracing a record company, a successful band, a string of uninspiring clothes shops, and a share in Britain's first dance radio station Kiss FM'.[45]

Notwithstanding these more recent examples of a concern with autonomy in the music business, controlling the means of production has fallen away somewhat as an issue in the politics of 'indie' music. A number of factors have probably contributed to this. The music industry has consolidated itself since the early 1980s, being now a $30 billion industry carved up among just six multinational giants, which leaves little room for independents.[46] These six companies (Sony, Polygram, Time Warner, EMI, Matsushita and BMG) all have interests which span both hardware and 'software' in music reproduction, not to mention links with other elements of the entertainment industry and elsewhere, such as the military. Against this background, what defines a label as independent has become less clear-cut than in the fanzine rhetoric of the early 1980s, and also more pragmatic. Truly independent labels still exist, many catering to the burgeoning CD re-issue market.[47] At the level of high volume sales, though, it is difficult to be successful without capital from the majors. Creation, perhaps the most visible independent label of the 1990s, is part owned by Sony, yet retains control over its own output and has independent distribution. Other apparently independent labels might in fact be wholly owned by a major, a case of the majors protecting their market share by ensuring themselves a presence in any new 'scene' – as they did with both punk and 'progressive rock' beforehand.[48] I've even been told that BMG is independent; given that BMG is one of the big six majors, the important question becomes no longer 'independents or majors?' but 'independent from what?'

If independence as an end in itself is no longer the crucial issue, it nevertheless remains valid to look for signs of the independent ethic, or access aesthetic, within what is still identified as 'indie' music. Indie and rave bands have, for example, been closely linked to campaigns against roadbuilding and against the Criminal Justice Act of 1994, both of which challenge increasing State-control over people's lives and environment (in the broadest sense of that word). This has hopefully led to some degree to a re-politicization of pop music that extends beyond merely fighting for the right to pa-a-a-rty.

Enthusiasts of the Internet will also be heartened by the growing numbers of bands setting up World Wide Web pages and using electronic mail (e-mail) to communicate directly with fans. While at one level this represents merely a new opportunity to perpetuate the star/fan divide, many artists have made their music available for downloading free of charge on the Internet, a development which could potentially realize the independent ethic that each band issues its own music unmediated by record labels, although the music industry too is looking at how it can exploit this medium. In addition, at least a few artists (notably Chumbawamba) use their web pages to put across their political views. It is important not to lose touch here with the irony that the increased access afforded by the Internet is itself severely limited: despite the utopianism of much writing about the potential for computers to make information available to all, this 'all' includes only a small fraction of people in the West outside of government, academia and business, and a much tinier fraction in the developing world. Nevertheless, there are parallels here with the earlier activities I've been discussing.

Conclusion

The politics of music production have clearly changed in the almost two decades since independent records first began to flourish, reflecting in part the changing structure of the music industry itself. Whilst it's unclear whether or not contemporary musicians are as committed as their predecessors were to breaking down the boundaries between producer and consumer, it remains the case that change in the music industry continues to be closely connected to technological change, whether in computerized communications or in the opportunities offered by re-releasing back-catalogues on new formats.

The lesson from this case study is that anarchists need to address technology and culture simultaneously in our attempts to transform society. Furthermore, it shows that anarchist tendencies in culture can have lasting, if subtle, effects, which should be cause for (minor) optimism. The influence of the most radical early independents, like that of punk itself, is still visible in the pop music culture of the 1990s, even though it's little recognized. These bands and labels can claim responsibility for establishing the now instantly recognizable 'indie' style of music, and for giving an initial motivation to the major labels to develop strategies towards innovation, both musical and technological. As nostalgia comes to dominate the contemporary 'CD era' (this article being yet one more example), the kinds of records I've been discussing have in fact become eminently collectable in their original vinyl format (especially those with a wraparound A4 sheet for a sleeve). Hopefully the memories they trigger among collectors will allow the anarchist principles embodied in their production to irrupt alongside the music.

Notes

1. Thanks to Philip Johnson, who shared those times with me at a distance, for valuable comments on an earlier draft. Thanks also to Brian Rappert, Andrew Webster and Maria Thomas, and to Jon and Bar.

2. Directed by Brian Gibson, 1980.

3. Their music was generally a precursor of what's become known as 'indie', i.e. 'independent', a style typified in the 1990s by the 'Britpop' phenomenon.

4. This is, in fact, a first attempt to set out ideas I've been mulling over for several years. As such, it's very much a working paper about which I'd welcome comments.

5. Such a perspective can be found in Foucault (1984), Burnham (1983), Winner (1986), although these writers might not call themselves anarchists; see also extracts in Zerzan and Carnes (1991).

6. Pym (1990), p.5.

7. Hedgecock (1990).

8. Easterbrook in Zerzan and Carnes (1988).

9. Hedgecock (1990), p.5.

10. Abbey (1973).

11. See Bookchin 'Towards a Liberatory Technology' (1974).

12. Winner (1986).

13. Bookchin (1974), p.86.

14. Mumford (1975), p.52; inappropriately-gendered language in original.

15. Schwartz in Zerzan and Carnes (1988), p.178.

16. See Bijker (1995), Cowan (1983) for these examples.

17. Sakolsky (1992).

18. Home (1995), pp.37–8; see Frith (1983) for other examples.

19. See the biography of any band formed in the late 1970s for examples; for overviews see Savage (1991), and especially the irritating but informative Gimarc (1994).

20. Savage (1991), p.202.

21. Nevertheless, for many this was more akin to the 'stepping stone' approach – bands looking for gigs or a record deal discovered that for little more than the cost of producing a demo tape they could actually run off 500 or 1000 copies of a single, which would be far more impressive to send to promoters and record companies. The Skids' first single, 'Charles', for example, was on the No Bad label (1978) which released nothing else once the band had signed to Virgin. Similarly, the Rezillos released 'I Can't Stand My Baby' on Sensible Records (1977) before signing to Sire.

22. In 'State of Independents', *Independent*, 23 April 1992, p.14.

23. Included in Issue 89, November 1978.

24. *Zigzag*, 'Independent Label Catalogue 1980'.

25. *Zigzag*, 'Independent Label Catalogue' No. 4, August 1981.

26. In 'Wake up!', *Rolling Stone*, 24 July 1980.

27. See Lury (1993); Lash and Urry (1994).

28. See Frith (1983), for a more elaborate account of this process.

29. Ibid.

30. See Jay (1973) for a detailed discussion.

31. Wolin (1982), p.207.

32. Benjamin (1970), p.235.

33. Frith (1983).

34. Ibid.

35. Interview in *Jamming* fanzine, No. 6, early 1979, p.6.

36. Interview in *Common Knowledge* No. 1, 1979/1980, p.6.

37. *Cross Now* 2, Firework Edition, probably 1980.

38. *Common Knowledge* No. 1, pp.6–7.

39. Swell Maps, interviewed in *Things In General* No. 2, 1980, p.12.

40. In *Step By Step* 1, 1980.

41. Editorial, *NMX* fanzine, 23, 1982.

42. *Jamming* No. 6.

43. 'Introduction' to the 1981 'Cassette Book'.

44. *Allied Propaganda*, issue 7, Sept/Oct 1982.

45. Stuart Jeffries, 'The Jazzie B all and end all', *Guardian* 19 March 1992.

46. Much of the information in this paragraph comes from Episode 1 of the UK TV series *The Business*, first broadcast on BBC2, 26 June 1995.

47. Thanks to Philip Johnson for pointing this out.

48. See Frith (1983).

CHAPTER 8

Public Secret

Fredy Perlman and the Literature of Subversion

John Moore

Subversive literature appears to be a self-evident category of writing, but on closer inspection its subversiveness remains difficult to locate. This chapter examines the ways in which writing can be defined as subversive, in terms of both its textuality and its political content. Through an analysis of a passage by Fredy Perlman, the chapter demonstrates that subversive literature is generated through a synthesis of subversive political content and subversive literary form.

Introduction

It is commonly assumed that there exists a category of utterance called 'subversive literature'. On closer inspection, however, this category remains difficult to locate and identify. What makes a text subversive? Who defines a text as subversive and on what criteria? Are there specific textual elements that render a text subversive, or is subversiveness a category imposed from without? Given the use of the term in literature, is subversiveness confined to political texts or can it also be found in literary texts? These are some of the questions addressed here.

Literature and subversion

These days, subversion is everywhere, yet nowhere, pervasive, yet elusive. Notions of subversion abound in academic discourse and 'have become thoroughly inscribed in mass culture in the past few decades'.[1] And yet actual acts of subversion remain at a relatively low level: higher than the mass-mediated version of consensus reality would have us believe, but low enough to be contained so that the image of tranquillity and docility can be maintained.

There is thus a huge gulf between the widespread idea of subversion and the relatively scarce practice of politically subversive acts. This is due to the slipperiness of the concept of subversion. Lacking any firm definition, subversion can have a number of meanings, some of which overlap. In different discursive orders, subversion often acquires different meanings. Frequently, these meanings are only vestigially politicized and yet the use of 'subversion' as a signifier inevitably entails political implications.

This is particularly the case with literary criticism. In *Techniques of Subversion in Modern Literature: Transgression, Abjection, and the Carnivalesque,* M. Keith Booker considers the appropriation of the term 'subversion' in contemporary literary critical theory. Booker's title is in itself significant in that it clearly conflates notions of subversion and transgression: the latter becomes a technique of the former. Violation and infringement thus become equivalents, or tools for the effectuation, of overturning, overthrowing or destroying power.[2] Booker suggests:

> *Transgression and creativity have been inextricably linked throughout the history of Western culture. And since at least the time of the Russian Formalists, it has been common to suggest that the transgression of boundaries is an essential feature of literariness. But the Russian Formalists were principally concerned with the ways in which literature violated the expectations brought about by the dominant conventions of literature itself. Their critics, such as Mikhail Bakhtin, have argued that the Formalist treatment of literature as a 'closed, purely literary series'* . . . *prevents the exploration of the truly important transgressive energies of literature, which are directed not at other literature but at dominant institutions and ideologies in the real world of politics and history. There is exciting potential in this suggestion that literature can have a genuine political impact, and it is no accident that Bakhtin has risen to such prominence in contemporary literary criticism.*[3]

Booker allows the identification of the key process in the formation of subversion as a concept in contemporary literary theory. The Russian Formalists define transgression as the violation of literary conventions and cultural expectations. For many literary critics, as with Booker, there is a slippage of meaning so that transgression is regarded as subversive. The two terms become interchangeable. Bakhtin, for such critics, reinforces the notion that literature can be transgressive in a political sense and hence can be subversive. However, many critics maintain the Formalist definition of transgression (and therefore subversion) but attach to it the cachet associated with political subversion. In short, for such critics, challenging textual convention and reader expectation becomes in itself politically subversive. Although only conventions are questioned, the assumption arises that such questioning is tantamount to subverting social control structures. Challenging convention becomes a politically subversive act, a contribution to the struggle against oppression. Indeed, for many academic critics, in the absence of any other political engagement, such transgressive reading becomes their only contribution. Such readings are not seen as part of a wider political project, but as sufficient in themselves.

The result of such uses of the term subversion is a proliferating perception of subversiveness in literature. Women's literature comes to be seen as subversive because it challenges reader expectation of female behaviour and *therefore* threatens patriarchal control structures. Gay writing is regarded as subversive because it challenges conventional heterosexual representations of gay people and *therefore* threatens heterosexist power structures. Black texts are characterized as subversive because they question white conventions of depicting black experience and *therefore* threaten racist social hierarchies. And so on almost ad *infinitum*. Booker's comments on this process are again pertinent:

> *Amidst this hubbub, the notion that literature can be genuinely transgressive in a political sense has risen from anathema to apotheosis, a development that is, in general, to be applauded. However, given the apparent ease with which transgression has been adopted as an 'official' mode of literary discourse in recent years, one might legitimately ask what it is that is being transgressed against in 'transgressive' literature. Many of the works that have been acclaimed as politically effective in this century have been so difficult and complex that only professional scholars seem to be able to recognise their radical potential, while these scholars themselves tend to work within a heavily institutionalised university environment that has in itself — especially in North America — proved remarkably ill-suited as a locus for political action.*[4]

Booker's comments point to anxieties aroused by realizing that literary subversiveness and subversive readings actually occur within contexts of official permission. Transgressive reading becomes a hegemonic ideology in literary and cultural studies, but worryingly only in institutions sponsored by the State and corporate capitalism, i.e., those very institutions that such readings are intended to subvert. This anxiety produces further worries. Maybe 'transgressive fictions can provide images that might inspire and equip us to effect transgressions in the real world'. But equally they might do the opposite: 'Perhaps such fictions simply help us to tolerate injustices, sublimating our transgressive impulses into literature while pursuing a course of political quietism in the real world.'[5] In short, perhaps such readings are not subversive in a political sense at all; or only in the sense of co-opting the academic intellectual by encouraging illusions about the subversiveness and political significance of his/her work — a counter-subversion of the subversive individual. Marxism, feminism and deconstruction appear to be 'potentially subversive critical approaches', but 'Such subversive critical languages have virtually become the official mode of discourse in the academy (where it has become almost totally unacceptable not to sound subversive), while the academy itself has remained remarkably unchanged.'[6] Ironically, in short, a new orthodoxy has emerged — subversiveness — and like all orthodoxies it becomes oppressive. When the revolution comes to power, power wins and the revolution dies. When the doctrine of subversion comes to power, power wins and subversion dies; or, rather, stripped of all but its political aura, it is set up as a new idol in the halls of academe, so that political subversion may be banished.

This dire situation derives ultimately from the muddied way in which subversion is defined. As Booker comments:

> This situation is made all the more arduous by the difficulty in even defining transgression. After all, even the most transgressive works of literature do not in general immediately send their readers into the streets carrying banners and shouting slogans. Transgressive literature works more subtly, by gradually chipping away at certain modes of thinking that contribute to the perpetuation of oppressive political structures. As a result it is virtually impossible to document the actual political power of literature; about the only hard evidence we have of such power is the terror with which totalitarian regimes have traditionally regarded literary works that they deemed dangerous.[7]

Assuming that 'carrying banners and shouting slogans' signifies political activism, the fear here is that literature does not provoke such forms of subversion. So how can the presumed subversiveness of literature be gauged? If it has no concrete or immediate outcomes, how can transgressive texts legitimately claim to be subversive? Booker avers that such reading and writing work more subtly, i.e. in a more gradualist fashion, by eroding modes of thought that help perpetuate power structures. His emphasis lies on modes of thought, not modes of behaviour, and thus there is no indication that such erosion will eventuate in different social practices. But even in terms of thought, Booker admits that the erosion process remains imperceptible and therefore undocumentable. As a result, the grounds for the subversiveness of literature are subtly shifted.

Unable to measure literature's subversiveness in any other way, Booker turns to its repression by totalitarian regimes. In other words, subversiveness is no longer regarded as lodged in the text, nor in the eye of the writer, nor in the eye of the reader, nor in the interactions between text, writer and reader, nor even in the interactions between text, writer, reader and context. Literary subversion can only be gauged by the response of power structures, and only really by power structures in overtly repressive, totalitarian regimes. Such a move renders literature incapable of any significant subversive power except in totalitarian contexts. At this point, due to the lack of a firm definition of subversion, the argument of Booker and of other advocates of literary subversion, collapses in disarray. Literary subversion, as they configure it, is not subversive at all. Officially sanctioned, lacking documentability and concrete outcomes, and possibly acting as a method of co-opting intellectual resistance, transgressive reading's claim to subversiveness collapses in a welter of contradictions.

Politics and subversion

The problem with subversion as a category in critical discourse is founded on the lack of clear definition. This problem is compounded by the fact that the term also exists within a network of legal and political discourses. Furthermore, the legal and political meanings associated with the term have little connection with how the notion of subversion operates in literary discourse. The fact remains that in Western capitalist democracies – the context within which ideas of literary subversiveness have become prominent – no legal or political sanctions are attached to owning and/or reading texts deemed subversive by literary academics. Regardless of how such texts may be suppressed elsewhere, in capitalist democracies individuals are not prosecuted for engaging in transgressive readings or studying so-called subversive texts. On the contrary, they are often awarded degrees, academic positions, and scholarly recognition.

If literary critical notions of subversion are unclear, however, a similar situation is interestingly present in the case of legal and political definitions. In *Political Criminality: The Defiance and Defense of Authority*, Austin T. Turk argues that one of the defining characteristics of political 'criminality' is a lack of clear definition: 'Legal norms defining political offenses are exceptionally vague', even compared to 'the rubbery utility of conventional laws'.[8] 'Probably the most striking and incontestable characteristic of the political crime is its elusiveness', says another commentator.[9] Turk explains that this definitional vagueness is deliberate and politically motivated:

> Not only is it inherently difficult to specify the meanings of such terms as treason, sedition, and subversion, it is generally in the interest of authorities to leave themselves as much discretion as possible in dealing with intolerable political opposition. Implementation of political crime laws begins with the premise that the overriding objective is to destroy or at least neutralize intolerable opposition, and no legal restraint upon enforcement policies and practices is allowed to inhibit political policing to the point where such opposition has a serious chance of bringing about the destruction or radical transformation of the structure of power.[10]

The vagueness of the legal definition of subversion deliberately leaves scope for the State to respond to changes in the form of political resistance. Whatever the State deems as subversive at any juncture can be accommodated under the vague rubric of subversion. In this sense, subversion has no stable definition as a legal category and can be applied at will and as circumstances alter.

However, the history of the legal notion of subversion indicates that under this broad definitional umbrella, language – whether spoken or written – has formed the locus of anti-subversion laws. The example of the United States, the hegemonic capitalist democracy, remains instructive in this respect. Laws preventing sedition have a long history in the US, dating back almost to its foundation as a sovereign nation. But developments during the twentieth century are most pertinent in the present context.

On 15 June 1917, Congress passed the Espionage Act, a law which had no connection with espionage. This law made it a felony to make false statements or statements that might cause insubordination or disloyalty in the armed forces, or obstruct enlistment. Individuals found guilty under the law were subject to heavy fines and imprisonment of up to twenty years.

On 16 May 1918, Congress amended the Espionage Act and broadened its prohibitions. The amendment made it a felony, punishable by twenty years imprisonment,

> *when the United States is at war, [to] willfully utter, print, write or publish any disloyal, profane, scurrilous, or abusive language about the form of the government of the United States, or the Constitution of the United States, or the military or naval forces of the United States, or the uniform of the army or navy of the United States, or any language intended to bring the form of government of the United States, or the Constitution of the United States, or the military or naval forces of the United States, or the flag of the United States, or the uniform of the army or navy of the United States into contempt, scorn, contumely or disrepute.*[11]

This piece of wartime legislation, for all its verbiage, is clearly aimed not only at subversion generally, but at subversive language in particular. The nature of the utterances considered subversive are vague and open to legal debate. Nevertheless, subversion is clearly identified as a legal category on the basis of certain language uses.

Interestingly, a majority of states and territories followed the lead of the federal government and passed similar anti-sedition legislation. These laws were, significantly, commonly known as anti-anarchy or criminal syndicalism laws. As Stephen M. Kohn points out, however, there were differences between state and federal laws:

> *Unlike the federal anti-sedition laws, the state anti-anarchy or criminal syndicalism laws were not limited in their application to periods of declared war. The state sedition laws were also applicable during peacetime, and a majority of prosecutions under the state laws occurred after World War 1 ended.*[12]

> *Furthermore, federal and state laws uniformly upheld the constitutionality of these laws. In 1927, the US Supreme Court, in Whitney v. California, broadly interpreted the rights of states to criminalize the utterances of certain ideas, even if these utterances created no 'clear and present danger' to national security. The Court ruled that it was no longer even 'open to question' that a person could be prosecuted merely for 'utterances inimical' to 'organized government'.*[13]

Subversive language, originally a category restricted to wartime and dangers to national security, had now expanded to peacetime and practically any context. Earlier, in 1919, US Attorney General A. Mitchell Palmer – infamous for instigating the deportation of 'reds' after the First World War – had requested that Congress follow the lead of numerous states by passing legislation applicable in peacetime that would make 'sedition and seditious utterances and publications a crime'.[14] Congress declined on that occasion, but in 1940 it passed a peacetime federal anti-sedition law, commonly called the Smith Act. An even broader interpretation was given to this Act by federal courts than they had given to the Espionage Act.

It is true that in the 1950s and 1960s, the Supreme Court gradually narrowed the applicability of the peacetime sedition laws and even reversed the Whitney v. California decision. Still, Kohn concludes:

> *The Espionage Act, the Smith Act and most state criminal syndicalism laws are still in effect. Given the past history of these laws and the Supreme Court's failure to unequivocally declare such laws unconstitutional on their face, the future abusive application of sedition legislation is a realistic possibility.*[15]

Legislation regarding political crimes such as subversion is notoriously vague. Legal definitions of subversion are deliberately left as wide as possible. Nevertheless, a key element of anti-sedition legislation concerns the use of subversive language and as part of this, the publication of subversive literature. The legal grounds upon which a text may be regarded as subversive are uncertain, although they involve a politically motivated linguistic assault on the State and the form of government. Legislation which could be used to classify certain texts as subversive is in effect and could be invoked to determine and prosecute 'subversive literature'. Although vague, therefore, the legal category of subversive literature does exist in capitalist democracies such as the United States. But what constitutes the subversiveness of subversive literature in this instance remains purely at the determination of the courts. In other words, certain types of literature or language use are not seen as inherently subversive. The subversiveness of a text is imposed from outside.

The questions that remain to be answered are as follows: Is there anything inherent in a text which renders it subversive or capable of subversive interpretation? Are there any linguistic features or textual strategies that are innately subversive? And what is meant by the term subversive when it is applied in this manner? These are important questions for anarchists, given the anarchist project of subverting and ultimately abolishing all control structures. In order to investigate these questions, close attention will be paid to the opening passage of Fredy Perlman's *Against His-story, Against Leviathan!* (1983), arguably the most important anarchist text of the late twentieth century.[16]

The literature of subversion

> And we are here as on a darkling plain
> Swept with confused alarms of struggle and flight,
> Where ignorant armies clash by night.
>
> (M. Arnold)

> Here one can neither stand nor lie nor sit
> There is not even silence in the mountains
> But dry sterile thunder without rain . . .
>
> (T.S. Eliot)

The darkling plain is here. This is the waste land: England, America, Russia, China, Israel, France. . . .

And we are here as victims, or as spectators, or as perpetrators of tortures, massacres, poisonings, manipulations, despoliations.

Hic Rhodus! This is the place to jump, the place to dance! This is the wilderness! Was there ever any other? This is savagery! Do you call it freedom? This is barbarism! The struggle for survival is right here. Haven't we always known it? Isn't this a public secret? Hasn't it always been the big public secret?

It remains a secret. It is publicly known but not avowed. Publicly the wilderness is elsewhere, barbarism is abroad, savagery is on the face of the other. The dry sterile thunder without rain, the confused alarms of struggle and flight, are projected outward, into the great unknown, across the seas and over the mountains. We're on the side with the angels.

> A shape with lion body and the head of a man,
> A gaze blank and pitiless as the sun,
> Is moving its slow thighs . . .
>
> (W.B. Yeats)

. . . is moving its slow thighs against the projected wilderness, against the reflected barbarism, against the savage face that looks out of the pond, its motion emptying the pond, rending its banks, leaving an arid crater where there was life.[17]

This is the opening passage of Perlman's magnum opus. The first thing that strikes the reader is the nature of the discourse. The text is not written in the dry, abstract discourse of political science. If, as the second paragraph suggests, this is a political text, it is a political text with a difference. In the book, typeset by the author himself, the page – like the page at the beginning of every chapter in the volume – begins with an image by William Blake. The quotations from Arnold, Eliot and Yeats reinforce the sense that this is not a work of political but of literary discourse. More particularly, the range of references suggest that this text situates itself in relation to poetic discourse. And more specifically still, although an American work, the text is situated in relation to British literary discourse.[18]

The connections are rendered even clearer by the way in which Perlman interweaves the poetic discourse of his epigraphs with his opening sentences. The phrase 'darkling plain' in the opening sentence echoes Arnold's image, whereas the reference to 'the waste land' in the second sentence alludes to the title of the poem from which the Eliot extract derives. Perlman's list of countries echoes a passage from 'The Waste Land':

> **Jerusalem Athens Alexandria**
> **Vienna London**
> **Unreal**[19]

But whereas Eliot's list diachronically follows the urban centres of empire throughout history, Perlman's list synchronically enumerates the lands of current world powers. Moreover, whereas Eliot stresses the unreality of the cities and hence his distance from them, Perlman emphasizes in his second paragraph the harsh reality of the world powers, and his and our complicity in their horrors.

Moreover, as in a poem, what seems at first glance straightforward in Perlman's text is soon revealed as complex and ambiguous. The first three paragraphs are typified by a high degree of repetition: the word 'here' occurs three times, while the phrase 'This is' opens five sentences, setting up an extended sequence of semantic parallelisms. Moreover, the deixis – the orientation of these words in relation to time, place and personal participants – remains profoundly ambivalent. 'This', we are told, is the waste land, the place to jump, the place to dance, the wilderness, savagery, and barbarism. But where is 'this'? Where is 'here'? The cohesive devices in this passage encourage the reader to relate these terms to the list of world powers in the second sentence: 'This is the wilderness: England, America, Russia, China, Israel, France.'

However, this connection can only be made through the acceptance of paradox. According to hegemonic discourse, the enumerated nations are not sites of savagery and barbarism, but of civilization and progress. As the fourth paragraph indicates: 'Publicly the wilderness is elsewhere, barbarism is abroad, savagery is on the face of the other'. To accept the attribution of savagery to the civilized world, the reader must invert the binarisms which hierarchically privilege civilization over savagery. In short, the text attempts to subvert reader expectation concerning structures of cultural prestige.

In doing so, however, the text embroils the reader in a further paradox. When the text suggests that 'this' is the waste land, the wilderness, savagery, and barbarism, is the reader to regard these terms as pejorative or laudatory? Hegemonic discourse codes such terms as negative, but clearly the text challenges dominant codings. The question arises: is the text reclaiming these terms, ascribing to them positive meanings, or is it interchanging the terms of civilization and savagery in order to suggest that the civilized world is really barbaric, while the primitive world is marked by civility?

The evidence is contradictory. At one point, for example, the text maintains: 'This is the wilderness! Was there ever any other?' This could be read as a positive reclamation of notions of the wild and undomesticated for the docile, domesticated populace of the dominant world powers, an assertion of an underlying primitiveness against a veneer of civility characterized as restraint and control. Alternatively, due to the negative connotations associated with the wilderness in dominant discourse, this passage could be read as an indictment of the world powers for turning their lands into cultural, spiritual and ecological wastelands. In this reading, an implicit contrast occurs between the barrenness of civilization and the plenitude of the primitive. The howling wilderness projected on to the primitive by the civilized is seen, in a different sense, as actually inhering in civilization itself. Uncultivated and unimproved nature is not seen as wilderness: the industrial wasteland is the real wilderness.

Such conflicting evidence is also found elsewhere. For example, in the phrases 'This is savagery! Do you call it freedom?' and 'This is barbarism. The struggle for survival is right here'. Freedom and the struggle for survival are clearly incompatible, and yet both are seen as components of conditions characterized by synonymous terms, savagery and barbarism.

The reader, faced with overthrowing hegemonic binarisms, then confronted with a mélange of conflicting signals as to how to interpret key terms, is then dizzyingly opened to another possibility. That is, the deictic signifiers ('this', 'here') do not refer to referents in material reality, but in a self-referential fashion to the text itself. Wilderness and savagery – whether regarded as positive or negative conditions – are here in the text. 'And we are here as victims, or as spectators, or as perpetrators of tortures, massacres, poisonings, manipulations, despoliations.' 'We' are readers, and this passage indicates our range of possible responses to the text, both in terms of its historical (or more precisely, anti-historical) subject matter and in terms of its language and textual strategies.

This textual orientation directs attention to the issue of language-use in the passage. Such an emphasis seems appropriate in a text which openly proclaims its affiliation with poetic discourse. The fact remains that the third paragraph constitutes the locus of difficulty in the passage, and this paragraph is characterized by its exceptional use of foregrounded textual features.

Difference in this paragraph is marked from the beginning with the use of a Latin phrase – *Hic Rhodus!* – which can be interpreted in a number of ways when placed in its present context.[20] But the paragraph is also marked as overcoded by its plentiful use of punctuation marks, particularly question marks and exclamation marks. The use of exclamation marks signifies surprise and revelation. The question marks indicate enquiry, but as the paragraph continues they increasingly indicate that the questions are rhetorical, and therefore that the reader has understood the point being made and is invited to agree with it.

The distribution of exclamation and question marks in the paragraph is also important. The paragraph begins with three sentences ending in exclamation marks. There then follow four sentences in which questions are alternated with answering statements ending with exclamation marks. The turning point occurs with the only sentence in the paragraph which ends with a plain full stop. The paragraph then closes with three rhetorical questions, each of which is answered in the following paragraph. The distribution of punctuation thus suggests a shift from revelation through questioning to certainty and presumed agreement.

The question remains, however, of who is speaking in this paragraph. The paragraph could be seen as the transcription of an interior dialogue, but equally it could be regarded as a exterior dialogue or even as a polyvocal text. The shift from the singular 'you' ('Do you call it freedom?') to the plural 'we' ('Haven't we always known it?') remains indicative of the dialogic nature of the text at this juncture.

The third paragraph is a rite of passage, a transition point between dominant discourses on civilization and the primitive on the one hand, and a subversion of those discourses on the other. On the far side of the divide, the primitive is posed as the realm of freedom and community, and pitted against civilization, a site recast as the realm of domination and control. And like many rites of passage, this paragraph is a rough ride. To get the reader so far, so quickly, the text assaults the reader, descending into incoherence and multivalence to stun the reader into fresh perception.

For Julia Kristeva, in *Revolution in Poetic Language*, this moment of incoherence, this refusal of meaning, constitutes the revolutionary aspect of poetic discourse, the site at which the insurrectionary energies of poetry are unleashed. The contradiction between coherence and incoherence produces a shattered discourse that draws attention to the artificiality of its construction, and hence to the social forces that govern the textual economy. This elicits a crisis, and this

crisis, explosion, or shattering reveals processes of signification – especially in poetic language and the 'prose' of such writers as Joyce and Artaud – that are usually repressed by socially useful discourse. By erupting from its repressed or marginalized place and by thus displacing established signifying practices, poetic discourse corresponds in its effects, in terms of the subject, to revolution in the socioeconomic order.[21]

Poetic discourse, in other words, can effectuate a subversive effect in the reader which corresponds to the subversion of the social order. In fact, however, Kristeva suggests that in particular cases there is an even closer relationship between the two forms of subversion.

Political writing, Kristeva indicates, foregrounds its discourse – its argument, its theses – at the expense of its heterogeneous contradiction, 'which "poets" have made it their task to explore'.[22] But she suggests that in reading political works one should listen for both elements:

> *This should not be understood as a 'joining' of the two sides, designed to constitute some ideal totality: instead the two sides shed light on one another; they restore the subject's [i.e., the reader's] internal/external motility and thus his [sic] jouissance, but in this case through the risk involved in his social conflict. They restore his freedom, but only within the implacable logical constraints of his political struggle. This means that the question of the second stage of heterogeneous contradiction, namely, that of the interpretant or meaning in which this contradiction will irrupt, is of crucial importance.*[23]

The subversive thrust of political writing remains limited, even when its heterogeneous contradiction – its refusal of signifying closure, its affirmation of hermeneutic heterogeneity and internal contradiction as a rejection of governance – is restored to it. Political discourse thus conceived frees subversion in the subject, but only by placing the subject under the sign and interdict of subversion as it is defined by the State. Hence, the necessity of a second stage of heterogeneous contradiction, in which subversion and the subversive self irrupts in insurrection.

For Kristeva, this insurrection occurs through a synthesis of heterogeneous contradiction and a comprehensive critique of the control complex:

> *In capitalist society, where class struggle unsettles all institutions and where every subject and discourse are [sic] ultimately determined by their position in production and politics, to keep heterogeneous contradiction within a simply subjective representation is to make it inaudible or complicitous with dominant bourgeois ideology. Although the latter can accept experimental subjectivism, it can only barely tolerate – or will reject altogether – the critique of its own foundations. Combining heterogeneous contradiction, whose mechanism the text possesses, with revolutionary critique of the established order . . . this is precisely what the dominant ideology and its various mechanisms of liberalism, oppression, and defense find intolerable. It is also what is most difficult. In other words, the moment of the semantic and ideological binding of drive rejection should be a binding in and through analytical – and revolutionary –*

discourse, removing the subject from signifying experience in order to situate him [sic] within the revolutionary changes in social relations and close to their various protagonists. Although, to do this, heterogeneous contradiction must accept symbolic theses, they should be rooted in practice and in the analytical – and revolutionary – discourses that shake contemporary society to its foundations. The signifying process, whose heterogeneous contradiction is the moment of a fierce struggle, should be inscribed according to a historical logic in this representational narrative, which itself attests to the historical process underway in revolutionary class struggles. Narrative is one of the forms of binding, sublimation, and repression of the drive charge against the curbs imposed by community structures. As such, and to the extent that the text plays with it, it should be able to take on the narrative of a revolutionary project.[24]

Although framed in Marxist terms, this passage articulates the process undertaken by Perlman's *Against His-story, Against Leviathan!* in general, and by its opening passage in microcosm. Perlman's text combines the anarchist critique – the thoroughgoing critique which more than any other 'shake[s] contemporary society to its foundations' – with the heterogeneous contradiction 'which "poets" have made it their task to explore'. In other words, the text combines revolutionary content with revolutionary form, political content and literary style. As a result of this synthesis of political and poetic discourse, Perlman has created a text that is subversive in both senses of the word. His text satisfies literary notions of subversion through its transgression of convention and expectation. But it also meets the requirements of political and legal definitions of subversion, as no purely literary text ever could, as its radical content could clearly fall under existing anti-sedition laws in the United States. Moreover, the subversiveness of Perlman's book is not dependent on external definition, whether sympathetically evoked by transgressive reading or repressively invoked by State legislation. Perlman has achieved what Kristeva characterized as 'what is most difficult'. He has written a piece of genuinely subversive literature.

Conclusion

The category of 'subversive literature' needs to be used with precision and care. Those who would write subversive literature would be well advised to pay attention to Kristeva's notion of heterogeneous contradiction, and perhaps will currently find no finer exemplification of it than Perlman's radical textuality. Those who would write about subversive literature would be well advised to revise and integrate their praxis.

One of the leading characteristics of post-modernity remains a tendency to domesticate elements of radical praxis through co-optation and recuperation. Some of the techniques used to achieve this goal are very subtle and insidious indeed. The domestication of radical thought and textuality within academia through permitted usage of the rhetoric of subversion remains one of those techniques. Structures of authority stand to benefit from such permissive practices, not merely by learning about strategies of subversion and resistance, but also by containing those strategies within the confines of academia. Those who would promote subversive literature in particular and social subversion in general should be aware of this issue and understand its implications for their practice.

But if such people are truly to resist recuperation, they must extend the terrains of their intervention. To be effective, subversive literature cannot be severed from subversive practice, subversive thought cannot be severed from subversive action. If the ivory tower – even the subversive ivory tower – is to fall, then the scholar needs to become the insurgent scholar, integrating radical thought with radical action. On such a terrain, writers of subversive literature and scholars of subversive literature might find a common ground. Both might find a new, shared identity and common practice by retrieving an old category and infusing it with new significance. Both might find that, after all, they are revolutionary agitators.

Notes

1. Booker (1991), p.9.

2. I am drawing here on dictionary definitions of the two terms. The *Concise Oxford Dictionary* (1975) defines 'transgress' as 'violate, infringe, (commandment, law)' and subvert as 'overturn, upset, effect destruction or overthrow of, (religion, monarchy, the constitution, principle, morality)'.

3. Booker (1991), p.3.

4. Ibid., p.3.

5. Ibid., p.5.

6. Ibid., pp.8–9.

7. Ibid., p.4.

8. Turk (1982), pp.56 and 54.

9. Allen (1974), p.26.

10. Turk (1982), p.62.

11. Cited in Kohn (1994), p.9.

12. Ibid., p.21.

13. Ibid., p.21.

14. Cited in Ibid. p.26.

15. Ibid., p.22.

16. In *Against His-story, Against Leviathan!*, Perlman writes a visionary chronicle of human life from prehistory until the present day. The text recounts the path of human life from the state of nature through centuries of domination and revolt, and projects a renewed anarchic future. The villain of the narrative is Leviathan, the monster of power and domination, the megamachine of Western civilization. Leviathan wrenches people out of mythic or cyclical time into the linearity of history, or his (i.e. Leviathan's) story. But this process is not accepted passively, and the text recounts the human side of His-story, the repeated attempts to destroy or abandon Leviathan in order to reconstitute or return to the condition of anarchy.

17. Perlman (1983), pp. 1–2. The quotations are taken from Matthew Arnold's 'Dover Beach' (1867), T.S. Eliot's 'The Waste Land' (1922), and W.B Yeats's 'The Second Coming' (1920).

18. Yeats, of course, was Irish, and Eliot an anglophile American who spent most of his life in Britain. Both are conventionally subsumed, in rather imperialist fashion,

into the tradition of English literature, where language use and nationality meet when convenient.

19. Eliot (1969), p.73.

20. *Hic Rhodus!*: 'This is Rhodes!' The Latin phrase signals the introduction of the 'This is' formula and the hence the equivocal deixis examined above. But what does 'Rhodes' connote in this phrase? In the classical world, Rhodes was known for the Colossus, a gigantic statue of the god Apollo that bestrode the entrance to the island's port. Later in *Against His-story, Against Leviathan!*, Perlman draws upon the image developed by Thomas Hobbes, who depicted Leviathan as a vast human-shaped figure, whose body and limbs are made up of multitudes of men and women: 'Hobbes will picture the Leviathan as an artificial English man: masculine, blond, with a crown on its head, a scepter in one hand and a sword in the other, its body composed of myriads of faceless human beings, zeks' (p.26). The reference to the Colossus of Rhodes could therefore be interpreted as an early image of Leviathan as a gigantic human figure, particularly given that the statue was one of the Seven Wonders of the ancient world, and thus symbolizes the 'achievements' of the civilization that Perlman's text assails. Rhodes inevitably calls to mind Greece, the so-called cradle of civilization, but the use of a Latin phrase evokes Rome, and thus the two earliest phases of Western civilization are invoked and linked by juxtaposition with the contemporary world powers listed in the opening paragraph of Perlman's book.

However, if the image of the bronze Colossus is intended to be evoked, this image contrasts forcefully with the sentence that succeeds it: 'This is the place to jump, the place to dance!' The image of rigidity and stasis suggested by the statue is contradicted by the plasticity of images of dance and vigorous movement. 'This' place, then, the arena of civilization but also of the text, emerges as a site of contradiction, a site of Leviathanic dominance but also of freedom and autonomy.

21. Payne (1993), p.165.

22. Kristeva (1984), p.190.

23. Ibid., p.190. The notion of the heterogeneous contradiction can, then, be clarified thus. For Kristeva, the political text can be seen as promoting subversion through its content: it recommends subversion, but the coherence of its discourse indicates its lawfulness. In contrast, the literary text can be seen as enacting subversion through its form and style: its content may be apolitical, but the shattered nature of its discourse – its heterogeneous contradiction – indicates its subversiveness. As will become apparent below, Kristeva perceives a dialogical interaction between the subversive content of politics and the subversive form of literature in the truly subversive text.

24. Ibid., pp.190–1.

Part III

If Not Now, When?

CHAPTER 9

The Responsible Anarchist

Transport, Consumerism and the Future[1]

Jon Purkis

This chapter argues that by approaching transport and consumerism from a radical environmental perspective, anarchism can advance its philosophical premises and principles, moving them out of the nineteenth century and into the twenty-first. It proposes that of particular importance are questions of personal responsibility, collective action and ethics.

Introduction

It is the mid-1990s. Environmental activists throw themselves in front of bulldozers to stop roads being built through areas of natural beauty, take on the might of McDonald's in the High Court, reclaim city centres for pedestrians and cyclists, and move around the countryside harried by the law as modern-day nomads. In the media and in certain areas of business, the words 'consumer' and 'ethical' become associated with one another and talk of 'boycotts' achieves a currency not seen since the anti-apartheid movement of the late 1980s. Representative democracy is declared irrelevant and meaningless by a whole generation of potential voters, opting instead for a new kind of politics based around self-determination, community, and ethical living. A new world view struggles to emerge. At the cutting edge of ecological campaigning, from the darkest Brixton squat to the treehouses hanging above the jaws of the latest motorway monster, people are getting on with the time-honoured tradition of doing it for themselves.

In contemporary British politics there are new networks beginning to form, mostly connected to the environmental movement, that have much to offer the theory and practice of anarchism. Many of those described above are part of a political lineage that extends back at least as far as the late 1960s and which, it has been argued, contains a strong anarchist current.[2] One of the most distinctive features about the movements of the 1990s has been the evolution of a particular critique which challenges many of the premises behind what is assumed to be a 'good life' in modern Western democracies. This critique operates on many levels: how we travel; what and how much we consume; the relationship between our 'leisure' society and less prosperous parts of the world; the lack of information about and control over events which shape our lives; and injustices to other people. Each aspect is permeated with a sense that we can change the world on a day-to-day basis by adopting certain ethical and political practices as part of our lifestyle. Moreover, it is also a vital part of conceptualizing the future, particularly in relation to planetary survival, social justice, and the creation of sustainable communities.

The intention here is to take two themes – transport and consumerism – which are under-theorized by anarchists, but which are central to the concerns of this new political configuration, and place them both within a contemporary sociological and political context for the purposes of looking to the future. In the process, an argument will be offered for a broadening of the feminist slogan 'the personal is political' – hence the notion of the 'responsible anarchist'.

Transport and anarchism

For many years the anarchist position on transport, if such a thing can be claimed to have existed, has been to follow what can loosely be described as a socialist one. This position has demanded the right for equal access to clean, safe and cheap transport, but frequently conceptualized it as an after-thought to more grandiose schemes such as 'the revolutionary process', 'land use' or 'the city'. Emphasis has tended to be placed on the collectivization of the buses, ships and trains, with perhaps some individualistic concessions to motor cars and bikes. The end result of this type of thinking has often been an eulogization of how great it was when the anarchists ran the trains on time during the Spanish Civil War of the late 1930s.

Following this line of reasoning is to buy into an anarchism which no longer describes or theorizes the world within which we live at the end of the twentieth century. Furthermore, this kind of analysis assumes transport to be *solely* a means of linking Place A with Place B, the consequences of which are to ignore a number of social, psychological and environmental factors which affect our perception of travel. By assessing transport in more holistic terms, it becomes possible to integrate it more comprehensively into an anarchist vision of transforming contemporary society. Yet, in order to understand this, it is important to contextualize the anarchist thinking which the argument is trying to move beyond.

Anarchism is a product of Modernist political sensibilities, arguing for a transformation of existing societies through revolution, based on a historical analysis that condemns all hierarchical systems yet also believes in the advancement of human societies through technological and scientific progress. In the late nineteenth century, the primary concerns of anarchism were the injustices of industrialization, based mostly on certain ways of work. It is hardly surprising then, given the common historical roots of anarchism and socialism, that they each have treated transport as a means to an end within the 'wider' revolutionary context of transforming an unjust industrial world. Similarly, it also is understandable that 'the politics of transport' was largely confined to addressing the conditions of working in the transport sector and the profits gained by transport operators.

In the latter half of the twentieth century a number of shifts in Western thought have increasingly undermined the assumptions of this Modernist vision of progress, and an anarchist analysis based solely on the plight of the Western working classes has looked increasingly tenuous. The emergence of new political discourses such as feminism and ecology, often combined with a new post-colonial awareness, has posed a challenge to previously dominant descriptions of the world in political theory. In many instances, anarchists have failed to respond to these new critiques and have thus appeared theoretically unsophisticated as a result. In this respect, to talk of transport – or any other aspect of contemporary life – purely in terms of the experience of a nineteenth-century ideal type of anarchist is a barrier to both the theory and practice of anarchism.

Without wishing to devalue the many struggles which take place in more labour-related anarchist contexts (over wages, conditions, etc.), the challenge which the steady destruction of our planet poses means that while we do have to take note of 'the jobs issue', ultimately a work-based analysis is not elaborate enough. Moreover, wider questions of needs – of our children, the Third World and the ecosystem – require addressing and theorizing above and beyond the instrumentalism of what is in the pay packet of a worker at a car factory.[3]

Although the Green Movement of the 1980s and early 1990s can fairly claim credit for starting to galvanize anarchist thinking on transport, there are two lesser known earlier contributions to the debate. First, Paul Goodman cut across the quasi-socialistic industrial vision, writing that 'the first question about transport is not private cars and highways versus public transportation, but why the trip altogether?'[4] Also relevant is the Situationist concept of psychogeography. This posits the idea that people experience space in a very alienated manner – one constrained by the regulation of work, sleep and entertainment – and are unable to map personal mobility in terms of their own desires. The Situationists counter these constraints by advocating that people might relate to their immediate physical environment in terms of 'a purposeless and yet attentive meander through urban landscapes'.[5] This is something which I will return to in my section on the consumption of spaces and places.

What these examples of early thinking on transport suggest is that anarchists were beginning to add a psychological dimension to their analysis of Western societies. This similarly characterized the emerging perspective of ecology, which in the 1970s began to evolve a notion of 'holism' – the interconnectedness of all natural and social phenomena – with a more flexible view of cause and effect in political systems. This was a much more fluid theory of change and societal development than those which came out of the Modernist era. Although these ideas were suited to the often anti-determinist analysis of history which has typified anarchism, its potential still remains at best only partially fulfilled.

To illustrate this, I will briefly mention Colin Ward's book *Freedom to Go: After the Motor Age* and discuss some of its implications. Ward is one of the only anarchists to have bothered to treat transport on its own terms in recent years.[6] Ward's basic argument is that the car is to the twentieth century what the railways were to the nineteenth and canals were to the eighteenth: the pinnacle of technological mobility. The difference lies in how the car fosters a sense of individualism which we – including anarchists! – have become seduced by, and as a result believe that we have a right to travel as and when we want to. Although for some people the car could be perceived as the ultimate decentralization of transport because of its apparent flexibility to suit individual needs, there are, he argues, hidden costs. For example: in Britain the car is annually responsible for around four thousand deaths; governments and business prioritize it above the needs and health of communities; it runs on oil, an unsustainable energy source which pollutes at every stage of its processing and use; and the car industry is controlled by interest groups who have little incentive to protect the environment.[7]

Ward's book, which came out in 1991 before the anti-roads/car movement really gained momentum, is immensely reader-friendly and a brilliant primer on the issues, but it is also symptomatic of a number of problems with anarchist 'theorizing' on these matters. First, apart from his usual high standard of finding examples of mutual aid across the world – such as the collective taxis in poorer parts of Latin American cities – he self-consciously concludes on a things-which-the-government-could-do-to-revolutionize-transport basis, which read very much like the literature which the British Green Party and Non-Governmental Organizations (NGOs) like Friends of the Earth have been circulating for years. So, although Ward's suggestions are highly commendable in themselves, they do raise the more general question of what constitutes a *specifically anarchist* analysis of transport.

Second, although he draws attention to the question of anarchists taking responsibility for their 'freedoms', he stops short of looking at the ramifications which our transport choices might have beyond the boundaries of the British Isles, such as shipping and air travel because of 'their endless complexities'.[8] Now, given that most anarchists pride themselves on the fact that they claim to oppose power wherever it manifests itself, it should follow that wherever even a complicated power relationship exists, so should an anarchist analysis. Since anarchism has always proffered the maxim that the means should be commensurate with the ends, then within reason our behaviour should not, for instance, wantonly disregard someone else's freedom in the interests of our own. One would therefore assume that this did not suddenly stop applying the minute one stepped onto an aeroplane or cross-Channel ferry, even if such notions seemed a little inappropriate for the situation. This is the point where Ward ducks Goodman's aforementioned nod to the Green Movement ('why the journey at all?'), commenting that he 'deliberately refrain(s) from any discussion of the desirability of changing our ways of living so as to reduce the need for transport, whether of people or goods'.[9] Again, this is an area where groups within the Green Movement have actually been making progress, suggesting that there are both individual and collective ways of shaping the future – on this very issue.

Although many collectivist anarchists are hostile to the idea of the individual as agent of change, this may well be a prime opportunity for some revisionism, particularly since the issue of transport is becoming so associated with personal lifestyle choices. Moreover, it also raises a more general question: namely, just how do contemporary anarchists envisage change? Historically, radical political theory, anarchist or not, is fond of pitting a simplistic notion of revolutionary change against the ineffectiveness of liberal reformism, with the individual allowed only a few brushstrokes on the canvas of history, mainly it seems because the individual is seen to be associated with bourgeois philosophies. Yet, without some sort of acknowledgement that the complexities of the late twentieth century require more than these mechanistic platitudes, we might as well return to an anarchism more befitting the nineteenth century.

In the next section I want to embrace both this sense of complexity and the idea of the individual as an agent of change by considering consumerism from an anarchist perspective – as an issue in its own right, but also as a means of understanding how we can begin to conceptualize transport more broadly.

Anarchism and consumerism

During the late 1980s and 1990s sociologists, political theorists and commentators began to pay considerable attention to the activity of consumption. Although the subject had received attention as long ago as the 1920s,[10] a combination of factors brought about this new interest, including: the collapse of Soviet-style Communism and the emergence of the idea of the consumer as a 'storm-trooper . . . of freedom' for the gurus of the New Right;[11] an increased globalization of culture, particularly through satellite communications technology; a decline in the Puritan ethic of frugality and deferred gratification; and the spread of the new temples of the West – the out-of-town hypermarkets – and the public's apparent desire to shop there rather than in the high streets of their local towns.

The Left's response to this phenomenon was mostly to either write it off as irrelevant and divisive or to attempt some kind of analytical synthesis based on an acknowledgement that the 'market' was creating new forms of identity and associations, which weren't so easily locatable in a straightforward, economically deterministic paradigm.[12] Many on the Left felt that addressing consumerism was symptomatic of the debate about post-modernism[13] and that its apparent preoccupation with individualistic narcissism removed the focus from the study of wider historical (read economic) struggles, and therefore it was tantamount to political conservatism.

A similar charge might also be levelled at many anarchists who have drawn their inspiration from the Situationist's concept of 'the Spectacle'. This theory, first articulated by Guy Debord in the late 1950s, claimed that the ideology of capitalist consumer society had penetrated so deeply into people's consciousness that all their experiences and relationships with each other had become mediated by images.[14] The Situationist legacy has, on the one hand, left a whole style of image subversion (subvertising) and powerful critique of the emptiness of consumerism (even to the extent of influencing bands like the Sex Pistols); yet on the other, it universalized people's experience without explaining how they had been co-opted by the Spectacle. The question of what kind of consumerism might be acceptable in a future society was never asked.

Simplicity of analysis was also characteristic of the hard-hitting tabloid politics of *Class War* during the 1980s, whose main success was to put gentrification (aka yuppification) on the radical political map. To all intents and purposes this was an attack on the greed of the new Thatcherite rich rather than on consumption *per se*, yet it did draw attention to the sheer excess of some people, and did politicize the trashing of a Mercedes-Benz! However, the connection to transport is tenuous since *Class War* was opposing prestige cars because they were owned by yuppie invaders, not because cars kill the planet. Furthermore, much of the rhetoric employed by *Class War* was and is very similar to what class-struggle groups have always said (i.e. that capitalism is oppressive and it's time for the dispossessed to fight back).

If the emergence of the Green Movement can be seen to have galvanized the general issue of transport, then it can also take credit for raising the issues of consumption, on not dissimilar terms. Although environmental movements in the 1970s had begun to challenge the reasons behind the growth-obsessed consumer culture of the West, the following decade saw the ecological stakes being raised, and the interrelationships between different aspects of environmental destruction becoming more regular subjects for discussion. Whether the issue was the plunder of the tropical rainforests, the dubious logic behind nuclear power, the discovery of the hole in the ozone layer or the direct relationship between industrial production and global warming, the international scope of the problems of industrial development became very clear. By the 1990s the sense of urgency, combined with a growing disillusionment with the increasing hierarchies of the environmental pioneers of the 1970s such as Friends of the Earth and Greenpeace, had spawned a 'new' generation of eco-activists in Britain, who, through their grassroots direct action, also began to evolve a new agenda on consumerism and lifestyle.

Meanwhile, on a more mainstream level, matters were more complex, with the emergence of the 'green consumer' during the 1980s being a challenge to the excesses of the free market philosophy which characterized that decade, especially in Britain, yet equally being part of it. Regardless of this contradiction, a particular vocabulary evolved, with which it became possible for people to distinguish between the 'good' product and the 'bad' product on a reasonably unsophisticated level.[15] The other (concurrently evolving) 'alternative' movements of ethical consumerism and fair trading further developed the sense that modern capitalism should become more accountable to the public. These movements have subsequently had a profound influence on the strategies of modern business, and the criteria upon which producers are judged has become steadily more sophisticated. Moreover, this sophistication now manifests itself in the aforementioned direct-action networks at the radical end of the Green Movement, particularly Earth First! (UK), anti-roads protesters and animal liberationists, who advocate a completely different way of living to that currently celebrated by Western advertisers. As well as these movements being essentially anarchist in structure, they also offer what really is the closest thing to an anarchistic critique of consumption.[16]

What these groups advocate is living a lifestyle which is as free as possible from products or services which involve exploitation or oppression in their processing, distribution and consumption. Such theory becomes translated into action individually and collectively. At an individual level, personal choices are made: on what goods or services are purchased, based on a wide range of ethical criteria;[17] how and where one travels; where one banks (if at all); and how money is earned (and spent). At the collective level, the environmental protests of the 1990s have involved the development and use of dramatic and innovative techniques of protest against companies or organizations involved in exploiting social and natural eco-systems. A recent example of protest on a transport-related issue concerned the extension of the M3 motorway through an ancient historical site and area of outstanding natural beauty in the South of England – Twyford Down – during the period 1992–3. Political action was taken against the Department of Transport, the road builders and their contractors, annual general meetings of shareholders, the parent company of the security firm involved, and even the prestigious Winchester public school who had sold the land in the first instance. Many products or services were boycotted as a result, offices (and even cricket pitches!) were occupied, meetings were interrupted, as well as daily incursions being made on to the site of the road itself. Many of the radical opponents of the road extension created a camp on Twyford Down itself and celebrated a more 'natural' existence without the clutter of a conventional materialist lifestyle.[18] The theatrical, humorous, and non-violent nature of radical environmental protest has also served to appeal to the media, and made the protest tactics of the Left and some anarchist groups seem staid and dated in comparison.

As mentioned before, historically and analytically anarchists have attempted to oppose power wherever it has appeared, even though this has mostly been in an economic context. Radical greens are in effect doing the same thing which anarchists have always claimed to do, albeit from a different perspective. It is a moot point whether or not anything in 'official' anarchist history – outside of the great historical events such as those of 1968 in France and elsewhere – has seen quite the level of sophistication of campaigning tactics as those practised by contemporary radical environmentalists.

Of course, it would be fatuous to suggest that historically anarchists have somehow ignored a whole range of moral matters which relate to lifestyle, but there still seems to be a taboo around theorizing about them. This might either be a generational thing – that 'older' anarchist theorists are out of touch with the 'younger' grassroots activists – or that anarchists are stubbornly hanging on to a macho class politics which (similar to some Left groups) sees itself as 'above' diversionary issues.[19] It is interesting then to realise that even in 'official' anarchist history there are people who have utilized non-economically determined ways of understanding oppression and used it in their writings and actions. For instance, the idea that a human liberation must also involve animal liberation goes at least as far back as Louise Michel during the time of the 1871 Paris Commune, and there are plenty of examples of vegetarian anarchists from the nineteenth century.[20]

Philosophically, this reluctance to theorize about lifestyle-related matters is perhaps best understood in terms of how anarchists throughout history have posited a view of 'the revolution'. Usually, this has suggested a distribution of resources using the highest standard of living experienced in a particular country or geographical area as some kind of benchmark. The kind of suffering which might underpin such a standard of living is rarely theorized, and more often than not the argument focuses instead on the technological systems which could reduce the need for monotonous work in the specific Western society in question. Consequently, there is a high level of abstraction about trading patterns, and no international dimension to speak of. Somehow, there seems a notion, shared by many socialists, that, come the glorious day, everyone will share out the spoils and have a nice cosy right-on lifestyle, with a decent TV, hi-fi, fridge-freezer, washing machine and car – with no questions asked. Apart from the fairytale illusion of the nineteenth-century European insurrectionary model, this belief is based on profoundly naïve ecological assumptions.

Since the early 1970s there have been a number of studies[21] which have questioned the sustainability of the lifestyles 'enjoyed' by all but the very poorest people in the rich countries of the world. Computer projections of the drain on raw materials and land-use that primarily supports the Western lifestyle, the doubling of world population by the middle of the next century, the ability of the Earth to soak up pollution and so forth, suggest that ecological and social catastrophe on a global scale are only a matter of time unless major changes are made. Such claims used to be called alarmist and are still controversial, but particularly since the United Nations Conference on the Environment and Development ('the Earth Summit') in Rio in 1992, theorists and commentators are waking up to the uncomfortable fact that in order to save the planet, the rich countries will have to reduce their levels of consumption. Many political organizations and NGOs shy away from saying this because it is tantamount to political suicide, although Friends of the Earth have recently begun to address the issue.[22]

So far I have suggested that in terms of the official anarchist movement, the critique which exists on the consumption question is either slightly off the mark, over-simplistic or borrowed from other movements. However, with a little imagination, anarchism can benefit enormously from theorizing about consumption, principally because it raises questions which ought to be of interest to all political radicals.

First, by using consumption as a theoretical tool, anarchist theory can add an extra layer of analysis to what is currently seen to constitute oppression in contemporary society and the extent to which our lives are wrapped up in it. Anarchism has been and still is sociologically simple when it comes to unravelling complex power relations, and too often falls back on economic determinism. In the case of a phenomenon such as consumption, this simply will not work: it may well be a consequence of late capitalism, but as Gabriel and Lang (1995) point out 'consumerism is the outcome of a complex interplay of forces – political ideology, production, class relations, international trade, economic theory, cultural and moral values'.[23] Consequently, it is possible that at every stage in the production, transportation, advertising and retailing of any mass-marketed commodity – from toothbrush to four-wheel drive car – there can lie a huge variety of injustices. That such things are acknowledged only in sweeping rhetoric within anarchism suggests that there is a lack of analysis of the Third World and development issues within the anarchist movement generally.

Second, it is not case that the psychological need to acquire, to possess and to individually stake material claims is specific to capitalism. Obviously, any highly industrialized society, regardless of ideological persuasion, will have the capacity to manufacture many products which are additional to those needed for subsistence survival. So, which ones will we need, and will it be still reasonable to have a few useless gadgets rolling off the production line, if it makes people happy? Anarchists are fond of the rhetoric of 'each according to their needs', but this is a very old maxim and a complex society requires a more comprehensive theory of need fulfilment than seems currently available in anarchist literature.[24]

Third, treating consumers as active rather than passive participants opens up a whole area of resistance to oppression, and clearly this is not just specific to the environmental movement. It is undoubtedly true that the general level of awareness of the population of consumer rights issues is greater than it has ever been, owing mainly to the sheer availability of information. So, although this may well be occurring within the legal confines of democratic society, the diversity of challenges to consumer culture is extensive. Whether this takes the form of product boycotts, subvertising, court cases such as the McLibel one,[25] groups fighting for changes in safety regulations, design dangers or even unhealthy products, the implications are that the power of State and capital is not as fixed and invulnerable as is often assumed.

Fourth, the critique of consumption offers a way of conceptualizing a future which acknowledges many of the basic anarchist concerns about power and oppression, yet doesn't pander to simplistic insurrectionary dreams. Historically anarchists have been preoccupied with not wanting to create blueprints of a future society, but the ecological crisis which we are facing requires more than a few thumbnail sketches. Of interest here is Howard Erhlich's concept of 'the transfer culture', where energies are put into building alternative institutions – a kind of community-based anarcho-syndicalism[26] – but based on strict ecological anarchist criteria.

Consequently, to raise the notion of the 'responsible anarchist' is not to sell some revolutionary ideal short. Rather, it is to examine the world on an individual *and* collective level with a view to minimizing social, ecological, and interpersonal exploitation on an everyday basis, wherever possible. This has an important difference to some socialist analyses: while many socialists see change occurring through economic forces which are subject to 'laws of history' which reify the individual, anarchists see themselves as agents of history, carrying out revolutionary ideals in a day-to-day sense. This is the difference between the nineteenth- and late twentieth-century views of political change, and the difference between deterministic/ mechanistic thought and something more holistic, active and flexible.

So far in this chapter I have suggested that anarchist theories of transport and consumption are lacking holistic analyses, particularly in relation to the global consequences of our actions. In this final section, I want to return to transport and explore the extent to which travel and consumption are linked.

Consumption of places and spaces: moving the debate on

The politics of yoghurt

One of the emerging dimensions of transport theory in the contemporary environmental movement is the extent to which we should not only be concerned about how we get around as individuals or collectives, but how the things which make up our lifestyle also get around. This is one of the areas where an analysis of consumption overlaps with an analysis of transport. It is also the point where we move beyond Ward's very isolationist view of 'freedom to go' within the British Isles, and venture into the complexities of the international trading system.

Perhaps one of the most significant characteristics of the modern Western lifestyle is the extent to which it relies on products from anywhere in the world, at any time, and irrespective of weather or season. Indeed, the opening up of new markets in the Pacific Rim and the former Eastern Bloc, together with the increasing threat which trading bloc agreements such as the General Agreement on Tariffs and Trade (GATT) pose to the Third World and the environment,[27] has ensured that there will be more, not less, of this kind of phenomenon in the future, unless we take action. The pursuit of free trade is therefore linked to the perpetuation of unsustainable and exploitative agricultural and industrial practices in the Third World, which underpin the lifestyle of the 'consumer classes'[28] of the West. One of the most innovative ways into this complicated national and international problem is the theory of 'food miles'.

Given that commodities generally, but food in particular, are travelling further from producer to consumer than ever before, various calculations can be made to assess the impact which a product has – on the people and eco-systems in the country of origin – as a result of its packaging and preservation, or in transportation. For instance, one German study found that to produce a 150g pot of yoghurt in one part of Germany for consumption in another, ingredients had to be transported from Poland and the Netherlands; the lid manufacturer was 300km away; and the final delivery of a truckful of yoghurts pumped out 400 litres of diesel, sulphur dioxide and other toxic contaminants into the air.[29] A few other complications might be added, such as the yoghurts being sold at a large out-of-town shopping centre which isn't very accessible by foot or public transport, and where poorly paid workers work in alienating conditions which do nothing for community relations.

The theoretical implications of such an analysis as far as I am concerned go beyond the mere ecological implications of a product's creation, to the notion of 'space' itself. The global society within which we live has taken (particularly long-distance) transport so much for granted, that the space which has been crossed to provide us with the products or services, has (like the social relations of cash crop commodities) been conveniently forgotten. Consequently there is a level at which we are, in effect, consuming places and spaces and yet have no concept of the evolution and history of what we are consuming. It is strange that in our postmodern world, where we try to minimize the amount of unpleasantness around us by acknowledging the way in which we marginalize people within our own societies (e.g., ethnic minorities) or the impact we have on the environment, that we ignore such fundamentals as what lands on our plates. A similar approach can be applied to how we spend our leisure time.

We are all in the Club 18–30

One of the most beautiful sights from the hills around the Pennine village where I live is the setting sun catching the vapour trails of the dozens of planes which fly over every hour, usually heading to and from North America. Many of these flights are part of the enormous leisure industry which has emerged in the last few decades, and which we have become so accustomed to that – cost permitting – we think nothing of popping over the Atlantic for a few days' holiday. Despite the fact that jet travel uses 40 per cent more fuel than cars to move us a kilometre,[30] we take it for granted. We expect it *now*, as a right, and this is something that is very rarely analysed, let alone challenged by political radicals, and anarchists are no exception. This might have something to do with anarchism being more preoccupied with work rather than leisure, or it might be that we all want to turn our critical faculties off at some point, and lying on a Florida beach is as good a place as any to do it!

When I wrote the first version of this chapter three years ago, I felt deeply troubled by the fact that people I knew were flying off to Greece for two weeks in the sun, and to get there were flying over an area of Europe which has seen more suffering than any since World War II. To me there seemed to be a process of reification of space involved – as though the land travelled over could be conveniently forgotten about – yet it was not an issue I felt able to do more than speculate on, as the practical and theoretical implications seemed enormous. For instance, if we don't travel because there is suffering in the world, then we will never experience other cultures, contact with which may both inform us and allow us to develop interculturally and interpersonally. Clearly, given the history of boycotts, there are individual actions which can be taken concerning oppressive regimes and enterprises, which can often lead to more collective courses of action. A situation such as that in the former Yugloslavia is clearly far too complex to deal with on the level of an individual boycott, but the notion of reification of space is an important one.

The idea that modernity has had dramatic effects on our perceptions of time and space is not a new one. The Marxist geographer David Harvey, for instance, discusses the notion of 'time–space compression', a condition whereby the acceleration of capitalist developments within the global economic system shapes and distorts geography and social relations to such an extent that it produces an almost schizophrenic state of mind.[31] This is a useful starting-point, particularly if one considers the element of speed in contemporary society, especially in the context of the leisure industry. Despite being one of the twentieth-century's greatest achievements, the speed with which we travel is also potentially very anti-social if undertaken in ways which are detrimental to our attitudes to ourselves, the planet and other cultures. Commenting on how speed is often a common metaphor both for travel and consumption, the writer Jay Griffiths observes how one of the consequences of speed is an attitude which is more concerned with the act of getting from place to place than either the terrain or cultures which are travelled over.[32] Clearly, there are problems with suggesting that particular social relations and phenomena are produced by specific technologies *per se*, but, if one thinks of all the possible consequences of instantanous travel by aeroplane to distant holiday resorts it might be a less attractive or beneficial proposition than it first appeared.

First then, on a psychological level, travelling in this manner merely encourages culture shock, as you are suddenly thrust – in a matter of hours – into situations which you might not be prepared for. A more measured, slower and more ecological way of travel might be by bus, ship or even bike (if you have the time), which in theory can put the traveller in contact with cultures both on the way to the eventual destination and upon arrival. Griffiths suggests that travel, like friendship and love, should be savoured at a reduced pace to avoid what the geographer and environmentalist John Whitelegg has called 'loss of place particularity'.[33] To take an extreme and amusing example of this: one of the nineteenth-century ancestors of the Situationists – the *flâneurs* – took this to farcial levels by taking turtles out walking on leashes to maximize their experience of the (urban) environment through which they were passing![34]

Second, much of what is offered by the international leisure industry is ecologically harmful to sensitive eco-systems (the Everglades in Florida are a case in point), is economically unsustainable (Himalayan trekking industries, for example) and is often geared to the expectations of Western cultural tastes rather than local needs (big game parks in Africa use more than their fair share of water, for instance). In this respect it is arguable that there is a double-dose of reification: not only are people potentially reifying the space in order to get to their destination, but often the point of being there is not to experience the native cultures at all but simply to sit in the sun and consume many of the experiences which they are already accustomed to at home.

Tourism, however, has suffered something of a backlash in the last decade or so, and there have been reactions to some of these consequences, such as the creation of the eco-tourist – someone who aims to have as little impact on the culture which they are visiting as is possible. In addition, various initiatives have been set up to promote more sustainable ways of life for the local populations, such as the fair-trade handicraft cooperatives in Thailand designed to help women provide for their villages without getting drawn into the sex industry.[35] Moreover, people are also beginning to think in terms of the leisure equivalent of food miles, with a view to helping us understand other aspects of the unsustainability of tourism. In 1992, Friends of the Earth Netherlands produced a discussion paper for the Earth Summit on what a future sustainable Northern lifestyle might be like if the needs of all the citizens of the world were taken into consideration. Projected for the year 2010, far enough away to allow time for the practicalities of change, transport is radically different, with each person in effect able to use one litre of fuel per day, and a flight to Rio only undertaken once every twenty years![36]

This kind of thinking should not be misunderstood as the politics of guilt, or a mandate for staying in one place, but rather as another area to be developed by anarchists, based on a responsible awareness of how we spend our leisure time. Inevitably, when we begin to apply some of this to the consumption of spaces and places in a more mundane day-to-day sense, similar questions do arise.

The politics of saying hello.

It should be clear by now that I am arguing against a simply instrumental view of transport – that transport is just a means of getting from A to B – and suggesting instead that we could conceptualize it more holistically. The notion that we could *make a community out of a journey,* for instance, would sit very comfortably with anarchist principles of the commensurability of means and ends. Since in our daily lives many of us do engage in methods of travelling which reify space and do not involve much community (such as driving a car to work on a motorway on our own), it seems that there is an immense potential for extending the concept beyond the romanticization of bus queues, fine things though they are. Although, there might well be good arguments for cycling, walking or taking a canal boat – such as the quality of experience to be had from savouring the cultures and environment more slowly as discussed above – we are not all privileged enough to have that amount of time in the here and now. Responsible activities that anarchists could, however, bear in mind are use of public transport where available, participation in lift-share schemes, the promotion of and participation in hitching and lift-giving, and for local communities to encourage children to walk or take the bus to school to reduce the danger and congestion caused by vehicles in the vicinity of schools. Many of these activities tie into community politics, and it is here that we can take a leaf out of the social ecologist's book. This, the most recent philosophical re-working of anarchism, bases itself on 'a comprehensive holistic conception of the self, society and nature'[37] and argues for the development of social, political and economic relations on a bio-regional basis. Although it is always dangerous to fetishize the small-scale community as the ultimate in human experience, and many contemporary networks do this, it may well be the case that in this context, the kind of quality and experience of community which I am arguing for can flourish. Furthermore, it becomes possible to revisit the concept of the transfer culture but on an ecological basis. So, as well as the construction of alternative institutions, based on collective and community transport systems, it is also possible to introduce a more individual dimension to this same theory.

Despite these possibilities, there remains a problem within some radical Green and social ecologist thinking on transport, in that they do not really consider how we might travel outside of our slightly idealized bio-region (assuming that we are living in one!). Clearly, even if we begin to recon-ceptualize the nature of our work to reduce the need for alienated means of travelling and also try to reduce our reliance on goods and services which are provided outside of our locality, how will we begin to think about moving around our country or continent or beyond to visit our friends and relatives? Fortunately, there are many examples of alternatives to the mainstream methods of assisting our longer distance (non-aeroplane) journeys which are epitomized by the alienating motorway service station chains. We can look for inspiration in some apparently unlikely places such as the community of the lorry driver whose world is a network of (ideally) friendly and cheap 'caffs', sleepover bunkhouses and bars, and citizen's band radio to provide us with a working model of how interest groups can and do organize across and in spite of geographical, economic and political constraints. Also, without wanting to glamorize the more marginal groups in society, for anarchists this kind of phenomenon is often associated with the so-called New Age Travellers and other postmodern 'tribes' or cultures who have their own networks to tap into when they are on the road. There is no reason why this aspect of an ecological transfer culture cannot exist for canal travellers, cyclists or hitchers. Even in the precarious world of the North American train-jumping 'hobo', there are networks of support catering for the down and outs, the wanderers, and those active in the informal economy.[38]

Looking for the responsible anarchist: some concluding observations

In anarchism, the need to acknowledge both the individual and the collective equally is perhaps more problematic than in any other political perspective. While it has always been a feature within some strains of anarchism to equate the personal with the political, even before the second wave of feminism, that of Emma Goldman, for example, there is also a lot of resistance to it on the grounds of being overly individualistic. It has been my aim in this chapter to assess some of the most enduring of anarchist principles – such as the relationship between means and ends, and the opposition to all forms of oppression – in terms of two politically very complex issues – transport and consumerism. Anarchism in many respects is still philosophically grounded in the nineteenth century, which is why the dualism of individual/collective remains so strong in the movement. The holistic analysis offered by many in the ecological movement, particularly at its most radical end, allows us to begin to transcend this dualism, or at the very least, to completely reconceptualize it. Sociologically, anarchism has a limited vision of the complexities of many aspects of the postmodern world, particularly regarding the ecological implications of how we live in the West, and the relationship between ourselves and the Third World. Next to the theoretical output of and practical suggestions from NGOs and other 'reformist' organizations, anarchism often looks at best naïve. Rather than ducking the question of what do we do about it, or, possibly worse, putting up insurrectionary fantasies, we have to embrace the fact that unless we face up to the reality of what we are doing to our world, we will be still using the same nineteenth-century theory and practice a hundred years from now on a very barren and sick planet.

Put simply then, the notion of the responsible anarchist draws on both the individualistic aspects of lifestyle choice which are celebrated (usually beyond the current possibilities and expectations of most ordinary people) in groups such as Earth First!, yet also (on a more communitarian level) endorses the adoption of patterns of consumption and transport which are self-organized, non-exploitative and completely sustainable. The responsible anarchist asks questions such as 'how much is enough?', 'what is the relationship between my lifestyle and the rest of the world?', 'what do we tell people in the Third World who want cars and a throwaway lifestyle?', and 'what will the twenty-first century transport system look like?'

Notes

1. Earlier versions of this chapter were given to the then-named Northern Anarchist Research Group on 5/12/92 in Bradford's 1 in 12 Club and to the Anarchist Research Group on 16/10/93 in London. I would like to thank all the people who attended these meetings for providing feedback in a very friendly and supportive manner. A distant thank you must be given to Andy Pratt for a talk he gave to the History Workshop in Newcastle in 1987 on 'Space and Social Control', which started me on this journey, even though I have not addressed social control at all. Many of the ideas here have been influenced by colleagues in the Manchester-based Enough group, and developed whilst campaigning for sustainable consumption. Personal thanks also to Chayley Collis and my co-editor James Bowen for their intelligent, thorough and entertaining comments.

2. Cahill (1992).

3. These arguments are somewhat similar to those used by the Peace Movement to deal with the 'jobs issue' when opposing the building of weapons systems. The debate in that instance revolves around converting the technologies to civil use, whereas here a different form of work altogether might be appropriate.

4. Goodman (1977), p.240.

5. Institute of Contemporary Arts (Boston) (1989), p.3.

6. A particularly striking analysis is given by libertarian socialist André Gorz (1980).

7. Ward (1991), p.36. See also Williams (1991).

8. Ward (1991), p.8.

9. Ibid., p.111.

10. Veblen (1925).

11. Gabriel and Lang (1995), p.16.

12. The most prominent and controversial example of this was the Communist Party of Great Britain's *New Times* manifesto, which acknowledged the value of other voices and actors involved in contemporary analysis, such as perspectives on race and gender. See Hall and Jacques (1989).

13. For an assessment of some of the debates on post-modernism and its politics see Squires (1993).

14. Debord (1987).

15. Gabriel and Lang (1995), p.163.

16. For more analysis of the emergence and significance of Earth First! see Purkis (1996), pp.197–217.

17. The most comprehensive guide followed by the British Green Movement generally is the magazine *Ethical Consumer*.

18. These people became known as the Donga tribe, named after ancient Celtic walkways which were destroyed to make the M3 extension. The apparent 'primitiveness' and nature-centredness of their activities are by no means simple and need to be understood in its context. See Plows (1995).

19. This is merely anecdotal. At several meetings in recent years organized by the Anarchist Research Group or its offshoot the (north of England-based) Anarchist Discussion Forum, I have been struck by the unwillingness of older anarchists to recognize the anarchism in the animal rights/liberation movement or the anti-roads movement, or to understand the implications of their critiques for lifestyle.

20. Jameel (1991).

21. See, for example, Meadows *et. al.* (1992); an update of their (1971) *The Limits to Growth* report commissioned by the Club of Rome's *Project on the Predicament of Mankind*.

22. *Earth Matters* (1995).

23. Gabriel and Lang (1995), p.26.

24. Two attempts to develop these questions are Doyal and Gough (1991) and the pamphlet *Never Enough* (1995).

25. At the time of writing, two members of London Greenpeace are battling with McDonald's in the High Court over the contents of a leaflet which accuses the multinational of a variety of environmental, health and human rights abuses. Already the longest civil case in English legal history, the media interest in this David and Goliath story has arguably put McDonald's in a no-win situation, regardless of the verdict.

26. Erhlich (1982).

27. One of the most important books in recent years on the insanity of these types of economic powermongering is Lang and Hines (1993).

28. See Durning (1992) *passim*.

29. This example, originally calculated by the Wuppertal Institute, Germany in 1993, is quoted in the media pack of the Sustainable Agriculture Food and Environment Alliance (SAFE, October 1994).

30. Durning (1992), p.85.

31. Harvey (1989), *passim*.

32. Griffiths (1996), p.11.

33. Ibid.

34. Institute of Contemporary Arts (1989), p.4.

35. Thanks to Fiona Weir for pointing this out.

36. Summarized in *Ethical Consumer*, Issue 27, 1994, pp.8–11.

37. Clark (1992), p.85.

38. Davis (1992).

CHAPTER 10

The Curse of the Drinking Classes[1]

James Bowen

This chapter discusses the development of modern attitudes to time-use and paid work by means of a short excursion through the history of work. It seeks to highlight many of the social and psychological problems and contradictions associated with employment, with particular reference to the work ethic, need-fulfilment, unemployment and leisure. The distinction is highlighted between William Morris's concepts of 'useful work' and 'useless toil'. It is proposed that the appropriate use of technology coupled with changing value-systems and a rejection of capitalism are essential for individual and social liberation and development, and for the creation of an ecologically sustainable anarchist society.

Introduction

Work, however we define it, is in a state of rapid change throughout the Western world. In the post-World War II period there has been a dramatic shift in emphasis in our society away from a kind of industrial/ manufacturing/agricultural subsistence for the majority to the relatively opulent throwaway consumer society 'enjoyed' by over half of the population of the First World. True, there still exist huge areas of poverty in the West, and the riches consumed here are often obtained through the economic oppression of people in other parts of the world; but, in the First World, for the majority at least, life is no longer just a hand-to-mouth existence. Accordingly, employment patterns and time-use patterns have changed to a situation whereby paid employment is no longer the main time-consuming activity of the waking hours, even for that ever decreasing minority in full-time employment. Such changes have been facilitated by technological innovation, the globalization of economies, changing employment roles for women, and changing perceptions of need. However, the following still remains true:

- Much paid employment is boring, unsatisfying, unchallenging, and is carried out purely for financial remuneration;

- Much of the most socially important work, such as caring for children, the sick and the elderly is unpaid and unacknowledged, and is mostly done by women;

- Millions of people are unemployed and are thus chasing after jobs which they would much rather not do, given the choice;

- Fourteen million children in the Third World die every year of hunger and of easily and cheaply preventable disease as a result of Western economic imperialism and First World over-consumption;[2]

- Currently popular individualistic and consumerist lifestyles are simply not an option for everyone because our planet cannot continue to absorb that kind of abuse.

Fortunately, all is not doom and gloom, since technological advances could make it possible to take human beings out of many boring, repetitive, dangerous, unpleasant and unnecessary jobs; at the same time, increased accessibility to information and the potential democratization of information sources and channels could open up innumerable previously unexplored possibilities for people in terms of education, invention, creativity, distribution and the like. If human activities were undertaken more for people instead of profit, it would be possible to meet the physiological and social needs of the whole human race, and this without the inhabitants of the First World having to endure a major reduction in living standards (although obviously changes in consumption patterns and an elimination of unthinking throwaway consumerism would be necessary).

As the act of working moves further away from the struggle to survive, possibilities should be opening up for us all to work less. Currently, more and more of our work-time is spent in the thankless task of putting extra profits in the pockets of those who have more than their fair share already (bosses, shareholders, etc. to whom we apparently owe a living just because they happen to be richer than us); instead, we *could* be working more for our own personal satisfaction and for the benefit of each other, both locally and globally. Often such arguments are portrayed as representing 'the politics of envy'; I like to think of it as more 'the politics of humanity', and in the longer term, given current world population projections and evidence of environmental damage, it is also going to become 'the politics of survival of the planet and its inhabitants'.

This chapter will look at these arguments in greater depth and will discuss current reasons for working and some of the ways in which we might look to working in both the immediate and more distant future, taking into account some less-than-straightforward concepts such as value, human need-fulfilment and quality of life.

An unreliable history of work

The English word work means – a kind of playing from which all the fun-juice has been squeezed.[3]

In many ways, defining exactly what work is should be a relatively straightforward task, at least from a Western capitalist perspective: it is that activity which you engage in for the purposes of earning your material means of survival in terms of goods and services, hopefully with a bit left over for luxuries too. Such a definition deliberately avoids any mention of *the usefulness* of the work, the *intrinsic value* of the product, the *social acceptability* of the work, or the *self-fulfilment* gained from the work, because these concepts are often apparently irrelevant. Western society appears to think that there is something sacred about having a job (particularly if you don't have one) and it doesn't matter how demeaning or irrelevant the work is: *at least you're not unemployed*! This work ethic is of course reinforced by the lack of alternatives to working, particularly for those not rich (or entrepreneurial/exploitative) enough to support themselves economically outside of formal paid employment. Obvious exceptions to this are, of course, those who are economically supported by a partner, often in exchange for domestic duties, childcare, emotional support, sex, and even love; and those who survive on the subsistence payments made available by the Welfare State. I will come back to these later, but first I will look at the historical development of work, particularly in terms of its apparent divorce from life itself.

Out of Eden

The idea of work, at least from a Judeo-Christian perspective, is bound up with Original Sin and Adam and Eve's expulsion from the Garden of Eden. As God's punishment, it suddenly became necessary to work at survival; but, climate, disease and dangerous beasts permitting, subsistence (at least in the cradle of humanity in and around the Nile valley) should have been possible without too much problem, leaving plenty of time for self-development, invention and populating the planet.

In the West it was not until the development of 'civilization' and the attendant problems associated with maintaining it under the Ancient Greeks that a full range of unpleasant tasks was devised and designated as work. However, the Greek citizens (along with the Ancient Egyptians and the Romans), being fairly smart (and just a little bit inhumane) brought in slaves to do all the work, while *they* got on with philosophy, self-actualization, politics, culture, warfare and the other things which constituted 'the good life'. Some kind of a work ethic did exist, but it seems that it was quite possible for the citizens to take the credit for the work done by their slaves. The principles behind this work ethic have still not died out.

For most of the rest of the planet, however, work was simply a matter of hunting, farming, domestic organization and creating the means for subsistence, with a minimum amount of trade and exchange, and with usually only a minimal number of non-productive members of society (such as nobility and clergy/spiritual leaders, as feudal society developed). It would be easy to get overly sentimental about this rural idyll, and to ignore the hardships of living a hand-to-mouth existence in, say, Dark Ages Britain (or many places in the modern developing world), but what it does have to recommend it is the fact of working a minimum number of hours for the need-fulfilment of family and community. In Christian religious terms, however, work now came to be regarded as nothing more than a means to an end and was often despised, and, since charity was regarded by the Catholic Church as the road to salvation, there was nothing inherently wrong with living upon the charity of others.[4]

The Protestant work ethic

Unfortunately, any cosy state of affairs that might have existed was interrupted by Martin Luther in 1517 when he pinned up his theses in the German town of Wittenberg, because he asserted that work was no longer just an inconvenience to be endured in life, but that it was actually God's will that you work hard in whatever job He had assigned for you. The other side of this, of course, was that if you didn't work hard or you tried to change or improve your work and conditions you were rejecting God's will and therefore undermining His Church – which kind of raises the stakes when it comes to industrial action or even looking for a new job!

As nation-states continued to develop throughout Europe in the modern period (after 1500), there became a greater need for the royalty, the nobility and the ruling classes to raise armies and to pay for more or less extravagant wars through taxation. Participation in value-producing activities and work became essential for the support of international and particularly colonial activities, with the logical down-side being that non-participation in this state of affairs could be regarded as betrayal of your fellow nationals, even treason. In England, for example, the first Poor Laws were passed during the reign of Elizabeth I (1558–1603) which formalized the developing social taboos about not working, poverty and vagrancy. Thus a culture had begun to develop which implicitly and explicitly reinforced a work ethic for all (except for the idle rich) in terms of the laws of God, the laws of the land and in the prevailing moral and social code.

Capitalism and citizenship

The advent of the Industrial Revolution obviously had an enormous impact on the type of work activities that people were involved in, as a 'secondary' (i.e. manufacturing and industrial) economy developed. The new industry and resultant economic system had a dramatic impact on the nature of the communities where most people lived due to massive migration to the cities (where the work was) and brought the end of much family-centred, agriculture-based cottage and rural industry. Now, instead of working to produce a small amount of excess to pay the nobility, the Church or the State, or for trade and barter, it became necessary for the newly formed working class to work most of their waking hours for a pittance of a wage in order to make a profit for their employer. Much of this work involved the direct manufacture and production of goods or the support of manufacture and heavy industry (e.g. coal mining to produce the power to run the factories).

Obviously the workers needed to be supervised, and the supervisors needed to be managed, and thus developed the culture of jobs for life and the creation of the career ladder for those aspiring to raise themselves above the common herd. The arguments around the unacceptability of a capitalist economic system are well rehearsed elsewhere, so I won't go into details here, but suffice it to say that this economic system is still very much alive and well and more highly developed today, even if the conditions of work and remuneration are usually considerably less barbaric than 200 years ago.

The migration of communities into an urban environment destroyed many of the old forms of social relationship (some good, some bad), but it also created new possibilities for community and social organization, often on a mass scale. The intellectual and social developments which created and were part of the Industrial Revolution were also closely bound up with ideas developing out of the Enlightenment concerning new forms of social organization. The wealthy and the powerful, never willing to concede more than they have to, were forced to give some ground as rationalist concepts of democracy, citizenship and universal (male) suffrage ('Liberté, égalité, fraternité') began to gain common currency. Thus the seeds of much modern political ideology were planted.

Most modern Western political ideologies of both the Left and Right emphasize the importance of paid work, the right to work, and even the workplace as the site of the class struggle between the capitalists and the workers. This obsession with paid work was exacerbated by the terrible hardships endured by many during the capitalist crises of the 1920s and 1930s, and although it does address some of the important social issues surrounding work, the emphasis is all wrong: it is not the lack of work that is a problem for most people; it is the poverty that this lack usually entails. This is a subject that I will return to later.

Shop till you drop!

The main thing that has changed in the capitalist world since World War II is that citizenship has become almost obsolete as we have become consumers. Working practices have changed and developed, but with three overriding trends running through all of the changes: first, the long-term trend is for working hours to have steadily decreased; second, with the aid of technology and innovation, production and economies have continued to grow; and third, a majority of people in the West have more disposable income than ever before. Overall, there is less need for human labour as machines replace the humans; as more of the work is part-time, on short-contracts, low-paid, boring, repetitive and unfulfilling, and is done (increasingly by women) with little or no job security; and/or we get people in the 'developing' world to do it for less money and in worse conditions. Indeed, many of the jobs that do exist are for the production of useless gimmicks, goods with built-in obsolescence, or services which are unnecessary. The only real growth industries in terms of employment are leisure and the 'human services', providing financial security for an uncertain future along with new ways of juggling and spending money, and in the areas of emotional, psychological and health support and 'caring' for people living more and more psychologically unhealthy, alienated lives.

This is of course not to say that we are moving away from some golden age in the past when the living was easy: modern advances in, say, healthcare have increased our chances of physically reaching previously-undreamed-of ripe old ages. My argument is that we can have the benefits of late twentieth-century society (increasing life expectancy, physical mobility, adequate shelter, variety of occupation and leisure, etc.) without many of the problems (alienated and unfulfilling work, stress and attendant health problems, dysfunctional communities, etc.). However, for this to be a real possibility, it is necessary to question the apparent liberation offered by the consumer society and to expose some of the inherent social problems created by such a society.

One logical conclusion of the consumer society is of course the culture of individualism (sometimes also interpreted on a family-as-economic-unit, but rarely any wider, level). At its most extreme, such a culture asserts the primacy of the economically self-supporting individual (or the (ideally male) bread-winner of the heterosexual family unit) who exists outside of any concepts of 'society', 'community' or 'human relationships'. Instead, the individual only relates to the outside world on an economic level, purchasing every kind of physical, nutritional, emotional, (sexual?), educational, etc. need in the global marketplace. For the lovers of the free market, a theoretical existence outside of human society is perhaps the ultimate goal (where the only love is that of Mammon); but for those of us living in the real world, such an alienated and inhuman set of relationships has to be seen as the cause of many more problems than it solves. Similarly, any such assumption of independence falls down as soon as we look at the networks of interdependence and social value systems regarding, say, emotional support, childcare, and even crime prevention.

Much of the work undertaken in our society is unrewarding, unfulfilling and alienating, and the resultant financial rewards offered by many jobs are simply a means to buy into a social system which is similarly unfulfilling and alienating, and which is, in the long term, increasingly unstable, particularly where social and economic inequality is on the increase.[5] Of course, people experience the benefits and the problems of our society in a range of different ways depending on the nature of and extent to which their social, emotional, occupational and physiological needs are fulfilled. However, in terms of satisfaction at work, there is a growing body of evidence to suggest that any concept regarding a high quality of life is dependent upon economic and emotional security as well as good human relationships and meaningful, autonomous, responsible work.[6]

It would seem useful, therefore, to look at a broad concept of need-fulfilment (in terms of physiological, emotional and social needs) in both a localized and more global sense in order to look at ways in which we might achieve a more egalitarian and liberated society in which freedom, equality, participation, environmental sustainability and humanity are the corner-stones. This is important since any social analysis and projection, if it is to be genuinely concerned with equality and freedom for all, both now and in the future, must account for what is necessary, what is desirable and what is actually feasible.

Human need

Despite many ideological protestations to the contrary,[7] basic human needs are universal, although not uniform. Doyal and Gough (1991) draw up a convincing list of these needs in *A Theory of Human Need*, stressing the fact that the 'satisfiers' of these needs will be different within different cultures, climates, at different times, and for different individuals. It is also important to recognize that need-fulfilment is not just physiological (food, water, clothing, shelter); that it is not simply about the avoidance of physical harm (in which case, Huxley's *Brave New World* would be a fine place to be); and, indeed, there is a strong element in need-fulfilment which recognizes that simply to survive is not enough. Rather, need-fulfilment is concerned with optima and the ability to thrive, to participate socially, to develop personally and to act autonomously. Furthermore, needs are not the same as wants: it is quite possible not to want what you need (a balanced diet perhaps), and even more common to want things which actually do you harm (too much booze and fags being the obvious example); but in the long term, it is not possible to survive without the following necessities of life which *must* be fulfilled to ensure the 'first order human needs' of health, autonomy, social participation, self actualization, etc.:

- nutritional food and clean water

- protective housing

- a non-hazardous work environment

- a non-hazardous physical environment

- appropriate health care

- security in childhood

- significant and appropriate primary relationships

- physical security

- economic security

- appropriate education

- safe birth control and child bearing.

It would be hoped that such a list of universal needs would be essentially quite uncontroversial, although there are a number of qualifications which need to be made: first, this list is not, and can never be seen as one having a hierarchy, since, say, having your health does not make up for being unable to participate fully in society. An example would be being physically healthy but illiterate in a highly literate society; similarly, security in childhood does not make up for homelessness in adulthood. Furthermore, if we are looking at that slippery and elusive concept 'quality of life', it has to be stressed that *more* is quite definitely not *better* in many cases (examples would be excessive vitamin A and D consumption, or simply over-eating, which are clearly damaging, as are overpowering personal relationships). I interpret the listed item 'economic security' in the broadest sense, being not simply based on having a regular monetary income, but more to mean having some kind of guaranteed access to the material means of life in the long term.

Now if these are the needs which have to be fulfilled, the next question is how to do it. On a global level, there are huge cross-cultural problems concerning the interpretation of need-fulfilment, particularly with regard to attitudes to, say, autonomy and mental illness, and perhaps more significantly with regard to autonomy and children. From an anarchist perspective, it is important to be aware of these factors, since cultures do have very different interpretations regarding people's (and particularly children's) rights and abilities to make decisions about what they want and need. This also has implications regarding Western (and particularly American) foreign policy too, in terms of impositions of 'democracy' or 'freedom' but only in terms which suit Western capitalism. This is not the place for an in-depth exploration of such issues, but it is essential that they don't get overlooked in discussions of need-fulfilment.

It would potentially be possible, even under the current capitalist economic system which dominates the world, to cater for the simple physiological needs of the world's population (nutritional food, clean water, clothing, shelter, warmth, appropriate health care) if profit at any price were not the sole objective of much trade and distribution. Far more problematic are the 'social' needs, particularly given the cultural significance and differences attached to many such needs. The area that I do want to concentrate on is that which concerns social participation, social usefulness and identity and the ways in which these relate to work and the ways in which these might develop as paid work becomes a less central feature of many people's lives. As I have discussed above, there are major problems, particularly in the West, but also in such places as Japan[8] concerning the social meaning of work, social usefulness, perceived idleness, and the necessity to 'stand on your own feet' (either as an individual or as a family unit).

Identity

The purpose of work and indeed of society in general is not simply to survive at a subsistence level and to hope that *everyone* else will too (although this wouldn't be a bad thing to aim for on a global level in the short term): the purpose of life and work is, surely, to thrive, to achieve personal satisfaction and fulfilment, to have healthy relationships with our fellow human beings, to ensure that *everyone* has similar possibilities, and to do all this causing the least suffering, inconvenience and environmental damage possible.

For many people, particularly those in non-professional and low paid positions, the activity which they undertake for financial renumeration occupies a reducing amount of their waking time. Even for those who do work long hours, the current economic tendency for short-term contracts means that this is often only a temporary state. It is thus hardly surprising that the extent to which identity and work are directly linked is decreasing, with many people identifying themselves much more with non-work and leisure activities.[9] The centrality (in terms of psychological meaning at least) of work in their lives is small and constantly decreasing, particularly in terms of those who work in part-time and unskilled positions, and this has been found to be even the case in those recently industrialized countries with a very strong work ethic (Japan, Israel, Singapore), especially among younger workers.[10]

The culture of 'a job for life' is no longer realistic, and there are also social changes regarding perceptions of unemployment: politicians no longer make pledges of full employment by such-and-such a date, but just suggest that unemployment is a bad thing and that they are trying to alleviate the problem. Macarov (1987) suggests that there is likely to come a time fairly soon when a 'critical mass' will be achieved (at perhaps 20 per cent official unemployment) at which time there will come a significant social shift with regard to perceptions of unemployment and the unemployed: it is postulated that society might even stop blaming individuals for an economic system beyond their control, and unemployment may become a lot more socially acceptable.[11]

What this ignores, of course, is that there are many more 'social' issues tied up with work regarding identity, participation and belonging, as well as issues of poverty surrounding unemployment. For many people, the question 'What do you do?', as well as seeking a social hook upon which to hang your identity, is also a request for an economic justification of your existence. This is changing as we become less and less a society of workers and more and more a society of consumers, but there are still important social values attached to the jobs that we do (or not) and the ways in which we materially pay for our existence.

This situation is inherently problematic, first because what we *do* is far more complex (and probably more interesting) than the paid work that we engage in; and second, because of the changing nature of work, it is quite likely that even if we are in paid employment, the nature of our work, and our employers, will change over time; and third, a reduction of work-centrality in people's lives along with an increasingly large non-working older population all feed into a weakening work ethic. In addition, there are implications for people who work but don't get paid for it (such as voluntary workers, carers, and of course housewives (and househusbands), as the 'Wages for housework' campaigns of the 1970s highlighted).[12] And of course, many people do things which they regard as more-or-less leisure activities (gardening, playing music and sports, child-minding, decorating, writing books on anarchism (!), for example) which others do for a living and get paid handsomely into the bargain (well, in some cases anyway).

So why work at all?

Not everyone who works is unfulfilled and alienated by everything about their work, but there is a great deal of evidence to suggest that the self-actualization and satisfaction that most people get from their work tend to be bound up more with their social relationships, the degree to which they are in control of their working environment, the extent to which they feel valued (sometimes manifested in the obvious satisfaction of receiving a fair day's pay for a fair day's work).[13] My purpose here is not to devalue work that people do to which they are committed, often in the face of economic and social adversity: for those who can honestly say that their work is fulfilling, interesting, inherently valuable (to them or 'society') valued (by them, society, customers/clients, the boss, etc.), never boring or demoralizing, that's fine! But for many, the work itself has little or no intrinsic value, and it is for the extrinsic benefits such as human contact, social position, status, income, structure and responsibility that they bother getting up in the morning at all. It is the exception rather than the rule, however, for most people to leap joyously out of bed in the mornings in order to go to work.

The point that I want to make is that there is nothing inherently more *valuable* or psychologically more fulfilling about time spent in paid employment than not, and on a psychological level it is important to get away from the mentality that believes in 'the religion of work'. There are enormous social pressures brought to bear on people from an early age to go out to work, to pay their way in the world, and to be seen to be doing something useful (even if the job is inherently useless). In spite of the satisfaction to be had from receiving a nice fat wage packet, it is important to get away from the idea that a job (or, even sadder, a wage packet) is the meaning of life. Obvious, even facetious, though it may be to ask, but if working and having a job are so fabulous, why do they have to pay us to do it? On a less flippant level, there is little doubt that most of the people who play the National Lottery (in Britain or elsewhere) occasionally permit themselves to dream of winning enough money to be able to give up working for ever. It is also fortunate, even inspirational, that most pensioners seem to find plenty to do with their idle, workless days.

However, the suggestion that we (i.e. those of us not stinking rich by accidents of birth, chance or even hard work) might all work a bit less, and make sure that what work we do is actually useful in some way is one which meets with cries of horror and dismay from most people confronted with this as a serious suggestion. It seems as though this is one of the remaining social taboos, and that the peddlars of such anti-social filth should be cast out for their heresy immediately. And yet, although it is commonplace for people, say, to take industrial action to protect their jobs, it is, I believe, unheard of for people to take similar industrial action if their working week is to be reduced without any loss of pay or worsening of conditions. Similarly, it is not all that common to hear of people complaining about how quickly the working day or week has come to an end and how they wish that they could put in some extra unpaid overtime just for the sheer joy of working.

Work Eat Consume Die – We have been conned![14]
The money earned in many conventional jobs does afford a certain degree of freedom for those employed and their dependants. In most Western countries, the majority of those with jobs are able to purchase not only enough food, clothing, heating, etc. for the whole family, but also there is often some left over for luxuries, entertainments, throwaway consumer goods and the like, even after paying off the bank loan, mortgage/rent, bills, repayments on the car/video/freezer/washing machine/holiday, etc. In an important sense, this is the essence of what social participation is all about: being able to do what other people do, to have what other people have, and not to be too stressed out about how you are going to pay for it all the time. Although much poverty research in Britain does indicate that there is an increasing 'underclass' who are, in economic terms, being left behind by the rest of the society (the more comfortably off 70 per cent), and who are therefore unable, on many levels, to participate socially,[15] a clear majority does work hard in order to play hard.

What is created among those who do work, however, is a self-perpetuating cycle in which many work hard to earn their leisure time and the means to enjoy it, but spend much of that leisure time compensating themselves for the fact that they have a job. Much economic activity, and indeed many of the things which people do or buy in their leisure time (clothing, travel, food, drugs, etc.) are in some ways only necessary to their lives because they have a job. Similarly, many of the 'conveniences' of modern life (fast food, supermarket shopping, some personal services) are only necessary or desirable because people feel that they already waste quite enough of their precious time at work as it is, or that they need to treat themselves or their loved ones. Many of these work-created features of society are, of course, also environmentally destructive, as well as (more contentiously) being socially destructive. Examples include the problems of packaging, transport and shelf-life (and its extension) of goods in supermarkets, as well as the destruction of towns and communities by anonymous out-of-town shopping complexes and the car culture, and the perpetuation of class and wage inequalities as everyone tries to juggle their work and finances to finish with a net profit.

Many of the problems which the poorer members of our society have relate to their economic exclusion and their inability to participate in 'the consumer society'. In a similar vein, much of the resentment felt by the rest of society concerning those who are economically disadvantaged is that, first, they might be 'getting something for nothing';[16] and second, they are letting the rest of society down by not taking part in everyday activities, and also that they are not doing their bit to keep the economy growing.[17] Of course, there is nothing glamorous about being too poor to be able to choose how to live, but it is also important to acknowledge the paucity of choices regarding time-use, energy-use and money-use that are open to many of those 'fortunate' enough to have even reasonably paid work.

Anarchism as a political ideology seeks the development of a society in which all human beings are able to live lives as free from external constraints and power structures as possible. The culture of work within the post-industrial Western world, and even more starkly in the developing world, is quite clearly a major constraint upon human freedom, particularly in conjunction with the economic constraints tied up with it. A great deal of human labour has little to do with the enhancement of people's lives or the fulfilment of human needs, and it is often the other features of work and the workplace (social relationships, participation, autonomy, responsibility) which give people's working lives meaning.

A central tenet of anarchist thought is that 'life, liberty and the pursuit of happiness'[18] are the goals of human life. A society based on work, consumerism and individualism, but which is actually unable to provide work for all who economically require it is inherently flawed. That much work creates environmentally and socially destructive products or necessitates destructive activities simply exacerbates this fact. It therefore seems only reasonable to advocate a society which not only permits a shift away from 'paid work as the meaning of life' but also actually strives to reduce the need for human labour as far as is possible. The futility and expense of most job creation schemes are already well known[19] and the number of real jobs is diminishing. Instead of perpetuating the increasingly unachievable farce of work for all as the central pillar of human life, it would seem a far more reasonable project to try to invent ourselves out of paid employment altogether. And how are we to achieve this fabulous 'workless world'? By accelerating processes which are already long established, namely the development of technology and the rationalization of organizations.

Of course, a lot of difficult questions immediately arise regarding the social and individual implications of technological innovation, as well as the usefulness of much of the work that people do. In the next sections, I will try to address these issues, particularly with regard to: what is possible; how to fulfil the human needs of social participation, belonging, and meaning of life if we don't actually work in conventional work situations; and I will even try to answer that favourite old chestnut about who is going to work in the sewers after the glorious revolution.

A technological disaster area?[20]

The apparent enemy of the workforce in the late twentieth century is, of course, technology, and a great deal of workplace unrest, industrial action and union activity seems to be based on the question of whether people or machines are to do the work. For the most part, companies which are thriving and profitable invest in their futures in terms of technological research and development (such as the roboticization of manufacturing plants and the computerization of telecommunications and information processing). As the technology becomes available, it becomes necessary to make people redundant, or to 'featherbed' their jobs until natural wastage reduces the workforce. Net profitability and the economy continue to grow. Shareholders and management, and sometimes even the remaining workforce benefit from this in material terms, and the gap between the 'haves' and the 'have-nots' widens as the dole queues grow. In some cases there is a requirement for those in work to work harder (more productively) and for longer hours. Of course, there are a number of new jobs available as a result of the 'new technology' but these are few and far between in comparison to the jobs that they have replaced.

The traditional answer to increased unemployment, and particularly that caused by technological innovation, is, of course, to make a series of demands to the profitable companies: that they take on new people; that they don't lay people off; that entrepreneurs initiate new business opportunities and 'create jobs' for those recently or not-so-recently made redundant; and that the increasing size of the 'cake' available (in terms of growth of GDP and GNP) be shared out among the population (the much vaunted but sadly still elusive 'trickle-down effect'). Economies continue to grow (regardless of the availability of 'useful' goods); some people get richer; some people struggle along at an average level of financial comfort; and a growing number of people fall into ever deepening poverty. And there are fewer and fewer full-time jobs to go round. On a social and psychological level, people do need to feel usefully occupied for some of their time,[21] but the real enemy of those who don't work is poverty.

The social problems which are created by capitalism, with its individualism and greed (poverty, unemployment, alienation) cannot be cured by a 'quick fix' of more consumer durables for those that can afford them, and to suggest that unemployment could be remedied by a market economy is an untenable argument. The argument that technology can provide an immediate cure-all is, of course, flawed, but, used appropriately, technology is potentially liberatory.

Bring back slavery!

Civilisation requires slaves. Unless there are slaves to do the ugly, horrible, uninteresting work, culture and contemplation become almost impossible. Human slavery is wrong, insecure and demoralising. On mechanical slavery, on the slavery of the machine, the future of the world depends.[22]

In our capitalist world most human labour falls effectively into three categories: the production of the physiological 'means of life'; the creation of wealth for big business, the wealthy, the greedy and the occasional self-starter; and the attempted patching-up and remedying of the social, health and environmental problems created in the pursuit of the above wealth creation. Obviously this is a fairly simplistic analysis of global economics, but the sad part is that it is essentially true. There is a tendency for work to be defined in terms of money, profit, productivity and pecuniary value. In the West at least, only something like 10 per cent of the population is in any way involved in the actual manufacture or production of goods or food; the rest of those in work are providing 'services' on a number of different levels, such as the direct distribution of the goods, through marketing, retailing etc., to the 'support services' of our society such as the carers, cleaners, telecommunications engineers, nurses, bus drivers, artists and teachers who also help our society to function as it does.

A great deal of the technological innovation which takes place is similarly geared towards the needs of that curious, but apparently independent, organism, the market. In response to this, much recent anarchist writing concerning technology has been, not without reason, almost entirely negative. Zerzan and Carnes's (1988) volume *Questioning Technology*, for example, is almost wholly dedicated to exposing the flaws, the potential abuses, and the anti-democratic nature of market-driven advances in technology, particularly with regard to information technology. The argument usually runs that the technology is created by organizations which are so large as to be indestructible, and that we the poor innocent victims of big bad capitalism are unable to do anything about it, so we should pretend that new technology does not exist. To me, such an argument is tantamount to giving up on trying to change the world, and, indeed, it is not dissimilar to that put forward on a political level by those so apathetic or dispirited in the face of governments' activities across the globe to bury their heads in the sand. Fortunately, the people involved in the 'Velvet Revolutions' in Eastern Europe and Black people in South Africa were not so defeatist and negative about their possibilities, despite the odds being stacked massively against them.[23]

Many of the fears expressed in Zerzan and Carnes are rightly grounded in a deep mistrust of big business. However, what is ignored is that, first, when something has been invented, it cannot be uninvented; second, that some, even many, advances achieved in the pursuit of filthy lucre, military advantage and power do also have immediate and beneficial human implications too (such as in medicine, transportation and the like); and third, and perhaps most importantly, that it is ultimately human beings who invent, operate, programme, mend and destroy the machines, and that those human beings are not necessarily 'in the pockets' of big business, governments, capitalism or whatever. Although there are important issues of class, race, gender and geographical location (as well as individual personality) regarding education, position and opportunity for affecting and changing aspects of our immediate and wider environments, it is also vital that we acknowledge our power as individuals, particularly when acting on a collective level. The possibilities of, for example, the 'information revolution' are as yet barely touched upon, let alone fully explored, and although governments, big business and the other traditional enemies of anarchism may use the technology to their own advantage, there are also enormous possibilities opening up with regard to practical, human-centred, fully democratic decision-making, the creation of 'culture', access to data, even the means of developing human relationships and communities. In short, I believe that it is essential that we explore and understand new technology as best we can, since it is only from a position of understanding that we will have any power over it.

The implications of new technology for work are of course similarly complex, since at the same time as new human possibilities are made available, ever more tedious jobs are also created. Although many of the more unfulfilling jobs are a direct result of economies of scale and the destruction of individuality in the production line of the workplace (from Silicon Valley to Sainsbury's), there is also the very real possibility that we could actually invent ourselves out of many of these jobs altogether. A large number of the jobs carried out in our society simply exist for the sole purpose of perpetuating the economic and social system, and it would be hoped that these would be the first to become redundant as we work towards a society based on respect, freedom and equality. In effect, what I am arguing for is a society in which the technology is the slave of humanity, not the other way round. The important point about this is that, in much the same way as the anarchist argument about power insists that it (i.e. power) should be decentralized with explicit societal structures to inhibit its abuse, so too with technology. Our relationship with technology (and those who know how to use it) must be approached with the same caution as our relationships with each other, and particularly with those who seek abusive power relationships over us: the only power which is legitimate in a relationship is that which is freely and accountably received and given.

What are we going to do if we don't have jobs?

Having safely established that it is inevitable that there is going to be quantitatively less paid work for us to do in the future, and that we might influence this situation by actually abolishing many of the jobs currently in existence, the question that always seems to arise is: 'What the hell are we going to do with all this free time?' The answer to this question was actually provided by William Morris during the 1880s when he differentiated between 'useful work' and 'useless toil'.[24] Most people seem to be quite capable of filling up their free time (and a fair bit of their work time) with activities of their own choosing. Admittedly, many of these activities are unlikely to move us directly forward into the anarchist utopia just yet (!) but perhaps part-time workers, the long-term unemployed, pensioners, non-employed parents and others who are not in formal full-time work can set an example for all of us regarding usefully filling our days. It is not all fun and games, of course, but most people find plenty to do with their holidays, weekends and time off, and 'phoning in sick' is more common than employers would like. It is also rare to find someone who laments their excessively long holidays.

Of course, not everyone is using their non-work time to do great social works – they are just as likely to be slumped in front of the television – but quite clearly there is not a problem with finding things to do outside of the formal job market. One of the sadder sights that I have seen, however, was an unemployed middle-aged man in the local dole office literally begging the clerk to give him something – anything – to do because he was so bored. This sort of problem is only likely to arise where unemployment is regarded as an illegitimate activity for a grown man to be involved in. Questions of status, participation, and even human contact arise with regard to those who do not do formal work, and these can really only be answered with the usual anarchist cop-out on the future that we don't quite know what form a more liberated society might take. Clearly it is necessary for something of a re-establishment of community outside of the workplace for people who currently get much of their status, participation and community from their job and work colleagues, and value-systems regarding wealth and property would also come under close scrutiny.

What is important, however, is that we start to develop, both in our formal work situations and outside, new attitudes and relationships to each other. One of the problems of much technological innovation is that it depersonalizes and dehumanizes our relationships with each other. A tension thus immediately appears in my argument for the use of appropriate technology wherever possible as potentially liberatory, since a great deal of technology that could remove jobs could also remove the human dimension from many of our interactions. On the other hand, however, this is only really problematic if we assume a world pretty much as it is now, but with, say, jobs such as supermarket checkout workers and bank clerks being made redundant by the technology. A world truly liberated from much useless toil would, however, hopefully also be liberated from the semi-human relationships offered by fleeting economic transactions, depersonalization, and, in the long term, capitalism itself.

So who's going to do the really shitty jobs then?

If work was carried out for the fulfilment of human material, social, emotional, educational[25] and other needs instead of for profit and the perpetuation of the *status quo*, clearly many of the jobs that people do would become unnecessary. A rationalization of work into that which is necessary or desirable, along with that which is not exploitative of other people, animals or the planet, would clearly necessitate a re-thinking of the values with which we regard work that is done. The first point, of course, is that nobody would have to work massively long hours doing work which they found undesirable unless they really wanted to, because there would be quantatively less work to do anyway. The second point is that many jobs that people currently find attractive or unattractive are based on indirect value systems regarding money, status or whatever. If such value systems were to change or become redundant,[26] it is not unreasonable to suggest that many currently low-status jobs would become far less undesirable, particularly if you didn't have to work long hours for a pittance. Basic gardening is hardly a high-status job, and yet millions of people spend hundreds of their valuable leisure-time hours gardening for the sheer enjoyment of it, so it can't be *inherently* that unpleasant a job!

However, the real crux of the matter is, of course, who is going to work in the sewers, sweep the streets, empty the dustbins, dig the coal, care for the very young, the old and the sick and a whole myriad of other perhaps undesirable but indisputably necessary jobs? The easy answer is 'we all are'; but this ignores a number of points: first, the unpleasantness of these jobs could immediately be reduced if each person had to do far fewer hours; second, it would be in these areas that we might look to applying our new, human-scale, democratic technology to make the work as pleasant (as opposed to profitable) as possible; third, if these (nursing, cleaning, sewage plant work, etc.) are such terrible jobs to do, why are they so under-valued and poorly paid in comparison to managing directors, money jugglers and the other people who, strangely enough, also tend to hold the purse strings? And fourth, I'm sure many coal miners, sewer workers, nurses and the like would find the actual work invloved in high-status, white-collar jobs like those of, say, accountants, personnel managers and politicians pretty unsavoury, unethical, soul-destroying and demeaning!

As anarchists, it is essential that we pose these difficult questions about the value systems of our society, particularly regarding the inherent value, benefit and pleasure resulting from our work and non-work activities. In the long term, we need to look at working for material need-fulfilment, personal satisfaction and pleasure, with a view to enhancing our personal relationships and our immediate and global environment, for now and for the future.

Conclusion

In this chapter I have chosen not to address issues of distribution of goods and welfare in our society and world, particularly in possible situations of global scarcity. I leave these to be addressed by others better able than myself. I have, however, sought to explore some of the realities and myths surrounding work from a Western perspective. I have argued that, essentially, much of the paid work that we do is unfulfilling, alienating and unnecessary in terms of material, social, individual and emotional needs, and yet a work ethic persists which glorifies the 'nobility' of work. I have argued that we should challenge this work ethic and use all of the technological and social means available to us to rid ourselves of the scourge of work which benefits capital and big business. In a post-scarcity world, the end result of such an argument is, of course, not that we should all be idle, but that we might put our energies into our own self-actualization and empowerment with a view to realigning and developing our relationships with each other and our environment for a more equitable and liberated world for everybody, including future generations.

The future is in the hands of all of us to to begin to empower ourselves and to reject the alienated relationships, lifestyles and work options available in the 1990s, and thus to challenge the present political and economic system. And news now comes from afar that people are already creating initiatives for a future where useless toil will be safely thrown away in the dustbin of history:

> *Tramps in Argentina are expected to gather in their hundreds in the beach resort of Mar del Plata this September. The aim of the meeting, which has been billed as their first national summit, is to combat the scourge of work and to campaign for 2 May to be declared the International Day of Idleness.*[27]

If the most dispossessed, powerless 'victims' in society can take the initiative, why not the rest of us?

Notes

1. Many of the ideas contained herein were developed when I was working with Roy Carr-Hill and John Lintott and subsequently developed at an Anarchist Discussion Forum meeting about three years ago. A big thank you to all those with whom I have argued, discussed, ranted and raved about the subject of work. Special thanks also to Jacqueline, Chayley and Jon for criticism, red pen and support.

2. WHO (1989).

3. Mitchell (1975), p.68.

4. See, for example, Heller (1991) and also Macarov (1987) Chapter 5.

5. See Mack and Lansley (1985), Oppenheim (1993).

6. See, for example, Hodson (1991), Olson and Schober (1993), Tepperman and Laasen (1990), plus almost any article relating to social indicators research since the mid-1970s.

7. See Doyal and Gough (1991), Chapters 1 and 2 for a full discussion.

8. See, for example, Misumi and Yamori (1991).

9. There is a whole body of research relating to the concept of the work ethic, often with conflicting conclusions being offered as to the meaning of work, its centrality and other implications of working and not working, e.g. (in no particular order) Pasour (1990), Congleton (1991), Gini and Sullivan (1987), Lipset (1992), Brook and Brook (1989), etc.

10. See, for example, Quintanilla and Wilpert (1991), Heller (1991), England (1991), England and Quintanilla (1989), Brook and Brook (1989), Drenth (1991).

11. Macarov (1987), p.32.

12. See, for example, Malos (1982) for an extensive introduction.

13. Hodson (1991); Macarov (1987).

14. Graffito appearing on Melrosegate in York, UK.

15. For example, Mack and Lansley (1985), Gosschalk and Frayman (1991), Oppenheim (1993).

16. Although in terms of the Welfare State, it is of course the rich and the middle classes that benefit most in terms of health care, education, mortgage relief, etc. See Bryson (1992).

17. The local Asda supermarket has 'Thank you for shopping' written in huge letters above the door. Could it be that they have stopped being partial about where people spend their money, just as long as they do?

18. See Goldman (1979), p.39.

19. Macarov (1987), provides a wide-ranging account of such schemes, dating them as far back as the Ancient Egyptians and the building of pyramids.

20. Macarov (1987), discusses the implications of technology for a work-centred society, but, I believe, does not explore the full global or socio-economic implications for a 'post-work' society.

21. Macarov (1987), discusses (in Chapter 3) many of the 'indirect' problems created by unemployment.

22. Oscar Wilde (1895). I am unsure of the source.

23. This is not to say that I think that capitalism has offered much more real freedom to the people of Eastern Europe, or that South Africa is now anything more liberated than a 'Western-style' democracy with a Black president and universal suffrage. (The poor are still poor and oppressed in both cases.) However, the point I want to make is that normal people can and do change the world.

24. William Morris in Richards (1983) pp.35–52.

25. A good introduction to anarchist educational theory is provided by Shotton (1993). See also *Lib ED* magazine.

26. This point is discussed by Tony Gibson in Richards (1983), pp.108–14, particularly in relation to 'social contempt' and 'social approval' of certain jobs in the (at the time of writing, 1952) newly-formed state of Israel.

27. *Independent*, 19 March 1996, p.21.

CHAPTER 11

Twenty-first Century Sex

Judy Greenway

New sexual identities are emerging at the end of the twentieth century, mostly practised by Lesbian and Gay and Women's groups rather than specifically by anarchists. Individuals in these groups transgress previously existing constructions of gender, identity and personal relationships. In addition, new theories about the body and developments in biotechnology and Virtual Reality suggest that sex in the twenty-first century will be different. This chapter examines some of the implications of these changes and how they might affect personal relationships.

Introduction

What is sexual freedom? If anarchism has anything to offer for the twenty-first century, it has to begin rethinking this question. New ways of thinking about sexuality in recent years have emerged not so much from anarchist theorists, many of whom are stuck in the 1960s as far as thinking (or fantasizing) about sex goes, as from the women's and gay and lesbian liberation movements, and their successor issue-based campaigns. Today, new sexual and social movements proliferate. The direct action and spectacular demonstrations of AIDS activists, Lesbian Avengers, OutRage, and feminists for and against pornography catch the headlines, while postmodern feminists and Queer theorists join science fiction authors and songwriters in speculation about the transcending of gender and sexual categories. Developments in biotechnology and Virtual Reality pose difficult questions about how we understand the boundaries and limitations of our bodies.

In this chapter I will look at some underlying implications of different approaches to sex and the body, and question whether new theories and new technologies pose a real challenge to existing power relationships. Will twenty-first-century sex really be different?

True natures

One night in the 1960s at a party, I was trapped against a wall by a drunken member of my local anarchist group. As I pushed him off me, he said bitterly, 'Call yourself an anarchist?' This attitude that sexual freedom meant women on demand was one of the factors propelling many of us a few years later into the first Women's Liberation groups, where we were able to begin formulating demands on our own terms. There is a long history of association between anarchism and sexual freedom, but sexual freedom means different things to different people at different times, and has complex connections to ideas about nature, bodies, gender, power, and social organization. The concept of freedom, though it can seem like an absolute, is shaped by specific social experiences of constraint.

Although many anarchists have led entirely conventional sexual lives, a theory which rejects authority implies at the least a rejection of formal marriage, seen as State/religious interference in human relationships. Critics of anarchism have always claimed that anarchism would mean sexual licence, the absence of restraint, shameless women and irresponsible men indulging every passing lust. In such images, which mingle fascination and disgust, sexual order and political order are tied (or handcuffed) together. Some anarchists, particularly women and gay men, have also linked sexual and political order, using the language of equality, reciprocity, autonomy and democracy to develop a critique of power relationships between men and women and to try and work out a practice of everyday anarchism.

For well over a century, such anarchists have been criticizing marriage and experimenting with alternatives. They have focused on economic, household and childrearing arrangements – how best to structure personal relationships.[1] Underlying much of the discussion, however, is a model of an instinctive self which is repressed by social convention. Love, passion, and sexuality are understood as natural feelings which should ideally be unconstrained. Our natural selves are repressed and distorted by social restrictions, both external and internalized, so sexual freedom is not just freedom from Church or State intervention, but is about self-expression, liberating our true natures. Such ideas have led some anarchists to be among the pioneers for sexual education, for birth control and for the acceptance of sexual diversity, including homosexuality.[2]

In the years since World War II, these things, though still controversial, have become part of the mainstream of most Western cultures. Sex, love, and childbearing – never as securely tied to marriage as they were meant to be – have become increasingly deinstitutionalized. Serial monogamy is commonplace. Sexual pleasure as a basic human need is taken for granted, and every woman's magazine gives advice on how to achieve it. Post-war contraceptive technologies, particularly the Pill, are claimed to have separated sex from reproduction, making sexual liberation possible for heterosexual women. Although the rhetoric of sexual libertarianism is no longer as popular as it was, the imagery of sexual transgression has become a marketing cliché. The explanation for these changes may lie in demographic and economic shifts and complex social developments, but the way in which they are widely understood and debated is still in terms of natural sexualities.

Leaving the twentieth century: sexual anarchies

> We have decided to take up the struggle against capitalist oppression where it is most deeply rooted – in the quick of our body. It is the space of the body, with all the desires that it produces, that we want to liberate from the occupying forces. . . . 'Revolutionary consciousness' is a mystification so long as it doesn't pass through <u>the revolutionary body</u>, the body which produces the conditions of its own liberation. It's women in revolt against male power – implanted for centuries in their own bodies; homosexuals in revolt against terroristic normality; the young in revolt against the pathological authority of adults.[3]

In the new social and sexual movements of the late twentieth century, with their creative confusion of debate and activity, sexual politics and sex-as-politics are taken for granted; the meanings of sex and politics, however, are not. I want to argue that strategies of visibility, transgression, prefiguration and transformation are key, but problematic, aspects of both theory and practice around sexuality and the politics of the body.

Visibility

A politics of visibility raises questions about what is taken for granted and what is missing from the social picture, and about how that picture is constructed. In 1969, the Miss World competition in London was disrupted by women calling themselves Mis-Conception, Mis-Placed and Mis-Fit.[4] For a while the term 'sex object' became part of everyday language, and the organizers of beauty contests went on the defensive. In smudgily duplicated pamphlets, French Situationist theories – or at least slogans – were recycled in debates about women both as consumers of the Spectacle and as spectacular consumables.

'We're here, we're queer, and we're not going shopping' went the chant on one of the earliest British Gay Liberation marches down London's Oxford Street in the late 1970s. A small contingent of drag queens teetered into Selfridges, to shock not to shop. (Now to be queer *is* to go shopping, if the rise of gay consumer culture is anything to go by.) Some fifteen years later, gay activist group OutRage was disrupting church services to denounce religious hypocrisy. In the USA, fire-eating Lesbian Avengers rode into town on motorbikes, while their tamer British counterparts made themselves noticed by riding around on top of a bus with balloons. In such actions, visibility is in itself political, asserting the presence of what has usually been rendered invisible, disrupting the spectacle of normality. Today, when every British soap opera has its lesbian or gay characters, it seems that after decades of activism, lesbians and gays have succeeded in making themselves visible within the mainstream (however temporarily).

The debate now is about the range of representations and how these have been shaped for a (presumed) heterosexual audience. When a tiny segment of urban lesbian and gays are cast by advertising executives as style leaders, their images used to sell ballgowns and spirits, jeans and perfume, they are not disrupting the spectacle but becoming one.[5]

Making a spectacle of themselves has been on the agenda as a means of empowerment for successive generations of young women, too. Material Girl Madonna may have just been playing with conventionally pornographic images of the sexual woman, but from Seventies Punk to the Riot Grrls, in music, comics, and the informal theatre of the streets and clubs, traditional notions of femininity and female sexuality have been challenged and rejected. Not just attitude, but *Bad Attitude*;[6] being good or nice is now the fate worse than death. Often moralistic feminists are cast along with straight society as the enemies of sexual self-expression, while feminists against censorship represent themselves as a sexual vanguard, and declare pornography to be a site to be reclaimed by women. The full debate about what constitutes pornography and its effects is too complex to enter into here, but feminist critiques of sexual libertarianism are not necessarily anti-sexual or pro-censorship: they can be about trying to transform the power relationships involved, making these visible. Anarchist feminist activists, like USA's Nikki Craft and the Outlaws for Social Responsibility, argue that:

> *Sex is not obscene. The real obscenity is the marketing of women as products. . . . We are in favour of nudity and sensuality. . . . There is a difference between a genuine love, acceptance and empowerment of the body, and the marketing of women and exploitation of women that is the trademark of pornography. . . . We advocate and commit civil disobedience.*[7]

Silence = death

Dissent from mainstream representations of the body, sexuality and gender, through direct action and the creation of alternative representations, has also been an important part of AIDS activism, which particularly in the USA has emphasized the importance of visibility and participation for those affected by AIDS and HIV. As well as challenges to the medical and scientific research establishments, health education work by activist groups has given a new urgency to debates about sexual identities and definitions. 'With each daily restraint and frustration, capitalism imposes its norms . . . it thrusts its roots into our bowels . . . confiscating our organs, diverting our vital functions, maiming our pleasures.'[8]

But what is it, exactly, that has been invisible, Mis-Represented, silenced? When the Situationists painted 'Speak your desires' on Paris walls, when the women's health movement brought out *Our Bodies, Ourselves*,[9] when gays and lesbians chanted, '2-4-6-8, Is your girlfriend really straight?', the implication was that there are genuine desires, natural bodies, true sexualities, to be revealed and asserted against the repression, misconceptions and misconstructions of an oppressive society. When lesbians abseiled into the House of Lords, or people with AIDS invaded medical conferences and demanded to speak from the platform, they may have been, as Simon Watney says, constructing 'an effective theatre of images . . . seducing the voyeuristic mass media, invading "public space"';[10] they were also publicly claiming an identity.

For all the intensive debates among feminists and Queer theorists about the shortcomings of identity politics, and the discussions in academic circles about Michel Foucault's argument that there is no inner sexuality or true self to be discovered, the old ideas persist. Can there be a vision of liberation if there is nothing there to be liberated?

Transgression

Transgression, the deliberate and visible breaking of social rules, also raises difficult questions for a politics of sexuality. The boundary between public and private, constantly being renegotiated, and central to liberal sex reforms, seems to be under attack from the new generation of 'in your face' sexual libertarians claiming the right to do what they want where they want. At its simplest, transgressive sexual behaviour or appearance is seen as important for its shock value – the old game of scandalizing the bourgeoisie. But shock can become its own value, requiring a constant supply of shockees. If one thing becomes acceptable, then a new unacceptability has to be found. This use of transgression depends on its opposition to existing values, so cannot be about broad social change, even though it may result in changing the boundaries of permissibility (e.g., the mainstreaming of images formerly confined to top shelf pornography). Transgression in this sense is about the pleasure of self-expression – a self-defined, in differentiation from a dominant, other. For instance, in a recent interview, lesbian photographer Della Grace talks about how her images explore our fear of otherness (who is the 'our' here?), then goes on to tell of an encounter with a hostile neighbour who was:

> very upset that I was in the garden photographing three naked, scarred, bald, tattooed and pierced dykes. . . . Afterwards I was, like, shave me. I needed to have my head completely bald. I didn't want to be associated with her brand of normalcy.[11]

Even when sexual transgression seems to be about creating new versions of sexuality, the language of the 'true self' recurs. Speaking our desires is seen as revealing an inner truth, with assertions that take the form: this is who I really am, and this is how I will live it out. Sometimes, for instance, in the debates about the limits of consensual sado-masochism, its defenders use the traditional rhetoric of civil liberties, maintaining the public/private distinction. Other groups and individuals reject the notion of tolerance, and demand more (for instance, the right to public sex, or self-mutilation): see me; accept me; make it possible for me to live out my desires; realize your own. 'It is the space of the body that we want to liberate from the occupying forces. It is in this way that we want to work for the liberation of social space: there is no frontier between the two.'[12] Transgression can work in a more complex way, using disruption, a version of the Situationist *détournement*, with the aim of rendering visible both to participants and observers power relations which are normally hidden. When Nikki Craft was arrested in 1981 for exposing her breasts on a beach, and supporters demonstrated topless outside the courtroom, she argued:

> We're living in a society that sells women's breasts in topless bars, in advertising and pornography, and then attempts at the same time to deny them rights over their own bodies. I wish women would demand control at every level.[13]

In England in the mid-1990s a woman who tries to breast-feed her baby in public can still be abused on buses or asked to leave a restaurant. Where does this fit on the spectrum of normality and transgression?

Prefiguration

Prefiguration, the demonstration or rehearsal or sample of how life could be in a better world is usually but not always transgressive. Often it is about experimenting with different ways of living, from the anarchist colonies of the late nineteenth century and the communes of the 1960s and 1970s, to the New Age travellers of the 1990s. Attempts are made, with varying degrees of success, to challenge dominant forms of sexual relationship. Non-monogamy, serial monogamy, anonymous sex, celibacy, polymorphous perversity have all at some point been argued for as ways of breaking down internalized oppression and relating to one another in a non-capitalist and/or non-patriarchal manner. The importance of friendship has been asserted over the isolation of coupledom, and the chosen family replaces blood ties. The stereotypical lone mothers and lonely homosexuals who serve as warnings to those who live outside conventional family structures may have support networks unimaginable to those who have not had to create their own communities.[14]

Whether sexuality can be the basis for rather than an aspect of community has been a central debate for lesbian and gay activists. Most recently, originating in the USA and drawing on rhetoric from Third World nationalism, the concept of a Queer Nation has been used in attempts to draw together groups of sexual outsiders, men and women, black and white, gay and non-gay (but definitely not straight), in an inclusive movement. The language of nationalism is one most anarchists would reject as rooted in a history of definition through exclusion and domination. However, the idea of an imagined community based less on shared identity than on shared oppression, or sexual otherness, has more to offer.[15] In particular, it makes possible the move from organization based on affinity groups, to the development of coalitions, working with difference rather than by separation.[16] How far this is really prefigurative is questionable: a community based on shared oppression may come to need oppression in order to maintain its identity. An emphasis on difference and diversity may end up fossilizing the sexual/social categories of a particular moment in time (see some equal opportunities checklists for examples). And the celebration of difference can obscure inequalities in power, which is a major reason why it is so hard for groups like Queer Nation to sustain themselves over time. What can be prefigurative, however, is not the specific composition of particular communities or organizations, but the creative attempt to live and work in new ways; the process rather than the result. (Seeing it like this can also undercut the pessimism that often follows painful failures.)

Transformation

Prefiguration is about more than making a safe space for yourself (important though that is). Both the disruptions of transgression and the experiments of prefiguration can be part of an attempt to transform a whole society. Whether or not sexuality and sexual relationships are seen as central to social change, they must be part of it. It is easy to see (after many illustrative failures of attempts to live a new life) how both external factors such as economic insecurity and internal ones such as emotional insecurity help to reinforce the sexual *status quo*. Rather than leading to pessimism, these connections can inspire attempts to rethink the ways in which change is possible. Although single-issue campaigns focusing on legislation concerning the body and sexual behaviour are to that extent reformist, they generate new constituencies, and enable new and more radical questions to be raised about sex, society, and the State. The conflicts and contradictions of campaigns aimed at a broader notion of sexual liberation allow difficult questions to be asked about the shaping of our desires and fantasies, and the extent to which they can be separated from the society which produces them.

Imagining the twenty-first century

Chaos: the order of the day

Postmodernist theory, making its breakthrough from academic subculture to style magazines, claims to challenge the idea of authoritative forms of knowledge, and rejects traditional ways of understanding and explaining the world, or even the possibility of doing so. Although it puts anarchism as a world view in the dustbin of history along with every other ism (except postmodern/ism – perhaps best seen as the dustbin itself), the rejection of hierarchy and authority, the emphasis on diversity can be seen as anarchism under an alias: theoretical outlawry. The association between anarchism and chaos, which has so often been a source of irritation and disavowal for anarchists, becomes a virtue when chaos theory is proposed on T-shirts and greeting cards as a paradigm of postmodern life. If anarchism can after all be thought of as an approach, a critique, a set of questions to be asked about power relations, rather than a theory or set of answers, then perhaps it can escape the fate of yesterday's discarded ideologies.[17]

Postmodern bodies and sexualities

In postmodernist rhetoric, fixed identities become fluid, boundaries dissolve, fragmentation replaces illusions of wholeness, nothing is natural and everything is constructed. If ideas about human nature no longer seem an adequate basis for discussing sexual and social possibilities, the approach of the twenty-first century has seen dramatic changes in ways of understanding the body. If the Pill made sex possible without reproduction, new reproductive technologies are making reproduction possible without sex.[18] If woman's body has been conceptualized by traditionalists and by many feminist theorists as reproductive body, what happens when that link is broken? Will there be 'women' in the twenty-first century? Or 'men'? (Are men conceptualized in bodily terms in the same way as women?) Medical technologies seem to promise the deconstruction and reconstruction of bodies, genders, sexualities, which appear at the same time utterly interwoven and yet capable of separation. In terms of bodily transformation, sex-change surgery was only a start; now the taking of hormones to produce what some proponents describe as a third sex, or the use of plastic surgery as a radical aesthetic statement suggest the limitless possibilities of high technology. Orlan, the French performance artist who broadcasts the surgical transformation of her body on live video link says: 'The body itself is an object for redesign. It is redundant, failing to meet the demands of the modern world. My work raises questions about its status in our society and the future for coming generations.'[19] The body is conceptualized as matter, as personal property to be remodeled. And not just by medical professionals – there is a thriving do-it-yourself and artisanal culture as well, of bodybuilding, tattooing and piercing, while therapists provide the interior redesign.

Recent developments in genetics and biotechnology, not just the crossing of species to create new kinds of animals, or the exchange of human with non-human genes, but the very idea of biological engineering and genetic recombination pose new challenges to the boundaries between humans and other animals.[20] Meanwhile, cyborg theorists claim that the human/machine distinction is finally on its way out with the latest developments in information technology.

Why should our bodies start or end at the skin? On a computer network there is no ultimate distinction between the human and mechanical components. The Cartesian mind/body, machine/organism, male/female/life/death distinctions are meaningless . . . in cyberspace. We are all hybrids, mosaics, chimaeras.[21]

In this scenario, your grandmother's pacemaker or hearing aid makes her a cyborg without knowing it, using technology to overcome bodily limitations. Her grandchildren are already beginning to be conscious cyborgs, welcoming the dissolution of boundaries in a world without limits. And sex? In Sadie Plant's story 'Cybersex' she writes:

the telecom's revolution is accompanied by a sexual revolution that is making old style masculinity increasingly obsolete. To be sure, this is a quieter change than the great 'liberation' of the 1960s, but only because it is more widespread, diffuser, diverse, and so difficult to name and define. 'Queer' is one way of putting it, but even this has limits when dealing with 1990's galaxy of explorations of sexuality and experiments with – and beyond – sex. Dance and drugs began to rival the sexual experience altogether, and there were years of lesbian chic, fashionable S&M and a widespread interest in piercing and tattooing all of which contributed to a new willingness to experiment with the human organism and what it can do and feel. Normality became obsolete.[22]

And if normality is obsolete, transgression becomes the new normality. Does this kind of theorizing challenge or transform existing power relations, or does it mask them with yet another fantasy of power and control?

Postfeminism and postanarchism?

Fantasy and cyberspace

What is missing from visions like these is any sense of history or social or economic context. Experiments 'with – and beyond – sex' are not new. Their fashion and visibility in the 1990s are shaped by factors such as responses to the threat of AIDS, commercial imperatives, and socio-economic developments which make possible the places and spaces where such changes can happen for small numbers of people. Experimentation with 'the human organism and what it can do and feel' has a long and terrible history, which has marked the very fantasies which are claimed as liberatory. For chains and black leather to have their power as sexual fetishes, they have to have been used in non-fantasized, non–consenting situations. Subversion? Or is that claim itself a fantasy of power and control, of imaginary freedoms unaffected by social constraints?

Technological developments are accorded enormous power: 'Virtual reality is a space that is neither real in the old sense nor is it nothing nor is it fantasy. . . . That alone is devastating to the whole philosophical world view and undermines all the gender and power relations.'[23] In cyberspace, you can represent yourself as whatever gender, race, or bodily conformation you choose, and engage in virtual encounters with others who may be playing the same games. Sexualized interactions have become common, and the first allegations of virtual adultery are about to hit the divorce courts in the USA. Is this the imagination in power? Yes, the Internet can provide a space where people can experiment with identities, fantasize other worlds and perhaps thereby change their own. But so can the printed word or traditional storytelling.[24] Women, people with disabilities, and Black people using the Internet have been subjected to abuse and harassment. The fact that they could disguise themselves, or that their abusers can, seems to miss the point, which is that it is the imagined reality of the body which invites the replication of off-line power relations. Whatever identity we construct for ourselves on the Net is rooted in what we understand ourselves and others to be in the bodies hunched over the keyboard.

Liberatory technologies?

The idea of the integrity of the human body, problematic though it is, has been useful as a way of arguing against medical approaches which treat the body as a collection of parts. Theories about the dissolution of bodily boundaries look rather different from the perspective of Indian peasants forced by poverty to sell their kidneys, working-class women in the United States acting as surrogate mothers for the rich, or middle-aged women having unnecessary hysterectomies. Virtual Reality is hardly accessible to those whose labour in the other kind of reality produces the raw materials for the computers and the food for their operators. No theory of the liberatory powers of technology can afford to overlook or downplay the conditions of its production and consumption.

This is more than a question of asking who gets left out or made invisible in these imaginings of the future. There is also the point that technology embodies social relations and would itself need to be transformed as part of a wider process of social transformation.[25] Too often, new forms of technological and biological determinism are masquerading as fluidity. If biology is not destiny, why do we need to change our bodies with drugs or surgery, or pretend we have a different one in cyberspace in order to challenge existing notions of sex and gender? The idea that technology will do away with the social relations which produce it is to look for a technological fix for problems which need to be addressed in far more complex ways.

The issue is not technology on the one hand versus nature on the other. Where does the technology come from? How are our understandings of it produced? Who designed it, who made it, who uses it, what and who is excluded by it?

Fantasizing about the future is itself an important kind of prefiguration. If we want actively to transform the world, imagination is crucial. But fantasies that deny the limitations of our bodies are not transcending the

Cartesian split between mind and body, they are reinforcing it. Undermining existing power and gender relations needs an understanding of the way they, too, are embedded in a material reality which is all too resistant to our attempts to change it. What will twenty-first-century sex be like? I don't know. The question is not whether there is a true inner sexuality to be liberated, but which ways of understanding ourselves make it possible to act with some chance of bringing about positive changes. The dreams of the future are embedded in the power relations of the present. A materialist, embodied anarchism will try to encompass both.

Notes

1. Greenway (1993).

2. Haaland (1993) illustrates these themes in her study of Emma Goldman.

3. Wicked Messengers, (n.d., though probably mid-1970s).

4. O'Sullivan (1988).

5. I am not suggesting that it is a negative development to have such images in the mainstream – far from it – simply that it raises contradictions about the notion of disrupting the normal.

6. *Bad Attitude* is a 'radical women's newspaper' with a strong anarchist feminist input, published irregularly in London since 1992.

7. Quoted in lootens and henry (1985), p.7.

8. Wicked Messengers.

9. Boston Women's Health Collective (1978)

10. Simon Watney in Carter and Watney (1989), quoted in Boffin and Gupta (1990), p.164.

11. Quoted in Gray (1996).

12. Wicked Messengers.

13. lootens and henry (1985), p.7.

14. Weeks, Donovan and Heaphy (1995 and 1996).

15. The idea of imagined community is taken from Anderson (1991) who uses it as a way of understanding how nationalism is constructed.

16. Reagon (1983).

17. To argue *for* anarchism as an approach, though, is to assert a value for it which has no place in a fully fledged postmodernist perspective. But then neither does postmodernism.

18. See for example Spallone (1989), and Van Dyck (1995). Thanks to the students in my class on Women, Health and Reproduction who have helped me to formulate these issues.

19. Quoted in Armstrong (1995), p.90.

20. Spallone (1989).

21. Armstrong (1995), p. 90

22. Plant (1994/5), p.92.

23. Plant, quoted in Grant (1994).

24. For example, Piercy (1993) is an inspiring science-fiction exploration of the potential of biological and computer technologies.

25. Albury and Schwartz (1982).

CHAPTER 12

Echoes from the Future

Colin Wisely

Inspired by a conversation with a psychiatrist on the nature of interpretations of history, this chapter presents five essays which interlink to explore possible future outcomes for contemporary society with regard to crime, drug-use, work, bigotry and interpersonal relationships. The first two essays draw on pessimistic visions, whilst the final two explore more optimistic outcomes. The third essay presents a picture of an unending drama, constantly replayed against the changing back-cloth of time.

The nightmare of inevitable decline

There is a nightmare vision which haunts me. This persistent terror began the night my mother called me down at the age of 10 to show me a programme that I will never forget. On the television screen were images far more frightening than any I had hitherto encountered even in my worst dreams: images of grim-faced men in black uniforms sporting Death's head insignia and piteous figures dressed in stripy rags with the faces of the dead. Ever since then I have been consistently woken at night by a dream in which I hear the sounds of dogs barking and loud knocking at the door.

In looking towards the twenty-first century, one thing that all libertarians must face is the reality of this nightmare's return to our planet. The miasma of evil which circles this planet, descending here and there, is forever with us: Cambodia, Rwanda, Bosnia, Tibet and numerous other countries echo to the sounds of angry shouts in the night and the lamentations of those who survive to grieve for their dead. As the deserts creep and populations are increasingly displaced by ecological catastrophe, as nation states continue to implode and capital globalizes, the rights of the individual will inevitably decline. Can it really be true that we have seen the future and that it lies somewhere between Phillip K. Dick's bleak environmental disaster 'Do Androids Dream of Electric Sheep?' where the protagonists see the ownership of a living animal as a status symbol and Spielberg's vision of women huddled shivering with fear beneath showers which will either dispense freezing water or clouds of death?

There is now very little doubt, even amongst liberal observers of the international economic system such as Will Hutton,[1] that the Welfare State has had its day. At best, the post-war social-democratic high-wire act was but an illusion doing just enough to sufficiently convince those in the West that equality really did exist. At its worst, the grand illusion hid, behind the veneer of compassion, the vision of our brothers and sisters in the underdeveloped nations starving and suffering while we in the West have been bought for baubles. With the proceeds of this form of modern slavery, humanity has not advanced one jot. Still, the time may come when people in the industrialized West look back on the measly welfare handout as if it were a king's ransom.

The shadow of war has already fallen over Europe: the collapse of the Eastern European nations, and in particular the horrors of the former Yugoslavia may in turn come to pass a little closer to home. The comets which are crossing our late twentieth-century skies may, as the late-seventeenth-century poet John Milton wrote in 'Paradise Lost' 'shake war and pestilence from horrid hair'. Will the bigots come to seek us out as they have already done with others like us in the mountain villages and towns of Bosnia?

Disease, of course, is ever present in human society, and only the most optimistic or foolish would dare to dream of the eradication of illness. Increasingly we are being forced to re-examine our concept of health. The average lifespan of a Russian has declined rapidly since the death of the Soviet Empire.[2] Life has become so hard for the poor in Russia that some now hanker for the return of the communists once so despised. The fact that it is alcohol that is fuelling the decline in life expectancy for Russian men in particular gives us one more frightening echo from the future. As Western medicine continues to obsessively pander to the whims of capital, we can be sure that our bloated post-industrial hearts, filled with the fatty tissues of excess, will always take precedence over the emaciated bodies of infants from another continent.

It is a calculated but probably fairly accurate guess that alcohol and drug problems will become the major public health crisis of the next century. In the face of enormous global climatic, economic and demographic changes, what hope will we be able to offer the confused and bewildered people of our future to prevent them from seeking oblivion in the bottle, pill and needle? Unfortunately, as we are beginning to realize now, those who seek oblivion through these means often add to miseries, not only of their own but to those of others around them as well. Of course the governments of the twenty-first century, those that still have any remaining vestiges of authority or power, will only add to these problems by fuelling them with idiosyncratic hypocrisy. Trapped between a self-imposed, moralistic anti-drugs stance and the realities of uncontrollable mass-narcotized behaviour, governments across the world will respond simply by locking more and more of these unfortunate individuals up. Which leads me neatly back to the banging on the door!

Prison populations in America and England are rising rapidly along with the proliferation of laws which impede individual rights and liberties in the face of accumulated wealth and prosperity. I wonder what will happen when we no longer have the resources to continue filling those jails. I wonder how the world will look from inside the walled citadels that the bourgeoisie are presently building, defended by their private armies. Will they take their last look at a sky that will be God knows what colour and ask themselves where they went wrong? When the famine and disease finally reach the walls and razor wire of the technological bubbles created in the desert, I wonder what they will say as they in turn have to watch their children die, just as many will have done before them. Indeed, many did today, even as you read this. Will there be a time for sighing and a last moment for regret as the last representatives of our once-triumphant species confront extinction?

Computer networks will not fill the seas again. Robotic technology and even genetic discoveries will not have the power to make barren earth bear fruit. As the climate plummets into increasingly unstable cycles of change and the last survivors cling on to survival with their fingertips, I wonder if they will even remember us. Will they recall how their mothers and fathers fought one another simply to live for another day and to feed their families? The knocking on the door will have finished long before this time.

Edward Gibbon, the eminent eighteenth-century historian who documented the end of the Roman Empire, expressed interest in the ancients' superstitious fear of a comet which crossed the night sky in AD531. In observing that the comet returned every 575 years, Gibbon could only wonder who in AD2256 would be viewing the return of the comet which was the herald of a period of disaster during the reign of Justinian. Gibbon could not have known how incredibly optimistic he was being in assuming that we would still be interested in the stars. There will be no time for the luxury of cosmology or for a future successor to Gibbon in a world where even the sunshine brings death.

The triumph of authority

Communism as the ultimate evil has always been the spectre haunting property owners, as it threatens the very root of their class position and superior status. The Soviet, Chinese, and Cuban revolutions were traumas to Western élites, and the on-going conflicts and the well-publicised abuses of Communist states have contributed to elevating opposition to communism to a first principle of Western ideology and politics. This ideology helps mobilize the populace against an enemy, and because the concept is fuzzy it can be used against anybody advocating policies that threaten property interests or support accommodation with Communist states or radicalism. It therefore helps fragment the left and labor movements and serves as a political control mechanism. If the triumph of communism is the worst imaginable result, the support of fascism abroad is justified as a lesser evil.

(Edward S. Herman and Noam Chomsky, drawn from *A-infos*, a list server on the Internet for anarchist information)

The great solution to the burgeoning problem of crime in the twenty-first century was simply to look to the past. As key figures such as Franco, Mussolini and Hitler had attempted during the tempestuous twentieth century to restore the ancient values of Rome to the era of the rabble, so their successors during the subsequent period successfully vanquished the apologists for the child abuser and the robber. Better solutions would be found for these problematic elements. One of the greatest triumphs of the National Renewal Party in its initial glorious phase was the elimination of not only crime but of all the criminal classes. Acquisitive crime relating to drugs, delinquency and alcoholism threatened to undermine the very foundations of civilization. These problems above all others greatly troubled the minds of our early leadership. Terrible atrocities committed on a daily basis struck fear into the hearts of the people of that time. Who could have foreseen that the solution was so simple?

For the first few decades of the twenty-first century, after the acceptance that our foolish experiment with liberal democracy had ended, a period of strife and general civil war reigned. Between 2023 and 2034 the conflict raged across the globe. The principle of leadership paved the way for solutions so long yearned for by citizens of all nations. What was to be done with the scum that robbed our houses day and night, peddling white death to our children and spreading diseases without a care across the planet? Now that we had finally swept the liberal élite from their white houses and their citadels of depravity we were finally able to take control of the gangsters and thieves that crawled upon our streets. The idea seemed simple but effective: of course! Make the criminals pay! Furthermore, their toils could act as a means of reducing the tax-payer's burden. What better opportunity for those law-abiding citizens to vent their frustration and anger at the behaviour of these villains than to see justice acted out most poetically.

The establishment of the first gladiatorial prisons during the late 2030s proved an enormous hit. The first competitions between prisons took place in American stadia, but soon the idea caught on in Europe and the East. Shows were sold out months in advance as queues stretched for miles. Television companies fought for the rights to broadcast the events. Spectacles of criminals trained in hand-to-hand combat became the new mass entertainment. The old sports waned when faced with this new martial competition. It didn't take long for the more progressive prison authorities to recognize the potential to be realized in the entertainment business. In fact, ever since the executions of prisoners had been televised in the old USA, prison authorities had realized this interest in the form of extra income. Prisons in themselves rapidly became self-funding institutions and with their newfound wealth greater and more fulfilling spectacles were prepared to slake the people's thirst for justice. Justice at last could be seen to be done, as the sex abuser was castrated before a crowd and the millions who watched the weekly broadcast from their living rooms gave graphic evidence of the public's support for the policy. Games were themed, drawing from many historical sources. The classical themes, however, always proved the most popular and nothing thrilled the crowds more than to see two men armed with short swords fighting to the death. Research proved conclusively that these innovations led to a rapid decline in offending in every country in which the games were initiated. It is now from the vantage point of our peaceful twenty-second century that we can look back and thank those innovators for their gifts.

Obituary: Antonio Falcone (1997–2033)

> *We have always lived in slums and holes in the wall. We will know how to accommodate ourselves for a time. For, you must not forget, that we can also build these palaces and cities, here in Spain and in America and everywhere. We, the workers. We can build others to take their place. And better ones. We are not in the least afraid of ruins. We are going to inherit the earth. There is not the slightest doubt about that. The bourgeoisie might blast and ruin its own world before it leaves the stage of history. We carry a new world here, in our hearts. That world is growing in this minute.*

> **Buenaventura Durruti (1896–1936)[3]**

Antonio Falcone, who died last Thursday aged 36, was one of my friends and comrades. Formerly one of the active lights and leading militants of our revolutionary movement, Falcone will long be remembered for the part that he played in inspiring the people during the twenties and thirties of this century.

Antonio Falcone's childhood in a northern Italian port seemed impossibly romantic to me, the dry Northern European. Falcone's personal experiences of impoverished urban communities working together to overcome the odds inspired him in his lifelong belief in libertarian co-operation. I remember Falcone telling me one day about his memories of the streets where in his description: 'As many doors were open, you had a mother behind each.' For Falcone, even the way that the denizens of the slums would co-operate to dry their washing by throwing lines from one tenement block window to another helped to develop the web of reciprocity that drew the poor together and gave them strength.

There is no doubt that Falcone's father's early death in 2011 plunged his family into a crisis which would continue to haunt Falcone for the rest of his life and simultaneously provide him with his inspiration and sense of injustice which drove his revolutionary commitment. The complete destruction of all welfare systems throughout European countries during this period meant that those who were vulnerable were left to the winds of fate. The 14-year-old Falcone survived and fed his family by introducing sailors to prostitutes and selling cannabis on the ports. It was because of this that he spent his first period in prison, having been arrested for selling cannabis. Prisons are always grim places, but there is no doubt that the worst examples of prisons in Europe can be found in Italy. During a brief stay at the age of 18, Falcone became conscious of the terrible repression of prisoners and in particular the role of one prison officer in perpetuating the sadistic and brutal regime. In perhaps his first political act, Falcone conducted a referendum amongst the prisoners in order to determine what had to be done about this prison official. All but two of the prisoners voted that justice should be done. On leaving the prison, Falcone made his first contacts with the Anarchist resistance movement based in Milan, and with the help of his comrades assassinated the prison official. It is a mark of the deep respect that Falcone had for all life that this event haunted him for the rest of his days. 'Even the enemy have children and those that love them,' he would say.

Social unrest throughout the whole of Europe at around this time was so profound that movement across the continent could take weeks as borders were shut and opened and roads were closed and opened. The ability of anarchist network members to appear, however, seemingly at will at any point in Europe at a day's notice became legendary. The infrastructure that had been built during the early years of the twenty-first century certainly began to pay dividends.

It was perhaps Falcone's most famous exploits during the late 2020s that are most notable in terms of their power of political propaganda. In conjunction with the Nostros group of revolutionaries named after Durutti's comrades, a series of daring bank robberies were conducted throughout Europe. In their early deliberations, the group decided not to attempt to conceal their identities, deciding that they needed to show by deed that they did not fear the authorities. All the robberies were therefore conducted without masks. In order to show the people that the rulers and robbers who governed the State were not untouchable, the Nostros also decided that at each robbery they would call the local forces of law and order and invite them to the scene of the crime. Amazingly, the Nostros continued their campaign for more than two years before they were all finally killed or captured. Newspapers and television stations across the globe could not ignore such brazen acts, and the gun battles that took place at each bank have now gone down into folklore.

In some ways Falcone's worst stroke of fate was to fall alive into the hands of his pursuers. After his bloody body had been publicly pulled from the vehicle in front of the world's assembled press by officers whose hands trembled with fear at the sight of the legend, there were no surprises in what was to happen next. A show trial, followed by attempts to discredit Falcone's reputation failed to diminish his support amongst those people he had grown up with in the holes in the wall from Naples to Dublin. All that was left to do for the vengeful state was to crush his spirit. Years of solitary confinement eroded my friend's capacity to cope and somehow, despite being unable even to embrace his family on their regular visits, Falcone developed a heroin addiction. The shame of this fact kept Falcone silent as to his subtle assassins, but on his release it was discovered also that Falcone was HIV-positive. Whilst speculation remains as to the exact way in which Falcone contracted the virus, it is true that the virus quickly finished the job that countless law enforcers had failed to do over the years.

The courage and selflessness of my friend and all his comrades cannot be diminished by his death or those of the others. Falcone's actions will continue to inspire others at this most crucial phase of world history. Where Falcone fell, ten others have already sprung up in his place, and where they fall ten more will take theirs. In this way we will emerge from the ruins to rebuild anew.

The Deptford Re-education Centre

In 1994 I had the task of speaking to the Market Deeping Lions, a group of local businessmen in Stamford, Lincolnshire, about drug use and abuse. Here I confess freely that it was in order to receive a sum of £1,000 for the drug treatment agency I happened to be working in at the time. A picture still exists of me, in some local newspaper archive, looking bemused as I receive a cheque from a strange-looking man in an ill-fitting suit whilst two young ballet dancers grimace cheerfully at the camera lens. Never was a soul bought more cheaply nor the consequences more painful. These Round Table warriors, so far removed from Arthur's noble knights, emerged from a form of human social organization with which I had had little contact previously. A brave ethnographer would find rich pickings in the little town of Market Deeping, as members' earnest attempts to correct my overly liberal views on the subject of drugs and drug users certainly gave me food for thought. It had been some time since anybody had suggested to me that we should drag them all out into the streets and shoot them! Prison was, after all, just like a holiday camp, and anyway the likes of me would just want to take them off on a holiday trip to the Costa del Sol if we were given half a chance.

It was pointed out to me in no uncertain terms that the emerging Asian economies, known as the Pacific Tigers, had taken the right response to the drug menace. I pondered to myself at the time that, yes indeed, judicially murdering the odd drug smuggler who is unfortunate or stupid enough to get caught is not a bad idea. In particular it is not a bad idea for the cynical assassins of all governments who secretly collude with the huge corporations that grow heroin in the East. Indeed, corruption and hypocrisy have been the proper way for governments and rulers throughout history.

Anyway, driven to distraction by the absolute crassness of debate, I consoled myself with a recurring delusion of grandeur which I cannot seem to shake. Returning in 2010 in a half-track wearing my red and black star at the head of the new Durruti column, I would round up the local members of the Market Deeping Lions and bring them back to the pub where we had once met. It crossed my mind during that autumnal evening, whilst I fielded increasingly more fascistic comments from the assembly, that one day perhaps, after sanity had finally triumphed, one of my first suggestions to a future workers' council of the North Peckham estate would be that we arrange some form of exchange between the residents of the estate and those good citizens of Stamford who had once worked so tirelessly for charity with not a second thought for their own advancement. I wondered how Phil, the garage owner from Stamford who had complained so bitterly of his cars having their stereos robbed, would fare after he and his wife had been on benefits for a year, living in a council estate with a lift that was filled with piss. After a while, though, they would not worry about the lift, for it would inevitably break down leaving them to climb seven storeys every time they wanted to leave the building. Of course his two young kids would fare well in those conditions because the cream will always rise to the top! After all, as Phil insists, it *is* in the genes. No doubt Phil, being the enterprising businessman that he was (or rather is), would find ways of making money even on the North Peckham estate. Just like other residents on the estate, Phil would rapidly come to his own conclusions about where fortunes could be made. Given the lack of other opportunities, he might find dealing in illicit substances appealing and the success of other locals would no doubt persuade Phil that he could make his way in this new world. Given Phil's formidable organizational skills and entrepreneurial spirit we can be sure that Phil would make enough to feed his family; even enough to make a small name for himself in the local area. He might even find himself being admired as a real king of the jungle. This local fame, however, could cause unwelcome attention: success has its price. A spell in our virtual prison lovingly crafted to recreate the prison system of the late twentieth century might also enlighten Phil as to some of the pitfalls that once befell his predecessors. Yes, vast wealth could be made, but beware

Phil — such enterprises would be 'virtually' frowned upon in our new anarchist republic.

How's about Terry, the honest chap that introduced me? Now Terry might be a 'Lion' but he certainly is no relation to a Pacific Tiger. He told me that he was a caring sort of bloke, concerned about the evils of this new drug menace which would one day come to claim his own children. I wonder how Terry would come along, transported to the Pypes Estate in Deptford, a grim and unforgiving area of South London with a similar social profile to the North Peckham estate. Terry, the successful retailer from Stamford! We will have to give him a job as a shelf-stacker at a nameless supermarket in Lewisham. We will have Black management of the store, latterly from the same flats that Terry has had to move into, and we will have all the shelf stackers as white middle-aged chaps like Terry, once from the affluent suburbs and hamlets of the Home Counties. Terry has always been a hard worker: he told me so. He had raised himself up from humble beginnings once so I am sure that he will do it again. Of course there will be no racism in this new supermarket organization that Terry works for — it's just that all of his superiors are Black. Of course, the place has an equal opportunities policy and Terry like everyone else can apply for promotion. Looking round, however, Terry notices that all the other shelf-stackers never seem to get promoted either — somehow or other they just cannot get off the nightshift. Who could blame Terry after a few years of hard work and honest toil if he wouldn't turn for solace to the bottle and perhaps something a little harder to help him numb the pain of disappointment and bitterness? How would his friends and family feel seeing such an honest decent hardworking bloke who'd given everything he'd got for the company getting taken for a ride every day till he could take it no longer? Of course, the day that Terry walked out on his wife in despair at being unable to provide properly for his family, we re-educators might relent from our tormenting of the poor soul: after all, the bad days will be over and no one will have to suffer these indignities for real any more. People would no longer watch him leave and sigh at the fecklessness of the underclass and wonder at the burden of another single mother on the welfare.

Part of the deal in accepting this sum of money on that autumn day in Stamford was that, along with my partner, we would attend a fund-raising show in the town. On the particular afternoon that we were forced to attend the gala, we sat through three hours of various forms of excruciating torture which ought to attract professional tormentors from across the globe in order to learn from the masters. The highlight of this event, however, was left to the children of the local bourgeoisie who gallantly performed a version of the Dying Swan which I would not wish on my worst enemy. In discussion with a friend subsequently I have wondered why it is that these smug, well-fed gents are in any way different from the denizens of estates. Perhaps they do deal in drugs themselves, do have drink problems, do beat their children and partners, do stare at the skies at night and wonder why, fall in love and betray each other. What is the difference then, I wonder? Well, the difference is that this group of people seldom seem to end up in prison for their misdemeanours, and if they do they will inevitably be treated more leniently than their counterparts from Deptford. These people can also make a big difference to the poorer people. They run the show, they sit in judgement over the rest of us, policy is determined according to their views and values. The Nazi art of the 1930s and 1940s is essentially bland, emphasizing mediocrity and 'normality'. Sitting in that dark room that day while the sun shone brightly in the blue sky outside, I finally began to understand where Hitler found his audience.

Visions from the bins

As Christ succinctly pointed out, anybody can love their own children: the real challenge is loving our enemy. In the true spirit of loving one's enemy, I wonder what future we can wish for our enemy's children as well as our own.

As human knowledge has increased over the last 200 years and our ability to harness ever more sophisticated models of the world around us has grown, science and technology have leaped forward. Our capacities now far outweigh our wisdom and like small children handed loaded weapons in the play room, a disaster seems all but inevitable. What, I often ask myself, would the world look like if we could harness this technology that we have created and put it to more constructive use? Dare we allow ourselves to imagine a world where our endeavours and inspiration are geared towards the alleviation of suffering and misery, not the selfish pursuit of wealth?

A recent article in a Marxist magazine had me raging as the writer argued in favour of the right to genetically test for defects in the foetus. What is the point of having a revolution if we are not aiming at perfection? the journalist seemed to argue. After all, isn't the goal of socialism ultimately to rid the world of suffering? It is exactly this sort of simplistic logic which led to the gulags and the death camps. We must not allow ourselves to be deceived by the utopian heresy of the Left and must deny vehemently the sterile paradise promised by the cult of political perfection. Surely our aim should be to strive towards a better way of organizing ourselves so that all may enjoy the fruits of our labour, not just those designated as worthy of partaking in the feast? Hamfistedly, the correspondent claimed that having an intellectual disability prevents an individual from truly living life to the full. God help us if this character ever gets in charge. With my short-sightedness, I might have been selected out before birth for not being able to see the architectural glory of our citizens' revolutionary future. This heresy has led us time and again to the brink of disaster. The best we can hope for is to work together to defeat those evils that human inspiration can vanquish. To quote Emma Goldman, 'If I can't dance I don't want to be part of your revolution.' If we cannot have people with Down's syndrome, then I prefer to take my chances with the capitalists. At least *they* still have enough space in their hearts for doubt and uncertainty about such matters.

My first contact with libertarian thought came at the age of 15 when an English teacher asked us to imagine the world without money. 'A world without money?', we asked. She might as well have suggested a world without water. People look at me with incredulity when I suggest it to them. This artificial system for the allocation and distribution of resources has achieved such status in our society that a classroom of children was not able to grasp the concept of being without it. How would the world look without money? Would we be able to allocate and distribute resources according to the needs of the community and individual? In the West I wonder how easy we would find it to give up those little privileges that we have become so accustomed to in order that our brothers and sisters in the shanty towns of Brazil could have sanitation and food on their plates. This will be the first sacrifice that we must make and certainly not the last.

The idea of Alan Clark, Conservative politician, darling of the English New Right, and one who has been 'economical with the truth' in the 'Arms to Iraq' affair, having to hand over his Range Rover to the local workers' council in order that they use it for childcare duties does indeed fill me with malicious glee. I sincerely hope that it will be me who has to explain patiently to him that his multi-million pound castle will be having a few more residents: perhaps the heroin-using young couple I once spent a pleasant day with in Liverpool, surviving in a flat where quite literally one would not have dreamed of swinging the proverbial cat. Of course Mr Clark claims not to care what foreigners do to each other, and I do not imagine he cares too much about these two. But maybe he will if they come to live with him. I want to think that after a while they might all get to like each other and that some day a visitor with an eye for the bizarre might be surprised by the idyllic scene of a former right-wing ideologue playing croquet on the lawn with a group of scousers sipping home-made wine and laughing uproariously at Alan's anecdotes.

And imagine the factories and manufacturing plants of the world producing products that are designed to last for decades and centuries! Capital demands that all produce must have a built-in obsolescence. 'After all, if the consumers stop buying the product then we will all be out of work,' they say. It always amazes me when I look at a light bulb to realize that the manufacturer introduces something into the filament that makes it blow every few months. What would we do with all those other factories if there was only one factory producing light bulbs that lasted for years? Take this simple proposition, apply it to the whole manufacturing process, give it a good shake so that the goal of production is for the improvement of humanity not the lining of pockets and we can only begin to imagine what would happen.

I was sitting at my desk at work the other day and I wondered what it would be like if every year I had to do a month cleaning the streets or running the bins, taking my share of the less glamorous tasks in society. Perhaps it would not be so bad. I used to wash dishes in restaurants at college and it never seemed so bad knowing that I only had to do it for a short while during my holidays. In fact I met some of the most interesting people in those sweaty kitchens. I certainly came to understand, like Orwell in *Down and Out in Paris and London*, that the kitchen porter is the lowest of the low, and gained a valuable insight into how one becomes invisible at the bottom of society. I will never forget the beautiful French waitress who eerily could look right through me as if I simply was not there. Equally I will also never forget the rock-climbing chef at the University of London who made each day a joy with his comedy routines and philosophical interludes. Most difficult experiences are generally bearable, knowing that there will be an end to them. The real suffering in life begins at the point that we realize there will never be an end. Seligman's rats learned helplessness in their cages, randomly receiving electric shocks until they slumped into despair and no longer even attempted to avoid the excruciating current.[4] Behind this cruel experiment there is deep truth for those who wish to learn from it: the same syndrome is frequently observed in our own species. Sociologists have commented on the effect of social isolation in the 'non working poor' communities of North America.[5] The effects of this isolation include depression, aggression, amotivation and generally a sense of helplessness which no doubt those rats would have much to say about, were they able to speak. Into this environment, children arrive every day from the ether, innocent and defenceless. For some of us a bit of drudgery probably would not be such a bad idea anyway, and for others the chance to escape from grinding poverty and day-long boredom might seem even better. I dreamed up the best novels of the 1980s beside that sink listening to the mad chef ranting from seven in the morning till seven every evening. Sadly the novels never actually got written. But maybe one day on the bins I will find my muse again.

I tried to imagine while writing this chapter how the village where until recently I lived might change if I could act out my daydream. I pictured each street employing its own chef rather than each individual household having to cook and wash the dishes every night. Maybe we could even take it in turns to do the dishes. We could all meet at the restaurant at the bottom of the street, somewhere where we could take the kids, unwind and catch up on the latest local gossip. Of course in my daydream we would never wish to compel people to become sociable, but then given the choice between eating out every night and having to cook, I know what most people would choose, even if they still had to do the dishes.

Now that money would be abolished, childcare would need to be reconceptualized also. The most important area of human endeavour would undergo its own revolution. Caring for one another's children in a more positive way might contribute to the breaking down of those isolated little nuclear units that we now call families in Britain. In opening up the opportunity for communal living, who knows what other changes might come about. With the abolition of wage slavery, other forms of work which currently receive no remuneration or status in society would at last be seen as valuable.

I have one further puzzle for this future society. Now that we have rid ourselves of property, wealth and inequity, what will we do with those who still have the craving for uniforms, shiny badges of office and fierce dogs? What can we say to the odd individual who may still wish to make the rest of our lives a misery? One question that always arises with friends after they have at least accepted that the concept of a world without money is theoretically possible and yet still remain unconverted to the beautiful illusion of liberty, is what do I intend to do with these people? What about the little Hitler who will find freedom just the place to plan his supremacist nightmare? Or the local village bully who likes to hurt for pleasure? Anarchists, mistakenly I believe, claim that these individuals will disappear come the glorious day. If we adopt this approach we fall into another utopian trap. Human nature will neither sweeten nor sour as the years pass. We delude ourselves if we think that we can return to the garden of Eden. What can and must change is our ability to build structures and shapes to cope with our dualistic nature; buildings which do not cause illness; hospitals that aim to improve the quality of life not just extend it; schools where children are taught *how* to think, not *what* to think; and communities which encourage our better nature. Kropotkin had time to reflect on the nature of jails, having spent many years observing them from the inside, as did many others in the pursuit of liberty at the end of the last century and the beginning of this one. In a famous speech in Paris, he mentions that a Swiss educationalist named Pestalozzi had founded an institute for orphaned and unwanted children during the last century. Pestalozzi apparently created genuinely liberated learning environments for these young people, as did Francisco Ferrer at the Modern School in Barcelona, where self-determination, social participation and the desire to learn thrived. Kropotkin proposes that we consider turning prisons into such establishments, so pleasant and enjoyable that the individuals therein would not even wish to escape. In fact the problem with them might be persuading the residents to leave. Prisons without walls! Inside the buildings and structures of these establishments, I leave the reader to imagine what sort of activities might be happening. There can be no doubt however that the residents of these places would be surrounded, perhaps for the first time in their lives, by an environment which would nourish their spirit rather than allow it to wither and die.

Notes

1. Hutton (1995).

2. Ryan (1995).

3. Paz (1976), p.314, quoted in Paz's excellent biography of Falcone's inspiration.

4. Seligman (1973), pp.43–8.

5. Liebow (1992).

Glossary

Adorno, Theodor (1903–69) – A leading exponent of **the Frankfurt School of Critical Theory**. Perhaps best known for his criticism of mass culture as impoverishing working-class consumers and for his theoretical investment in modernist high culture for its perceived auto-critique of its commodity status. He most fully explores his philosophy in *Negative Dialectics* (1966).

Alienation – A term developed in the early writings of Karl Marx to describe the lack of inherent value to workers of work undertaken for the profit of the bourgeoisie. Initially coined as a moral value, it was later developed as a scientific one, describing the alienation of work from life in an essentially economic sense. It is now often used in other contexts to describe many human, social, cultural and other activities where people interact as alienated units rather than human beings.

Anarcho-capitalism (or **Right-wing libertarianism**) – Individualistic and unprogressive political philosophy which believes that human society would be best served by the total elimination of the State, thus leaving all social development in the 'invisible hand(s)' of the free market. The theory is that everyone can pull themselves up by their bootstraps, and for any that fail, the rest of society will support them with voluntarily given charitable donations (or not).

Anarcho-primitivism – A critique of civilization, initially based on the work of the American writer and philosopher **Fredy Perlman**, which synthesizes an advanced analysis of the existing forms of power within society with a re-evaluation of the concept of the 'primitive'. It has been criticized for fetishizing the primitive and for failing to address economic factors.

Anarcho-syndicalism (also related to **Syndicalism** and **Revolutionary syndicalism**) – Political philosophy which rejects the State as a tool of capitalist oppression, and which advocates direct action and political and social organization based on the workplace under the direct democratic control of the workers. Developed by such thinkers as Georges Sorel, it was a particularly important movement in Southern Europe and the Americas before World War I, and was an important revolutionary tool in Spain in the 1930s.

Bakunin, Mikhail (1814–76) – Russian anarchist, most famous for his rejection of the Marxist model of 'Dictatorship of the Proletariat' and his criticisms of the Second International, as a result of which he has come to symbolize anti-authoritarianism among some anarchists. A complex and often contradictory theoretician, he is, however, rightly regarded as one of the major founders of modern anarchism, particularly due to his development of a 'collectivist' model of social organization.

Benjamin, Walter (1892–1940) – Highly regarded German literary critic and radical who, mainly because of his interest in popular culture and the relationship between art and technological mass production, has achieved a posthumous reputation for being less élitist about the study of culture than many of his contemporaries.

Bioregionalism – A term associated with the philosophy of **Social ecology**, which advocates the maximization of sustainable life within a specific geographical area (such as a river basin), using as many of the human and natural resources within it as is possible.

GLOSSARY

Bookchin, Murray (b.1921) – American eco-anarchist whose impact on anarchist thought in the last three decades has been second to none. He has written widely on many themes including the liberatory uses of technology, the Green movement, freedom and citizenship. Although some of his earlier works such as *Post-Scarcity Anarchism* (1971) and *The Ecology of Freedom* (1982) remain influential today, he is perhaps best known for the development of the philosophy of **Social ecology** and the creation of the Institute of Social Ecology in Vermont, USA.

Brecht, Bertolt (1898–1956) – German poet, playwright and communist. Connected with the **Dada** movement, he developed and presented a form of epic drama which deliberately avoided the conventions of theatrical illusion. His techniques of 'alienation' (not to be confused with Marx's definition) sought to defamiliarize the conventions of dramatical performance, usually in order to bring an audience to a political understanding of historical or class issues. A strong believer in the use of art as a forum for social, political and ideological comment, Brecht's theatre can be seen as a political form of **Modernism**.

Chaos Theory – A multi-disciplinary theory within the natural sciences which posits the idea that the order of matter and energy in the world is sufficiently complicated and interconnected to make predictions of cause and effect difficult. Its most popular association is that of a butterfly flapping its wings on one side of the globe and causing tidal waves on the other.

Chomsky, Noam (b.1928) – Highly prolific and influential American anarchist, initially famous for his linguistic theories, who has tirelessly worked to expose the hypocrisy and brutality behind Western (particularly American) foreign policies. He has paid considerable attention to the role of the modern media and their creation of the illusion of democratic debate.

Class War – British anarchist paper (with relatively massive circulation) and federated movement, renowned for its irreverent style, its hard-hitting polemic, its hatred for the Royal family and its glorification of violence. The paper uses a 'tabloid' style and 'popular' methods to criticize established power. Also criticized for its lack of analysis, the mindlessness of its violence and its fetishization of 'the working class'.

Communism – Political philosophy whose avowed aim is the creation of a classless, Stateless society in which property is held in common for the common good. For Marxists, Communism is the ultimate goal of political activity, whereas **Socialism** is the transitional phase before Communism can be adopted. Anarchists reject this Marxist model, arguing that the State will not wither away, but will become entrenched and self-perpetuating.

Conrad, Joseph (1857–1924) – Polish-born English writer, best known to anarchists for the lasting damage which his black-hatted and caped character Karl Yundt in *The Secret Agent* (1907) has done to the image of anarchism.

Conservatism – Political philosophy opposed to rapid change and innovation which holds great respect for historically important institutions such as the Church, the family and private property. Traditionally, Conservatives believe in the importance of a powerful State and for political pragmatism in favour of the needs of capital, often at the expense of human rights.

Crass – Now-defunct English anarchist punk band and record label. Initially associated with helping establish the Free Festival movement during the early 1970s, but best known for their hard-hitting anarcho-pacifist and feminist songs. Possibly the most influential of all the punk bands of the early 1980s, they also can claim the distinction of being discussed in the House of Commons at the height of the Falklands War in 1982, for their records *How Does It Feel (To Be The Mother Of A Thousand Dead)?* and *Sheep Farming in the Falklands*.

Dada – More explicitly political than succeeding avant-garde movements, Dada was a **nihilistic** artistic movement of the early twentieth century which flourished primarily in many major cities in Europe and the USA. Its visual and literary forms found inspiration in the bizarre, the irrational, the iconoclastic and the fantastic, and its protagonists developed it as an expression of disgust at bourgeois values and in vehement opposition to World War I.

Determinism – The pursuit of an idea to the point where it nullifies any other possible explanation. Often used pejoratively to suggest simplicity of analysis, it is a very general philosophical term which in this context tends to be associated with the interpretation of cultural phenomena, the explanation of historical change and the evolution of ideas.

Discourse – A theoretical method of examining the endurance of certain ideas across time and context.

DIY Culture – Lifestyle and cultural activities of oppositional and marginal groups which have gained high profile in the 1990s. Associated with squatting, anti-roads protests, rave culture, New-Age Travellers and related movements, DIY culture is often seen to embody anarchist principles.

Durruti, Buenaventura (1896–1936) – Spanish anarchist and revolutionary, he was one of the most distinguished military figures of the **Spanish Civil War**. Despite having written nothing, he has become a cult symbolic figure in anarchist circles for his unswerving belief in the righteousness of the cause.

Earth First! – Direct action-oriented grass-roots environmental movement, whose decentralist and non-hierarchical structures suggests anarchistic tendencies. Initially North American in the 1980s, but spread to Europe in the early 1990s, and has been involved in a variety of projects including defending wilderness areas from destructive development projects, opposing road building and questioning the sustainability of contemporary consumer societies.

The **Enlightenment** – Rationalist European intellectual movement of the seventeenth and eighteenth centuries which held that the goals of rational human beings were knowledge, freedom and happiness, and that these could be achieved by a synthesis of reason, God, nature and humanity. Rationalist thought developed critiques of the arbitrary, authoritarian nature of the State, and it was out of this movement that much modern, democratic, **Liberal**, **Socialist** and anarchist political philosophy emerged. Much Enlightenment philosophy is now taken for granted as common sense, as well as being criticized by **postmodernists**.

Existentialism – A philosophical movement concerned with relationship of human beings to their world in terms of individual self-development. The philosophy contests that humans are capable of becoming (or choosing not to become) whatever they like, essentially unfettered by anything more than their own creativity and desires.

Feminism – A series of theoretical positions which interpret history from a perspective that women have been systematically excluded or oppressed in a variety of social, political, sexual and economic ways.

Formalism – A term in literary criticism and art history which emphasizes form over content. Usually regarded by modern theorists as a conservative perspective, but has also been combined more radically with political theory by writers such as Mikhail Bakhtin.

Foucault, Michel (1926–84) – Historian of ideas, principally concerned with exploring concepts of truth, power and self. His innovative tracing of the genealogy of certain **discourses** – including madness, crime, punishment, knowledge, sexuality and medicine – has had a profound impact on the social sciences and political and cultural theory.

Frankfurt School of Critical Theory – Developed principally in the post-World War II period by **Adorno**, **Marcuse** and others, this theoretical school rejected past philosophy for its search for some ultimate human identity or primacy, arguing that to do so would be to 'reify' the human subject and render it subject to exploitation. The task of Critical Theory is to challenge all conceptual distinctions so that they cannot deform the true nature of reality. It is often seen as having turned Western **Marxism** away from direct engagement in politics towards academic and cultural issues.

Freedom – British anarchist paper (and anarchist publishing house), established in 1886. Essentially representing the respectable face of British anarchism, it is also often criticized for being too middle-class, liberal, etc.

Friends of the Earth – One of the main (international) environmental Non-Governmental-Organizations, founded in the early 1970s. Although well respected for its research and lobbying of governments, many anarchists and anarchistic groups such as **Earth First!** regard it as hierarchical and bureaucratic.

Gandhi, Mahatma (1869–1948) – Indian political leader, known for his organized campaigns of civil disobedience both against injustices of his own government and against British rule in India. Also against the caste system and materialism, his philosophies on peace and methods of protest have inspired many an anarchist over recent decades.

GLOSSARY

Godwin, William (1756–1836) – Writer and radical, usually acknowledged as the founder of British anarchism with his *Enquiry Concerning Political Justice* (1793), an extremely sober but radical book of its time. Also famous for being married to proto-feminist Mary Wollstonecraft and being the father of Mary Shelley.

Goldman, Emma (1869–1940) – Jewish-American anarchist famous for her tireless propaganda work for the anarchist cause in both Europe and the USA. Her goals of freedom, equality and living for pleasure instead of pain have been an inspiration to generations of anarchists, feminists and other radicals.

Goodman, Paul (1911–1972) – An innovative American anarchist educationalist with a strong interest in decentralization and community politics, who had an impact on the youth culture of the 1960s.

Gramsci, Antonio (1891–1937) – Italian communist theoretician who wrote at length while in prison for the last decade of his life. He has been an important influence on the development of cultural studies in Britain, with particular reference to the relationship between power, ideas and ideology and the ways in which they become manifested in culture. His validation of popular culture is regarded as highly important, standing in opposition to the **Frankfurt School**.

Grand narratives – Term used to describe self-contained and all-explanatory philosophies which are usually associated with a particular person (such as Marx – **Marxism**), and to which **postmodernist** writers are frequently hostile on the grounds of absolutism.

Greenpeace – The world's most famous environmental organization, who captured the popular imagination in the 1970s with their direct action against whaling and nuclear testing. Now in effect a multinational company, they are often criticized by anarchists for their hierarchical structure and lack of grass-roots activism.

Historical materialism – Marxist interpretation of history and society which suggests that it is objective economic factors and the work activities that people engage in that determine their 'consciousness', their interpretations of the world and their actions.

Home, Stewart (b.1963) – Idiosyncratic contemporary writer associated with the general anarchist milieu, despite his high-profile protestations that he is a communist. Well-known for taking controversial stances (most recently in a satirical critique of Green anarchists), he has published many 'pulp' novels in addition to his most serious work *The Assault on Culture: Utopian Movements from Lettrisme to Class War* (1988).

Kropotkin, Peter (1842–1921) – Russian prince, geographer and anarchist, particularly renowned for his writings on mutual aid in evolution, anarchist communism, Russian literature, history and geology. His ideas on decentralized communities have resonances in modern anarchist and **social ecology** movements.

Lib ED – British anarchist magazine, journal and book publishing collective 'for the liberation of learning', concerned with the distribution of ideas and information about alternatives in education both within the State sector and beyond.

Liberalism – Political philosophy which believes in the maximization of individual liberty and that the primary function of the State is to protect the rights of citizens. Liberalism is an ambiguous term, however, since at one extreme it can be interpreted as advocating totally unregulated *laissez-faire* capitalism (the market unfettered by the State); at the other extreme it is a basis of **Socialist** ideology, where the State is regarded as the defender of citizens' right and the provider and distributor of welfare.

Libertarianism (Right-wing) – see **Anarcho-capitalism**.

Marcuse, Herbert (1898–1979) – German-born US political philosopher, Freudian and Marxist who believed Western society to be unfree and repressive, that its technology had bought the complacency of the masses with material goods, and that it had kept kept them intellectually and spiritually captive. He was a highly inspirational thinker among student revolutionaries in the 1960s.

Marxism – Political philosophy developed by Karl Marx, Friedrich Engels and others which interprets history in terms of the tensions between the socio-economic classes. Capitalism is regarded as an inevitable phase in human development in which the majority (the proletariat) work to produce surplus value which is appropriated by the minority. The proletariat, it asserts, driven to rebel against this injustice by the extreme nature of their **alienation**, are historically destined to unite behind a common goal of healing the divisions within humanity and creating a classless society.

Marxism-Leninism – A form of **Marxism** which asserts that the proletariat are only able to organize and rebel against bourgeois society under the leadership/dictatorship of a professional class of revolutionaries.

May 1968 – A significant event in anarchist history, owing to the variety of spontaneous and leaderless occupations and experiments with new forms of political organization that took place. A huge general strike in France involving most social classes – initially sparked by student radicals – came close to toppling the regime of Charles de Gaulle. Other radical activities ensued in the USA, Germany and Britain, and although in the short term, few real political advances were achieved, the events of 1968 are regarded by anarchists as symbolically important regarding the rise of the New Left, in providing a basis for political criticism and change in modern Western democracies, and in moving political focus away from the relations of production towards a sense of the importance of consumption. Also seen as influential in the formation of modern environmental movements.

Metanarratives – A related term to **Grand Narratives**, but wider in scope and directed more at ideologies which cannot be attributed to one person (e.g. **Socialism**). Similarly under fire from **postmodernist** writers.

Michel, Louise (1830–1905) – French anarchist thinker, writer and teacher who was a leading figure in the Paris commune of 1871 and who was influential in the development of radical alternatives to State and authoritarian education.

Millenarianism – Doctrine arising out of Christian theology which has often been popular at times of rapid social change and which believes that good or catastrophic (or both) events are imminent, particularly with approach of numerically relevant historical dates. Due to its inherently fatalistic nature, millenarians are often involved in marginal and unconventional social movements.

Modernism – A defining philosophical sensibility of the late nineteenth and early twentieth century, arguably either rooted in **Enlightenment** principles or a reaction to them, it is associated with the emergence of the Social Sciences, the political theories of **Socialism** and anarchism and various artistic movements. Essentially a philosophical assault on orthodox 'realist' methods of cultural representation, it embraced the political and industrial turbulences of its time with a self-conscious style, but remained commited to the search for absolute truths.

Mutual Aid – A term coined by **Peter Kropotkin** to counter the competitive Darwinian model of evolution. Based on the premise that people are inherently social and co-operative, it has become a central tenet of the feasibility of anarchism as a form of social organization.

New Right – The collective name for the philosophers and commentators who developed the free-market policies behind the governments of Margaret Thatcher during the 1980s. At their most extreme, they can also be associated with **Anarcho-capitalism** and **Right-wing libertarianism**.

New Social Movements – A term used in the social sciences to describe non-Party political movements which have emerged since the 1960s. These have tended to focus on quality-of-life issues and universalistic moral sentiments, and the term has been most commonly associated with the peace, women's liberation, civil rights, environmental, Gay liberation and animal rights movements. These often use anarchist methods of organization in the pursuit of genuinely democratic participation.

Nihilism – Nineteenth-century political philosophy which initially rejected all forms of aestheticism and all forms of authority exercised by the State, Church and family, but which also developed a constructive aspect which advocated utilitarianism and scientific rationalism. Nihilists later (at the turn of the century) became associated with political violence and destruction.

Paris Commune (1871) – Regarded as one of 'the anarchist moments' in history, revolutionaries, **socialists** and anarchists came to power and influence in Paris by means of elections and popular movements, following the Franco-German war. A number of radical social and political reforms were called for (rejection of religion, 10-hour working day, etc.) but, after two months of the commune and the bloody suppression of other communes in France, government trops entered the city and slaughtered some 20,000 insurrectionist during '*la semaine sanglante*' (bloody week).

Perlman, Fredy (1934–84) – The main founder of the theory of **anarcho-primitivism**, he is best known for his work *Against His-story. Against Leviathan* (1983) but also was involved in publishing and printing with various radical Detroit organizations in the 1970s and 1980s.

Post-industrialism – A sociological term which maintains that the industrial configuration and associated social relationships of contemporary Western societies have undergone a qualititative transformation, moving away from manufacturing-based industries towards a more knowledge-based, service-based and flexible economic system.

Postmodernism – A series of different theories which challenge many of the philosophical premises of the **Enlightenment**. Extremely controversial, it emerged originally from architecture during the 1980s celebrating eclecticism, pastiche, popular culture and a philosophical iconoclasm, often to the point of relativism. Despite being hated by the traditional Left for its rejection of moral and political absolutes, it is welcomed by many – including some anarchists – for its theoretical openness, its opposition to determinism and its sense of humour.

Post-structuralism – The collective term for a series of influential theories which emerged from literary criticism and radical French philosophy during the 1970s, and which had their major impact on cultural studies and philosophy in the 1980s. Principally concerned with the dissolution and reconstitution of meanings and symbols, post-structuralism maintains that the historical 'subject' has become a fragmented and nomadic entity, often eluding definition. Like **postmodernism**, it is often seen to be far too relativistic, yet has been adopted as a cultural method for **feminists**, who see in its flexibility a space to redefine their experience.

Proudhon, Pierre-Joseph (1809–65) – French anarchist, printer and scholar who was the originator of the phrase 'property is theft'. Active during the tumultuous events of 1848, he put forward ideas for the transformation of society, believing essentially that, as humans become morally more mature, the restrictions of law and government become redundant and can be dispensed with.

Revolutionary syndicalism – see **Anarcho-syndicalism**.

Right-wing libertarianism – see **Anarcho-capitalism**.

Rousseau, Jean-Jacques (1712–78) – French political philosopher, educationist and writer who postulated (in *The Social Contract*) that every individual should surrender their rights to the collective 'general will' which is the sole source of legitimate sovereignty and which represents 'the common good'. His ideas were highly influential in progressive movements in France and elsewhere, particularly at the time of the Revolution of 1789.

Sex Pistols – Short-lived and much-hyped English punk rock band who put the word anarchy into the popular imagination, and helped to make punk fashionable. Best known for the songs *Anarchy in the UK* and *God save the Queen* (which was banned), their politics were more Nihilistic than anarchistic, although some of the band's artwork (by Jamie Reid) did draw on **Situationist** representations. At the time of writing the band have just reformed, eighteen years after splitting up.

Situationism – Political philosophy dating from the 1950s and 1960s which rejects much of modern technological and consumer society for its reduction of individuals into commodities, and which emphasizes **alienation** experienced through consumption as much as production. Essentially a synthesis of Marxist and anarchist thought and developed principally by Guy Debord and Raoul Vaneigem, Situationism succeeded in updating revolutionary political ideas for the post-World War II world with attacks on faceless bureacracy, commodification and the depersonalization and pacification of people in 'the **Spectacle**'.

Social ecology – An ecological philosophy, pioneered by **Murray Bookchin**, which gained critical attention in the late 1980s. It maintains that the domination of nature is rooted in humanity's domination of itself through hierarchical relationships and advocates an eco-centric organization of society based upon an integrated balance of human and natural eco-systems.

Socialism – Political philosophy which advocates the organization of society in which private property and the distribution of income are subject to control by means of a more or less powerful centralized State. Often interpreted by Communists as representing a transitional phase in which a strong State is necessary until genuine Communist organization becomes possible.

This is regarded by anarchists as naïve, because, they argue, the State is an inherently authoritarian structure with a tendency for self-perpetuation and bureaucracy.

Spanish Civil War (1936–39) – Probably the most historically important 'anarchist moment', in which Spanish society became polarized around the elected anarchist, socialist and republican Popular Front government and the fascist nationalist insurrectionaries. Despite the hardships of fighting German- and Italian-supported fascists on one side and being undermined by power-seeking Soviet-supported communists on the other, the achievements of the anarchists were many, and the anarchist movement claims this period as a practical example of anarchist principles being put into practice on a large scale, until the fascists' eventual victory in 1939.

The **Spectacle** – A key political term in the philosophical world view of the **Situationists**. Developed by Guy Debord in the late 1950s, it charged Western capitalism with having turned life into a representation of itself, mainly through the growth of mass consumerism. Rather than being seen as a series of images which have detrimental effects on people, the Spectacle can be best understood as a relationship between people which is mediated by images.

Surrealism – Visual and literary artistic movement which flourished between the two World Wars (1918–39), producing works of art which defied reason and which rejected the rationalism of recent Western history, science and art. Surrealist art sought to explore psychological and subconscious impulses by means of surprise, shock, chaotic imagery, impossible juxtaposition, suggestion and fantasy.

Sustainable Development – Ecological model of change which advocates that production and consumption in society be organized in such a way as to avoid harming or depriving future generations.

Syndicalism – see **Anarcho-syndicalism**.

Ward, Colin (b.1924) – Relatively high-profile English anarchist thinker, writing in the tradition of Kropotkin, who has succeeded in giving anarchism a respectability through his regular column in the *New Statesman and Society* and his eminently readable and practical books. His best known work is *Anarchy in Action* (1973), although more recently his *Freedom to Go: After the Motor Age* (1991) has attracted interest beyond the anarchist movement.

Warhol, Andy (1926–87) – American artist and filmmaker, pioneered 'pop art' in the 1960s and experimented with unusual and avant-garde film techniques in an attempt to eliminate the individuality of the artist. Later turning to portrait painting, he was regarded by 1960s' radicals as politically very important, particularly with regard to his representations of everyday objects in new ways and his multiple reproductions of images.

Bibliography

Abbey, E. *The Monkey Wrench Gang* (London: Robin Clark, 1973; 1991 rpt.).

Abel-Smith, B. 'Whose Welfare State?', *Conviction*, (London: 1958)

Adams, I. *Political ideology today* (Manchester: Manchester University Press, 1993).

Against Sleep and Nightmare (US alternative press – see *Anti Clock-wise*).

Albrecht, G. 'Ethics, Anarchy and Sustainable Development', *Anarchist Studies*, 2, 2, Autumn 1994.

Albury, D. and Schwartz, J. *Partial Progress* (London: Pluto, 1982).

Allen, F.A. *The Crimes of Politics: Political Dimensions of Criminal Justice* (Cambridge, MA.: Harvard University Press, 1974).

Anarchy in the UK (Slab-O-Concrete, PO Box 148, Hove, BN3 3DQ).

Anderson, B. *Imagined Communities* (London: Verso, 1991).

Anti Clock-wise (PO Box 175, Liverpool L69 8DX).

Armstrong, R. 'Cut along the Dotted Line. Orlan Interview' in *Dazed and Confused 17*, (1995).

Baudrillard, J. *Simulations* (New York: Semiotext, 1983).

Bad Attitude (121 Railton Road, London SE24).

Bakunin, M. 'God and the State' *Michael Bakunin: Selected Writings* (ed. and intro. A. Lehning, trans. by S. Cox and O. Stevens) (London: Jonathan Cape, 1973).

Bakunin, M. *Statism and Anarchy* (Cambridge: Cambridge University Press, 1990).

Barrot, J. and Martin, F. *Eclipse and Re-emergence of the Communist Movement* (Detroit, MI.: Black and Red, 1974).

Baviskar, A. *In the Belly of the River: Tribal Conflicts over Development in the Narmada Valley* (Oxford: Oxford University Press, 1995).

Benjamin, W. 'The Work of Art in the Age of Mechanical Reproduction' in *Illuminations* (London: Collins 1970; 1992 rpt.).

Berry, C.J. *Human Nature* (London: Macmillan, 1986).

Bijker, W. E., *Of Bicycles, Bakelites and Bulbs: Toward a Theory of Sociotechnical Change* (Cambridge, MA.: MIT Press, 1995).

Black, A. *Guilds and Civil Society in European Thought from the Twelfth Century to the Present* (London: Methuen, 1984).

Blackwell, T. and Seabrook, J. *A World Still to Win: The Reconstruction of the Post-War Working Class* (London: Faber & Faber, 1985).

Boffin, T. and Gupta, S. (eds) *Ecstatic Antibodies* (London: Rivers Oram, 1990).

Bondurant, J. V. *Conquest of Violence: The Gandhian Philosophy of Conflict* (revised edn.) (Berkeley, CA.: University of California Press, 1967).

Bookchin, M. *Post-Scarcity Anarchism* (London: Wildwood House, 1974).

Bookchin, M. *Towards an Ecological Society* (Montréal: Black Rose, 1980).

Bookchin, M. *The Limits of the City* (Montréal: Black Rose, 1986).

Bookchin, M. *Urbanization Without Cities* (Montréal: Black Rose, 1992).

Booker, M. K. *Techniques of Subversion in Modern Literature: Transgression, Abjection, and the Carnivalesque* (Gainesville, FL.: University of Florida Press, 1991).

Boston Women's Health Book Collective with A. Phillips, J. Rakusen, *Our Bodies, Ourselves* British edition (London: Penguin, 1978).

Brook, J. A. and Brook, R. A. 'Exploring the Meaning of Work and Nonwork', *Journal of Organizational Behavior*, Vol. 10, 1989, pp.169–78.

Brown, L.S. 'Anarchism, Existentialism and Human Nature: A Critique', *The Raven*, Vol. II No. 1, 1988, pp.49–60.

Brown, M. and May, J. '*The Greenpeace Story*' (London: Dorling Kindersley, 1989).

Bryson, L. *Welfare and the State: Who Benefits?* (London: Macmillan, 1992).

Burke, E. *Reflections on the Revolution in France* (Harmondsworth: Penguin, 1982).

Burnham, D. *The Rise of the Computer State* (London: Weidenfeld and Nicolson, 1983).

Buttle, N. 'Civil Disobedience and Punishment', *Political Studies*, 33, pp.649–56.

Bypass Zine: *Cross-Currents in the Under-the-Counter Culture* No.1 undated, early 1990s. (c/o 21 Cave St, Oxford, OX4 1BA).

Cahill, T. 'New Social Movements and Anarchism: a Green Perspective', paper to the Northern Anarchist Research Group (Bradford 19 September 1992).

Camatte, J. *Against Domestication* (pamphlet) (Ontario: Falling Sky Books, 1973).

Carter, Alan 'Towards a Green Political Theory', in, A. Dobson and P. Lucardie *The Politics of Nature: Explorations in Green Political Theory* (London: Routledge, 1993).

Carter, April *The Political Theory of Anarchism* (London: Routledge & Kegan Paul, 1971).

Carter, E. and Watney, S. (eds) *Taking Liberties: AIDS and Cultural Politics* (London: Serpents Tail, 1989).

Chomsky, N. *Necessary Illusions: Thought Control in Democratic Societies* (Boston, MA.: South End Press, 1989).

Clark, J. *The Anarchist Moment* (Montréal: Black Rose, 1984).

Clark, J. 'What is Social Ecology?', *Society and Nature*, Vol. 1, No. 1 (1992).

Class War Federation *The Heavy Stuff*, 2. (1988).

Class War: Britain's Most Unruly Tabloid (National Secretary, PO Box 3241, Faltley, Birmingham B8 3DP).

Cohen, C. *Civil Disobedience: Conscience, Tactics, and The Law* (New York: Columbia University Press, 1971).

Cohen, S. and Taylor, L. *Escape Attempts: The Theory and Practice of Resistance to Everyday Life* (London: Routledge, 2nd edition, 1992).

Congleton, R. D. 'The Economic Role of a Work Ethic', *Journal of Economic Behavior and Organization*, 15, 1991, pp.365–85.

Conrad, J. *The Secret Agent* (Harmondsworth: Penguin, 1978).

Cowan, R. S. *More Work for Mother: The Ironies of Household Technology from the Open Hearth to the Microwave* (London: Free Association Books, 1983).

Crowder, G. *Classical Anarchism: The Political Thought of Godwin, Proudhon, Bakunin and Kropotkin* (Oxford: Oxford University Press, 1991).

Dale, J. and Foster, P. *Feminists and State Welfare* (London: Routledge, 1986).

Davis, J. T. *Hobo*, BBC2 television documentary (Fine Cut Productions, 1992).

Debord, G. *The Society of the Spectacle* (London: Rebel Press, 1987).

Deleuze, G. and Guattari, F. *On the Line* (New York: Semiotexte, 1983).

DesJardins, J. *Environmental Ethics: An Introduction to Environmental Philosophy* (Belmont: Wadsworth Publishing, 1993).

Dick, P. *Do Androids Dream of Electric Sheep? (Bladerunner)* (St Albans: Granada, 1982).

Digby, A. *British Welfare Policy: Workhouse to Workfare* (London: Faber & Faber, 1989).

Dobson, A. *Green Political Thought: An Introduction* (London: HarperCollins, 2nd edition, 1995).

Dolgoff, S. (ed.) *Bakunin on Anarchy* (London: George Allen & Unwin, 1973).

Doyal, L. and Gough, I. *A Theory of Human Need* (Basingstoke: Macmillan, 1991).

Drenth, P.J.D. 'Work Meanings: A Conceptual, Semantic and Developmental Approach', *European Work and Organisational Psychologist*, 1 (2/3), 1991, pp.125–33.

Dreyfus, H. L. and Rabinow, P. *Michel Foucault: From Structuralism to Hermeneutics* (with an Afterword by Michel Foucault) (Brighton: Harvester Press, 1982).

Durning, A. *How Much is Enough? The Consumer Society and the Future of the Earth* (London: Earthscan, 1992).

Eagleton, T. *Literary Theory: An Introduction* (Oxford: Blackwell, 1983).

Earth First! *Earth Action Updates* (PO Box 9656, London N4 4YJ)

Earth Matters (Friends of the Earth members' magazine), No. 28,Winter 1995 (Friends of the Earth, 26–28 Underwood St., London N1 7JQ).

Easterbrook, G. 'The Heart of a New Machine' in J. Zerzan and A. Carnes (eds), *Questioning Technology: A Critical Anthology* (London: Freedom Press, 1988).

The Edinburgh Review (Edinburgh: Polygon/Edinburgh University Press, 1990).

Edwards, S. (ed.) *Selected Writings of Pierre-Joseph Proudhon* (London: Macmillan, 1970).

Eliot, T.S. *Complete Poems and Plays* (London: Faber & Faber, 1969).

England, G. W. 'The Meaning of Working in the USA: Recent Changes', *European Work and Organisational Psychologist*, 1 (2/3), 1991, pp.111–24.

England, G. W. and Quintanilla, S. A. R. 'Major Work Meaning Patterns in the National Labor Forces of Germany, Japan and the United States', *Advances in International Comparative Management*, Vol. 4, 1989, pp.77–94.

Erhlich, H. 'How to get from here to there: building a revolutionary transfer culture', *Social Anarchism*, 2 (2), 1982.

Ethical Consumer Research Association, *The Ethical Consumer Guide to Everyday Shopping*, (Manchester: ECRA publishing, 1993) (16 Nicholas St., Manchester M1 4EJ).

Ethical Consumer: Special Anti-Consumerism Issue 27, January 1994.

Fairclough, N. *Language and Power* (Harlow: Longman, 1989).

Fare Dodgers' Liberation Front *The Artful Dodger*, 1995 (Box FDLF, 121 Railton Road, London SE24 0LR).

Feminism and Nonviolence Study Group (FNSG) *Piecing it Together: Feminism and Nonviolence* (Buckleigh, IL.: FNSG, 1983).

Fiske, J. *Understanding Popular Culture* (London and New York: Routledge, 1992 [1989]).

Fo, D. *Accidental Death of an Anarchist* (London: Methuen, 1991).

Foreman, D. *Confessions of an Eco-Warrior* (New York: Harmony Books, 1991).

Foreman, D. and Haywood, B. (eds) *Ecodefense: A Field Guide to Monkeywrenching* (Tucson, AZ.: Ned Ludd Books, 2nd edition, 1985).

Fotopoulos, T. 'The Economic Foundations of an Ecological Society', in *Society and Nature: The International Journal of Political Ecology*, Vol.1, No. 3, 1993.

Foucault, M. 'Afterword on "*The Subject and Power*"' in H. Dreyfus, and P. Rabinow (eds), *Michel Foucault: From Structuralism to Hermeneutics* (Brighton: Harvester Press, 1982).

Foucault, M. *The Foucault Reader*, ed. P. Rabinow (London: Penguin, 1984).

Foucault, M. *The History of Sexuality. Vol.1: An Introduction* (New York: Vintage, 1980).

Freedom (84b Whitechapel High Street, London E1 7QX).

Frith, S. *Sound Effects: Youth, Leisure, and the Politics of Rock* (London: Constable, 1983).

Furniss, N and Tilton, T. *The Case for the Welfare State* (Bloomington and London: Indiana University Press, 1977).

Gabriel, Y. and T. Lang *The Unmanageable Consumer: Contemporary Consumption and its Fragmentations* (London: Sage, 1995).

Galtung, J. 'On the Meaning of Non-Violence', *Journal of Peace Research* Vol. II No. 3, 1965, pp.228–57.

Gamble, A. *An Introduction to Modern Social and Political Thought* (London: Macmillan, 1981).

Garber, M. *Vested Interests: Cross-Dressing and Cultural Anxiety* (New York: Routledge, 1992/Harmondsworth: Penguin, 1993).

George, B. and Defoe, M. (eds) *International New Wave Discography*. Vol. II 1982/83 (London/New York: Omnibus Press/One Ten Records, 1982).

George, V. and Wilding, P. *Ideology and Social Welfare* (London: Routledge, 1985).

George, V. and Wilding, P. *Welfare and Ideology* (Brighton: Harvester Wheatsheaf, 1994).

Gerver, N. 'What violence is', in A.K. Bierman and J. Gould (eds), *Philosophy for a New Generation* (London: Macmillan, 1968) pp.353–65.

Gibson, T. 'Who Will Do the Dirty Work?', in V. Richards, (ed.) *Why Work?* (London: Freedom Press, 1983).

Gimarc, G. *Punk Diary: 1970–1979* (London: Vintage, 1994).

Gini, A. R. and Sullivan, T. 'Work: The Process and the Person', *Journal of Business Ethics*, 6, 1987, pp.649–55.

Glasgow Anarchist Summer School, 'Popular Culture', mimeo (1993).

Godwin, W. (ed. I. Kramnick), *An Enquiry Concerning Political Justice* (Harmondsworth: Penguin, 1976).

Goldman, E. (ed. A. Kates Shulman) *Red Emma Speaks* (London: Wildwood House, 1979).

Gombin, R. *The Origins of Modern Leftism* (Harmondsworth: Penguin, 1975).

Gombin, R. *The Radical Tradition: A Study in Modern Revolutionary Thought* (New York: St Martin's Press, 1979).

Goodman, P. *Drawing the Line* (New York: Freelife Editions, 1977).

Goodway, D. (ed.) *For Anarchism: History, Theory and Practice* (London: Routledge, 1989).

Goodwin, B. *Using Political Ideas* (Chichester: John Wiley, 1992).

Gorz, A. 'Ideology of the Motor Car', *Ecology as Politics* (Montréal: Black Rose, 1980).

Gosschalk, B. and Frayman, H. 'The Changing Nature of Depravation in Britain - the Inner Cities Perspective'. Paper presented to ESOMAR conference, Seville, Spain, 1992.

Grant, L. 'Deadlier than the e-mail', *Guardian* 30 November 1994.

Gray, L. 'Me, My Surgeon and My Art', *Guardian* 2 April 1996.

Green Anarchist (BCM 1715, London WC1N 3XX).

Greenway, J. 'Sex, Politics and Housework' in C. Coates, *et al.* (eds) *Diggers and Dreamers 94/95* (Sheffield: Communes Network Publications, 1993).

Griffiths, J. 'Life of Strife', *Resurgence* No. 174, (Jan/Feb 1996).

Gross, T. *Fight for the Forest: Chico Mendes in His Own Words* (London: Latin American Bureau, 1989).

Guérin, D. *Anarchism: From Theory to Practice* (New York: Monthly Review Press, 1970).

Guerrilla Girls *Confessions of the Guerrilla Girls* (London: Pandora, 1995).

Guha, R. *The Unquiet Woods: Ecological Change and Peasant Resistance in the Himalayas* (Delhi: Oxford University Press, 1989).

The Guiness Who's Who of Indie and New Wave (London: Square 1, 2nd edition, 1995).

Haaland, B. *Emma Goldman: Sexuality and the Impurity of the State* (Montréal: Black Rose, 1993).

Hadley, R. and Hatch, S. *Social Welfare and the Failure of the State: Centralised Social Services and Participatory Alternatives* (London: George Allen & Unwin, 1981).

Hain, P. (ed.) *Community Politics* (London: John Calder, 1976).

Hall, S. and Jacques, M. *New Times* (London: Lawrence and Wishart, 1989).

Hargrove, E. 'Ecological Sabotage: Pranks or Terrorism?', *Environmental Ethics* 4, 1983, pp.291–2.

Harris, J. *Violence and Responsibility* (London: Routledge, 1980).

Harvey, D. *The Condition of Postmodernity* (Oxford: Basil Blackwell, 1989).

Hay, J.R. *The Origins of the Liberal Welfare Reforms 1906–1914* (London: Macmillan, 1975).

Hebdige, D. *Subculture: The Meaning of Style* (London: Methuen, 1979).

Hebditch, S. 'The Ideology of Grass Roots Action', in P. Hain, (ed.) *Community Politics* (London: John Calder, 1976).

Hedgecock, A. 'Virtual Reality: IT and the Retreat from Society', *Freedom* 51, 14 14 July 1990, pp.5–6.

Heller, F. 'Reassessing the Work Ethic: A New Look at Work and Other Activities', *European Work and Organisational Psychologist*, 1 (2/3), 1991, pp.147–60.

Henshaw, D. *Animal Warfare: The Story of the Animal Liberation Front* (London: Collins, 1989).

Herman, E. S. and Chomsky, N. *Manufacturing Consent: The Political Economy of the Mass Media* (New York: Random House, 1988).

Heywood, A. *Political Ideologies: An Introduction* (London: Macmillan, 1992).

Hobbes, T. *Leviathan* (Harmondsworth: Penguin, 1968).

Hodson, R. 'The Active Worker: Compliance and Autonomy in the Workplace', *Journal of Contemporary Ethnography*, Vol. 20, No.1, April 1991, pp.47–78.

Home, S. *The Assault on Culture: Utopian Currents from Lettrisme to Class War* (Stirling: AK Press, 1988).

Home, S. 'Organised Chaos', *Independent* 25 October 1994, p.2.22.

Home, S. *Cranked Up Really High: Genre Theory and Punk Rock* (Hove: CodeX, 1995).

Hutton, W. *The State We Are In* (London: Jonathan Cape, 1995).

Huxley, A. *Brave New World* (London: Chatto & Windus, 1984).

Institute of Contemporary Arts (Boston) Notes to the Situationist Exhibition, *On the Passage of a Few People through a Rather Brief Moment in Time* (1989).

Jameel, S. *Anarchism and Animal Rights*, paper given to Anarchist Research Group (London: 19 October 1991).

Jay, M. *The Dialectical Imagination: A History of the Frankfurt School and the Institute of Social Research 1923–1950* (London: Little, Brown and Co., 1973).

Jeffries, S. 'The Jazzie B all and end all', *Guardian*, 19 March 1992.

Joseph, K. and Sumption, J. *Equality* (London: John Murray, 1979)

Kelly, A. *Mikhail Bakunin: A Study in the Psychology and Politics of Utopianism* (Oxford: Clarendon Press, 1982).

Kerans, P., Drover, G. and Williams, D. *Welfare and Worker Participation* (London: Macmillan, 1988).

Knabb, K. *Situationist International Anthology* (Berkeley, CA.: Bureau of Public Secrets, 1981).

Kohn, S. M. *American Political Prisoners: Prosecutions Under the Espionage and Sedition Acts* (Westport, CN.: Praeger, 1994).

Kristeva, J. *Revolution in Poetic Language* (trans. M. Waller) (New York: Columbia University Press, 1984).

Kropotkin, P. *The State: Its Historic Role* (London: Freedom Press, 1987).

Kropotkin, P. *Mutual Aid: A Factor in Evolution* (London: Freedom Press, 1993).

Kropotkin, P. *The Conquest of Bread and Other Writings* (Cambridge: Cambridge University Press, 1995).

Lang, T. and Hines, C. *The New Protectionism: Protecting the Future against Free Trade* (London: Earthscan, 1993).

Lappé, F.M. and Collins, J. *World Hunger: 12 Myths* (London: Earthscan, 1988).

Lash, S. and Urry J. *Economies of Signs and Space* (London: Sage, 1994).

Leier, M. 'Anarchism and Existentialism: Much Ado about Being and Nothingness?' *Social Anarchism* 18, 1983, pp.33–40

Le Grand, J. *The Strategy of Equality: Redistribution and the Social Services* (London: George Allen & Unwin, 1982).

Lib ED magazine (Phoenix House, 170 Wells Road, Bristol, BS4 2AG).

Liebow, E. 'Tally's Corner: A study of Negro Streetcorner Men' in A. Harrell, and G. Peterson (eds), *Drugs, Crime and Social Isolation: Barriers to Urban Opportunity* (Washington, DC: The Urban Institute Press, 1992).

Lipset, S. M. 'The Work Ethic: Then and Now', *Journal of Labor Research*, Vol.XIII, No.1, Winter 1992, pp.45–54.

List, P. 'Some Philosophical Assessments of Environmental Disobedience'. Paper presented at the Royal Philosophical Society's conference on Philosophy and the Environment, Cardiff, May 1993.

lootens, t. and henry, a. 'Interview: Nikki Craft, Activist and outlaw' *off our backs* (Washington, DC, July 1985).

Lunn, E. *The Prophet of Community: The Romantic Socialism of Gustav Landauer* (Berkeley, CA.: University of California Press, 1973).

Lury, C. *Cultural Rights: Technology, Legality and Personality* (London: Routledge, 1993).

Lyotard, J, F. *The Postmodern Condition: A Report on Knowledge* (Manchester: Manchester University Press, 1984).

Macey, D. 'Obituary for Gilles Deleuze', *Guardian*, 7 November 1995.

Macarov, D. 'Quitting Time: The End of Work', *The International Journal of Sociology and Social Policy*, 1987, pp.5–181.

Mack, J. and Lansley, S. *Poor Britain* (London: Allen & Unwin, 1985).

Malos, E. (ed.) *The Politics of Housework* (London and New York: Allison & Busby, 1982).

Manes, C. *Green Rage: Radical Environmentalism and the Unmaking of Civilization* (Boston, MA.: Little, Brown and Company, 1990).

Marcuse, H. *One Dimensional Man* (London: Abacus, 1972).

Marshall, P. 'Human Nature and Anarchism', in D. Goodway (ed.), *For Anarchism: History, Theory and Practice* (London: Routledge, 1989).

Marshall, P. *Demanding the Impossible: A History of Anarchism* (London: HarperCollins, 1992).

Martell, L. *Ecology and Society: An Introduction* (Cambridge: Polity Press, 1994).

Martin, M. 'Eco-Sabotage and Civil Disobedience', *Environmental Ethics* 12, Winter 1990, pp.289–310.

Marx, K. *The First International and After: Political Writings, Volume 3* (Harmondsworth: Penguin, 1974).

Maximoff, G.P. (ed.) *The Political Philosophy of Bakunin: Scientific Anarchism* (Glencoe: Free Press, 1964).

McGuigan, J. *Cultural Populism* (London: Routledge, 1992).

McRobbie, A. *Feminism and Youth Culture: From Jackie to Just Seventeen* (Basingstoke: Macmillan, Youth Questions, 1991).

McRobbie, A. *Zoot Suits and Secondhand Dresses: An Anthology of Fashion and Music* (Basingstoke: Macmillan, 1989).

Meadows, D. L., Meadows, D. H. and Randers, J. *Beyond the Limits* (London: Earthscan, 1992).

Megill, A. *Prophets of Extremity: Nietzsche, Heidegger, Foucault, Derrida* (Berkeley, Los Angeles/London: University of California Press, 1985).

Miller, D. *Anarchism* (London: Dent, 1984).

Milton, J. 'Paradise Lost Book II', in *Prose Works and Poetical Works* (London: Henry G. Bohn, 1853).

Misumi, J. and Yamori, K. 'Values and Beyond: Training for Higher Work Centrality in Japan', *European Work and Organisational Psychologist*, 1 (2/3), 1991, pp.135–45.

Mitchell, A. *Man Friday* (London: Futura Publications Ltd., 1975).

The Moorish Orthodox Radio Crusade Collective *Radio Sermonettes* (New York: Libertarian Book Club, 1992).

Morris, W. 'Useful Work Versus Useless Toil' in V. Richards (ed.) *Why Work?* (London: Freedom Press, 1983).

Mr Social Control, *Away With All Cars* (pamphlet) (London: BM Jed, early 1990s).

Mumford, L. 'Authoritarian and Democratic Technics', reprinted in M. Kranzberg and H. Davenport (eds), *Technology and Culture: An Anthology* (New York: Meridian, 1975).

Naess, A. *Gandhi and Group Conflict: An Exploration of Satyagraha Theoretical Background* (Oslo: Universitetsforlaget, 1974).

Never Enough? A Critical look at Consumerism, Poverty and the Planet (1995), from 'Enough' c/o One World Centre, 6 Mount Street, Manchester, M2 5NS.

Newton, S. and Porter, D. *Modernization Frustrated: The Politics of Industrial Decline in Britain since 1900* (London: Unwin Hyman, 1988).

No! (PO Box 175, Liverpool L69 8DX).

O'Sullivan, S. 'From 1969' in A. Sebestyen (ed.), *'68, '78, '88: From Women's Liberation to Feminism* (Bridport: Prism Press, 1988).

Olsen, G. I. and Schober, B. 'The Satisfied Poor: Development of an Intervention-Oriented Theoretical Framework to Explain Satisfaction with a Life in Poverty', *Social Indicators Research*, 28, 1993, pp.173–93.

Oppenheim, C. *Poverty: The Facts* (London: Child Poverty Action Group, 1993).

Orwell, G. *Down and Out in London and Paris* (Harmondsworth: Penguin, 1974).

Oxley, G.W. *Poor Relief in England and Wales 1601–1834* (Newton Abott: David & Charles, 1974).

Parekh, B. 'Gandhi's Concept of Ahimsa', *Alternatives* 13, 1988, pp.195–217.

Pasour, E. C. Jr. 'External Effects and the Work Ethic: Does Society Gain when an Individual Works Harder?', *Economia delle scelte pubbliche*, 1, 1990.

Payne, M. *Reading Theory: An Introduction to Lacan, Derrida, and Kristeva* (Oxford: Blackwell, 1993).

Paz, A. *Durruti: The People Armed* (Montréal: Black Rose, 1976).

Perlman, F. *Against His-story, Against Leviathan!: An Essay* (Detroit, MI.: Black and Red, 1983).

Piercy, M. *Body of Glass* (London: Penguin, 1993).

Pierson, C. *Beyond the Welfare State: The New Political Economy of Welfare* (Cambridge: Polity Press, 1991).

Plant, R. *Modern Political Thought* (Oxford: Blackwell, 1991).

Plant, S. 'Cybersex' *Deadline*, December 94, January 95 (London: 1995).

Plant, S. *The Most Radical Gesture: The Situationist International in a Postmodern Age* (London: Routledge, 1992).

Plows, A. 'Eco-Philosophy and Popular Protest: The Significance and Implications of the Ideology and Actions of the Donga Tribe', in *Alternative Futures and Popular Protest Conference Papers Volume I* (Manchester: Manchester Metropolitan University, 1995).

Primoratz, I. 'What is Terrorism?', *Journal of Applied Philosophy* 7, 2, 1990, pp.129–38.

Proudhon, P.-J. *System of Economical Contradictions or The Philosophy of Misery Volume 1* (New York: Arno Press, 1972).

Proudhon, P.-J. *The Principle of Federation* (Toronto: University of Toronto Press, 1979).

Purchase, G. *Anarchism and Environmental Survival* (Tucson, AZ.: See Sharp Press, 1994).

Purkis, J. 'Daring to Dream: Idealism in the Philosophy, Organization and Campaigning Strategies of Earth First!', in C. Barker and P. Kennedy (eds), *To Make Another World: Studies in Protest and Collective Action* (Aldershot: Avebury, 1996).

Pym, D. 'Technology Versus the Social: or Illusion Versus Reality', *Freedom* 51, 18, 22 September 1990, p.5.

Queer with Class: The First Book of Homocult (Manchester: MS ED (The Talking Lesbian) Promotions, 1992).

Quintanilla, S.A.R. and Wilpert, B. 'Are Work Meanings Changing?', *European Work and Organisational Psychologist*, 1 (2/3), 1991, pp.91–109.

Raeburn, A. *The Militant Suffragette* (London: Michael Joseph, 1973)

Reagon, B. J. 'Coalition Politics: Turning the Century' in B. Smith (ed.), *Home Girls: A Black Feminist Anthology* (New York: Kitchen Table, 1983).

Revkin, A. *The Burning Season: The Murder of Chico Mendes and the Fight for the Amazon Rain Forest* (London: Collins, 1990).

Rich, B. *Mortgaging the Earth: The World Bank, Environmental Impoverishment and the Crisis of Development* (London: Earthscan, 1994).

Richards, V. (ed.) *Why Work?* (London: Freedom Press, 1983).

Rousseau, J.-J. *A Discourse on Inequality* (Harmondsworth: Penguin, 1984).

Roussopoulos, D. (ed.) *The City and Radical Social Change* (Montréal: Black Rose, 1982).

Rubinstein, W.D. *Wealth and Inequality in Britain* (London: Faber & Faber, 1986).

Ryan, M. 'Alcoholism and Rising Mortality in the Russian Federation', *British Medical Journal*, 11 April 1995.

Sakolsky, R. 'Anarchy on the Airwaves: A Brief History of the Micro-Radio Movement in the USA', *Social Anarchism* 17, 1992, pp.5–14.

Savage, J. *England's Dreaming: Sex Pistols and Punk Rock* (London: Faber & Faber, 1991).

Schochet, G. J. 'The Morality of Resisting the Penalty', in V. Held, *Philosophy and Political Action* (New York: Oxford University Press, 1972), pp.175–96.

Schwartz, E. S. 'Overkill: The Decline of Technology in Modern Civilization', in J. Zerzan and A. Carnes (eds), *Questioning Technology: A Critical Anthology* (London: Freedom Press, 1988).

Scruton, R. *A Dictionary of Political Thought* (London: Macmillan, 1982).

Seligman, M. 'Fall into Helplessness', *Psychology Today*, 7 (1973).

Sharp, G. *The Politics of Nonviolent Action* (Boston, MA.: Porter Sergeant, 1973).

Shiva, V. *Staying Alive: Women, Ecology and Development* (London: Zed Books, 1989).

Shotton, J. *No Master High Or Low: Libertarian Education and Schooling 1890–1900* (Bristol: Libertarian Education, 1993).

Simpson, M. 'Coming over all queer', *Deadline*, No. 60 (March 1994).

Slack, P. *Poverty and Policy in Tudor and Stuart England* (London: Longman, 1988).

Smart, P. 'Mill and Human Nature', in I. Forbes and S. Smith (eds), *Politics and Human Nature* (London: Pinter, 1983).

BIBLIOGRAPHY

Solanas, V. *SCUM Manifesto* (London: AIM and Phoenix Press, undated, late 1980s).

Spallone, P. *Beyond Conception: The New Politics of Reproduction* (London: Macmillan, 1989).

Sproat, P. 'Can the State be Terrorist?', *Terrorism* 14, 1991, pp. 19–29.

Squall 58 (PO Box 8959, London N12 5HW).

Squires, J. (ed.) *Principled Positions: Postmodernism and the Rediscovery of Value* (London: Lawrence and Wishart, 1993).

Storey, J. *An Introductory Guide to Cultural Theory and Popular Culture* (Hemel Hempstead: Harvester Wheatsheaf, 1993).

Sustainable Agriculture Food Environment Alliance (SAFE) *Food Miles*, Media Pack (10 October 1994).

Taylor, B.R. (ed.) *Ecological Resistance Movements: The Global Emergence of Radical and Popular Environmentalism* (Albany, NY: State University of New York Press, 1995)

Teichman, J. and Evans, K.C. *Philosophy: A Beginner's Guide* (Oxford: Blackwell, 1991).

Tepperman, L. and Laasen, H. 'The Future of Happiness', *Futures*, Vol. 22 No. 10, December 1990, pp.1059–70.

Test Card F: Television, Mythinformation and Social Control (Edinburgh: AK Press, 1994).

Thompson, E. P. *The Making of the English Working Class* (London: Penguin, 1968).

Turk, A. T. *Political Criminality: The Defiance and Defense of Authority* (Beverly Hills, CA: Sage, 1982).

Undercurrents (16b Cherwell St, Oxford, OX4 1BJ).

Van Dyck, J. *Manufacturing Babies and Public Consent* (New York: New York University Press, 1995).

Vaneigem, R. *The Revolution of Everyday Life* (Michigan: Left Bank Books and London: Rebel Press, 1983).

Veblen, T. *The Theory of the Leisure Class: An Economic Study of Institutions* (London: Allen and Unwin, 1925).

Walker, A. and Walker, C. *The Growing Divide: A Social Audit 1979–1987* (London: CPAG, 1987).

Wapner, P. 'In Defense of Banner Hangers: The Dark Green Politics of Greenpeace', in B.R. Taylor (ed.), *Ecological Resistance Movements: The Global Emergence of Radical and Popular Environmentalism* (Albany, NY.: State University of New York Press, 1995), pp.300–14.

Ward, C. *Anarchy in Action* (London: George Allen & Unwin, 1973).

Ward, C. *Freedom to Go: After the Motor Age* (London: Freedom Press, 1991).

Wardlow, G. *Political Terrorism* (Cambridge: Cambridge University Press, 1989).

Weeks, J., Donovan, C. and Heaphy, B., 'Programme Project Report: Families of Choice', in *Changing Britain*, 3 (London: ESRC, 1995).

Weeks, J., Donovan, C. and Heaphy, B. *Families of Choice: A Review of the Literature*, Research Report Series No. 2 (London: University of the South Bank, 1996).

Wells, D. A. 'Is "Just Violence" like "Just War"?', in *Social Theory and Practice* 1, 1970, pp.26–38.

Welsh, I. and McLeish, P. 'The European Road to Nowhere: Anarchism and Direct Action against the UK Roads Programme', *Anarchist Studies* 4, 1996, pp.27–44.

Wicked Messengers *Can You Feel Anything When I Do This? Away With the Murder of the Body* (London: Wicked Messengers, n.d.).

Williams, H. *Autogeddon* (London: Jonathan Cape, 1991).

Williamson, J. 'Interview with Jean Baudrillard', *Block 15*, 1989.

Willis, P. *Profane Culture* (London: Routledge & Kegan Paul, 1978).

Wilson, E. *The Myth of the British Monarchy* (London: Journeyman Press, 1989).

Winner, L. 'Mythinformation', in *The Whale and the Reactor* (Chicago, IL.: Chicago University Press, 1986).

Wolin, R. *Walter Benjamin: An Aesthetic of Redemption* (New York: Columbia University Press, 1982).

Wollen, P. *Raiding the Icebox: Reflections of Twentieth Century Culture* (London: Verso, 1993).

Woodcock, G. *Pierre-Joseph Proudhon: A Biography* (Montréal: Black Rose, 1972).

Woodcock, G. *Anarchism* (Harmondsworth: Penguin, 1975).

World Health Organisation *World Health Statistics Annual 1989* (Geneva, Switzerland: WHO, 1989).

Yeats, W.B. 'The Second Coming', in *The Works of WB Yeats* (Ware, Herts.: Wordsworth, 1994).

You What (one-off fanzine, date and publisher unknown, mid 1990s).

Zerzan, J. and Carnes, A. (eds) *Questioning Technology: A Critical Anthology* (London: Freedom Press, 1988).

Zerzan, J. and Carnes, A. (eds) *Questioning Technology: Tool, Toy or Tyrant?* (Philadelphia: New Society Publications, 1991)

Zigzag Cassette Book and *Zigzag Independent Label catalogue* (probably defunct, edited by Kris Needs, Phoenix Magazines, Leyton Buzzard).

Index